October Coup

OTHER LOTUS TITLES

Aitzaz Ahsan	*The Indus Saga: The Making of Pakistan*
Ajay Mansingh	*Firaq Gorakhpuri: The Poet of Pain & Ecstasy*
Amarinder Singh	*The Last Sunset: The Rise & Fall of the Lahore Durbar*
Anil Dharker	*Icons: Men & Women who Shaped Today's India*
Aruna Roy	*The RTI Story: Power to the People*
Bertil Falk	*Feroze: The Forgotten Gandhi*
Dinesh C. Sharma	*Indian Innovation, Not Jugaad: 100 Ideas That Transformed India*
Jenny Housego	*A Woven Life*
Kunal Purandare	*Ramakant Achrekar: A Biography*
Maj. Gen. Ian Cardozo	*Cartoos Saab: A Gorkha Soldier's Story of Bravery and Resolve*
Maj. Gen. Ian Cardozo	*Param Vir: Our Heroes in Battle*
Maj. Gen. Ian Cardozo	*The Sinking of INS Khukri: What Happened in 1971*
Monisha Rajesh	*Around India in 80 Trains*
Murlidhar C. Bhandare	*The Arc of Memory: My Life and Times*
Noorul Hasan	*Meena Kumari: The Poet*
Prateep K. Lahiri	*A Tide in the Affairs of Men: A Public Servant Remembers*
R.V. Smith	*Delhi: Unknown Tales of a City*
Rajika Bhandari	*The Raj on the Move: Story of the Dak Bungalow*
Ralph Russell	*The Famous Ghalib: The Sound of my Moving Pen*
S. Hussain Zaidi	*Dongri to Dubai*
Salman Akthar	*The Book of Emotions*
Shahrayar Khan	*Bhopal Connections: Vignettes of Royal Rule*
Shantanu Guha Ray	*Mahi: The Story of India's Most Successful Captain*
Sharmishta Gooptu	*Bengali Cinema: An Other Nation*
Shrabani Basu	*Spy Princess: The Life of Noor Inayat Khan*
Sobhana K. Nair	*Ram Vilas Paswan: The Weathervane of Indian Politics*
Thomas Weber	*Gandhi at First Sight*
Thomas Weber	*Going Native: Gandhi's Relationship with Western Women*
Vaibhav Purandare	*Sachin Tendulkar: A Definitive Biography*
Vappala Balachandran	*A Life in Shadow: The Secret Story of ACN Nambiar – A Forgotten Anti-Colonial Warrior*
Vir Sanghvi	*Men of Steel: India's Business Leaders in Candid Conversation*

FORTHCOMING TITLE

S. Natesh	*Iconic Trees of India*

October Coup

A MEMOIR OF THE STRUGGLE FOR HYDERABAD

Mohammed Hyder

LOTUS COLLECTION

ROLI BOOKS

Lotus Collection

First published in 2012
Third impression 2024

The Lotus Collection
An imprint of
Roli Books Pvt. Ltd
M-75, Greater Kailash II Market, New Delhi 110 048
Phone: ++91 (011) 4068 2000
E-mail: info@rolibooks.com
www.rolibooks.com
Also at Chennai & Mumbai

Cover: Kadambari Mishra
Layout: Sanjeev Mathpal
Production: Lavinia Rao

ISBN: 9788174368508

Typeset in Centaur MT by Roli Books Pvt. Ltd.
Printed in India at Repro India Ltd.

'Of the gods we believe and of the men we know, that by a necessary law of their nature they rule wherever they can. And it is not as if we were the first to make this law, or to act upon it when made: we found it existing before us and shall leave it to exist for ever after us; all we do is to make use of it, knowing that you and everybody else, having the same power as we have, would do the same as we do.'

– Thucydides, *History of the Peloponnesian War,* Chapter XVII

Contents

Editor's Note

In 1948, at one of the most difficult times in the history of Hyderabad, Mohammed Hyder was Collector of Osmanabad, one of the most politically sensitive districts of that state. This memoir is an edited version of the account of his collectorship written by him in Osmanabad Jail in July and August of 1949. His notebooks were typed up soon after his release in 1952, but not published at that time; presumably, he intended to first negotiate his professional future with the government. In 1960, rebuffed by the government, he put Osmanabad and everything connected with it behind him. But in July 1972, when the present editor – his son – offered him a shorter version of his work, his interest revived. He thoroughly reviewed it before his death in 1973, at fifty-eight.

Thus improved, the manuscript waited these long years for completion: Other preoccupations intervened. The remaining work of editing closely follows the 1972 version (the introduction and the concluding chapter were both added in 1972, with some additional material from his jail diaries). The last part of the book includes material from his trials in court, including the case that he brought against the government in 1957. This material constitutes a natural conclusion to the memoir, and provides documentary support for it.

Masood Hyder
New York
10 February 2012

The Beginning of the End

The question of Hyderabad was one of the major unresolved issues at the beginning of 1947: would Hyderabad accede to India by the time the latter gained independence, or would it stay out of the Indian Union altogether, as a sovereign state, or attempt to join Pakistan? For a time, the question loomed very large and it still remains on the agenda of the UN Security Council, more a historical relic than unfinished business. But in the beginning of 1947, the issue was no less worrying than Kashmir.

To look for the origins of this situation is to risk an infinite regress along the chain of cause and effect. Certainly, there were major causes, whose proper assessment would require a balanced historical analysis. Here, I propose to enumerate some of the more immediate causes. Even at the level of a fairly superficial overview, it becomes clear that the Hyderabad question had a certain degree of complexity, and given the contending historical, political and social forces, a peaceful and harmonious outcome was not assured.

As a factor contributing to the downward spiral, Hyderabad's relative isolation from the larger affairs of India figured somewhere at the top of the list. This could perhaps be traced to the exchanges between the viceroy of India, Lord Reading and the Nizam as far back as 1926, on the subject of Britain's paramountcy over Hyderabad. This famous clash subsequently dissuaded the ruler from taking a closer interest in Indian affairs. The Nizam's aloofness in the 1930s and 1940s adversely affected opinion in Delhi and in Hyderabad, at a time when trust and mutual confidence should have been cultivated by both sides. It also showed up the differences of outlook on the constitutional position of Hyderabad, which were to come to the fore in 1947. The British continued to assert paramountcy and the right to intervene in the internal affairs of all princely states; Hyderabad continued to regard itself as the greatest of the princely states, therefore expecting to be treated as a special case. And it began to anticipate the time when the British would depart.

In June 1947, when the new viceroy, Lord Mountbatten, announced his plan for the transfer of power, the idea that paramountcy would lapse was reconfirmed by Britain. In Hyderabad's case, it opened the way for the argument that the Nizam would revert to his original status of a sovereign prince, and could choose to assert his independence or accede either to India or Pakistan. Although the argument was legally sound, it was, in fact, quite unrealistic to expect that independent India would concede to Hyderabad what Britain had never allowed. Whoever ruled India would hold the view that Delhi would succeed London as the Paramount Power, and that Hyderabad could not possibly exist as an independent entity in the heart of the new Indian Union. But the Delhi perspective was not appreciated in Hyderabad.

At the level of popular politics there was one overwhelming fact to be taken into account: Hyderabad was predominantly Hindu, with Muslims representing some 20 per cent of the population. From one perspective, its political arrangements were self-evidently undemocratic, with an autocratic Muslim ruler at the head of the system, and a small, apparently reactionary Muslim ruling class dominating its administration and political life. From inside the system, the perception was entirely different. Hyderabad was viewed as a state blessed with a remarkably secular outlook, enjoying communal harmony, with a benign ruler concerned with the advancement of the poor and the protection of the oppressed; an excellent administration where recruitment was based on competition and advancement on merit; and an eclectic ruling elite, which included, besides Muslims, Hindus, Parsees, and others who had proudly assimilated into the distinctive culture of Hyderabad.

Which perception reflected the reality more accurately? It was all in the eye of the beholder. But those who subscribed to the second point of view were concerned that unless the inevitable transition to responsible government was handled with care, something of inestimable value might be lost.

Given these differences of perspective, the process by which the Muslims (or the ruling elites) were going to let go of their special position remained unclear. The main political beneficiary of any process of democratization, the Hyderabad State Congress, though espousing the same aims as the Indian National Congress, had a past in which it had proved ineffectual and a future that was likely to be equally unpromising, as long as it continued to be so poorly led. The state Congress leadership was, to say the least, unimpressive (with some honourable exceptions, such as Dr G.S. Melkote and Barrister Akbar Ali Khan). It had in the past made the wrong moves, such as initiating a civil disobedience movement in alliance with the Arya Samaj and the Hindu Mahasabha, parties less secular in outlook than the Congress. In the 1930s, Dr Lateef Sayeed had complained about the quality of Congress leadership in the state to Gandhi, with little effect. The ban against the Hyderabad State Congress was lifted in 1946, but it boycotted the legislative elections all the same, and at its meeting in Hyderabad city in June 1947, challenged the government to accede to its demands or face a mass civil disobedience movement. Then, having largely failed to get such a movement going, the state Congress leadership tried to enlist the sympathies of the neighbouring provinces. Returning from his tour of neighbouring provinces, the state Congress president, Swami Ramanand Tirth, courted arrest on 7 August 1947 by organizing a 'Join Indian Union Day'. However, the public response to this show of solidarity was so poor that the Swami had no audience for his speech. But he delivered himself up to the police all the same, for having breached the peace by hoisting the Indian flag. In short, the State Congress did not represent a very impressive movement and was reduced to an absurd spectacle, unable to mount an effective opposition to an efficient, authoritarian regime, despite its undeniable popularity among the Hindu majority of Hyderabad. Its utter reduction had, as we shall see, damaging results.

Meanwhile, the activities of communist elements in the Madras presidency were having repercussions inside Hyderabad, where the authorities had to take measures to suppress local Marxist activity and raids across the border. The communists had gone underground in 1943 after being banned, but their menace had only increased. By 1947, it was proving immensely difficult to contain the civil disobedience movement of the state Congress, while combating the communist incursions. Hyderabad had long borders and the state's modest law and order forces found themselves overstretched. It was under these circumstances that the Muslim party Majlis-e-Ittehad-ul-Muslimeen, also known as the Majlis, offered to set up a volunteer force, the Razakars, to help the authorities combat the threat on the borders of Hyderabad. This turned out to be a mixed blessing. Even at its best, the Razakar was a ramshackle outfit, largely ineffective as a help to the government's law and order forces, but a propaganda gift to the Congress party and other critics of the Hyderabad regime. Led by Syed Qasim Razvi, the Razakars gradually came to be seen as the private army of the Majlis, and the mouthpiece of the militant Islamic elements of the state.

By 1947, the Majlis had come a long way. Founded in 1927 as a cultural organization, it had long since assumed political overtones. In any case, it was never the same again after the untimely death of its brilliant and charismatic leader, Bahadur Yar Jung, in 1944, and increasingly became the vehicle for Muslim views, no longer tempered, it seemed, by responsible leadership.

Over and above all this was the government's handling of popular Muslim opinion. Muslim passions could be easily aroused and throughout this period, a factor weighing heavily on the government was the volatility of Muslim sentiment. There were many examples illustrating this fact. The editor of the local daily *Waqt*, Abdul Rahman Rais, launched a campaign against moderate elements in the government. Some time later, during the negotiations leading up to the Standstill Agreement, the press was so vicious in its attack on the constitutional adviser, Sir Walter Monckton, that he actually tendered his resignation (later withdrawn). The press did not even spare the prime minister. The public was willing to believe the worst. A state with a reputation for communal harmony seemed to be losing its equable political temper as Muslim opinion acquired an unprecedented stridency.

In Hyderabad, it was the Dichpally affair that most clearly illustrated the volatility of public opinion and the seeming lack of response from the government. It was alleged that the Dichpally Mission authorities had pulled down a mosque, a temporary structure with a thatched roof, located in the Leper's Asylum at Dichpally in Nizamabad district. This sent a wave of indignation sweeping through the Muslim population of Nizamabad. The local Majlis roused communal feelings and the Chattari government appeared slow to react. The council that was meeting at the time at Shah Manzil, the prime minister's residence, went about its business at a leisurely pace. The procrastination drew the Muslim crowds already gathering in the city to Shah Manzil, which they attempted to set on fire. The crowd then marched to the house of the minister of revenue and police, Sir Wilfrid Grigson, and set fire to it too, acting on the rumour that the mosque had been removed at his instructions. Prompt action could have prevented this senseless conflagration and possibly many future tragedies. The government's weakness or procrastination in dealing with the troublemakers only ensured many more such demonstrations and had a demoralizing effect on the civil service. Thus, an unremarkable event acquired certain significance, as an ominous precursor to Qasim Razvi's dramatic show of strength, regarded in some circles as a virtual coup d'etat.

The situation inside Hyderabad was exacerbated by external factors, most notably, the repercussions of Partition. In June 1947, the British announced their departure. Three months later, they were gone, having failed to anticipate the consequences of their precipitate withdrawal, which led to a massive exchange of populations between India and Pakistan, accompanied by a tremendous bloodbath, in which hundreds of thousands lost their lives. A thousand miles to the south, Hyderabad began receiving a flood of refugees, as frightened Muslims poured in thousands from neighbouring provinces, though southern India was generally calm during the period. Having experienced the trauma of partition, India developed an overriding concern with the possibility of fragmentation and chaos. Its determination to prevent a repetition of those horrors, and to pre-empt all further challenges to the integrity of India, without doubt influenced its negotiations with Hyderabad. The apparent fragility of the newborn Indian Union was certainly a factor in Hyderabad's calculations.

In June 1947, reacting to the Mountbatten plan for the independence of India and the creation of Pakistan, the Nizam announced that he intended to accede to neither India nor Pakistan, but would preserve the independence of his state. Nevertheless, the Hyderabad government continued to negotiate with Delhi (and not with Pakistan), and it was hoped that a Standstill Agreement would provide enough time to work out the details of whatever status Hyderabad eventually achieved. The negotiations were carried out in secret and continued in the months beyond India's independence on 15 August 1947. At one point, Qasim Razvi (returning from a visit to Delhi) unveiled a 'plot' to lead Hyderabad into accession. This caused quite a stir in Hyderabad, and the main negotiators, the Nawab of Chattari, Sir Walter Monckton, and Nawab Ali Nawaz Jung, came in for much criticism and were widely reviled. This episode, however, was just a curtain raiser to what was to follow.

Lord Mountbatten, the last viceroy of British India, stayed on as the first governor general of independent India, but it was understood that this would be a very short assignment. It was his fervent desire to settle the Hyderabad issue before leaving India. Spurred on by him, negotiations continued. By October 1947, the two sides appeared close to agreement. Shorn of all rhetoric, it amounted to this: India would consider a Standstill Agreement, on the understanding that Hyderabad would concede to the idea of accession. Provided Hyderabad agreed to join India, the latter was prepared to consider the modalities, the when and how of the matter. The draft agreement, reached after protracted negotiations, was brought back to Hyderabad in late October. The council approved the draft and recommended the agreement to the Nizam. In the early hours of the day that the Hyderabad delegation was to fly to Delhi, Qasim Razvi organized a massive demonstration. A large crowd surrounded the houses of the delegates, that is, the prime minister (the Nawab of Chattari), Sir Walter Monckton and Nawab Ali Nawaz Jung.

The delegation did not leave for Delhi and the draft agreement remained unsigned. This was a triumph for Qasim Razvi over the ruler, the government and the people of Hyderabad. The Ittehad leader had organized the show of strength with great care. In marked contrast to the unruly crowds that had in the past set fire to Shah Manzil, this huge gathering was disciplined and peaceful. Nothing untoward took place as the crowd gathered, or during the prolonged demonstration, or as it dispersed.

Of course, an event of such significance caused much reaction in contemporary government circles in Hyderabad. How was this demonstration accomplished? Why was no action taken when the Razakar volunteers had been moving about the whole night? When was the police commissioner informed? Why did the authorities not disperse the crowds? Did the government not desire swift action? Certainly, there were comments along these lines but little criticism. The consensus seemed to be that it would have been unwise to order the police or the army to take any sort of action against a peaceful demonstration. If the government had ordered such an action, it is not certain whether the army or the police would have carried it out, or fully executed it. This would have resulted in a worse outcome for the government. And however much the militant attitude of the Majlis, or the weakness of the government came in for blame, it was not felt that the civil service had a hand in the affair. Many such insinuations gained currency later, but this was not a point of criticism at the time. Among those early critics were Mulla Abdul Basith, Fareed Mirza, Baquer Ali Mirza and a few others, whose stand on the issue won widespread admiration. It took great courage to criticize the government in power and the Ittehad, whose star was clearly in the ascendant. Notably, Delhi kept aloof throughout the crisis. What would have happened if India had condemned the event as a coup and insisted on a constitutional process? But the moment passed. The crisis subsided as quickly as it had arisen, taking with it any possibility of an early intervention.

It was clear even then that this event marked a turning point. For some, it was the beginning of the end. Still others, more optimistic, argued that given India's preoccupations and assuming Pakistan's support and Britain's sympathy, Hyderabad could yet be swept into a tumultuous independence. It had a strong case in law and the best constitutional lawyer in the British Empire to back it up: Hyderabad had only to seize the day. This is how things appeared at the time. There was, in other words, an element of rational calculation in drawing back from accession, not just a blind response to extremist passion.

If there was calculation in the reluctance to sign the Standstill Agreement, the basis on which it was made soon began to erode. The position of Hyderabad did not improve; that of India did. While appearing to back off in the face of the great demonstration against the Standstill Agreement, the Hyderabad government nevertheless signed it one month later, on 29 November 1947. There were no changes in the terms on offer, the Indian government and Mountbatten refusing to countenance any. In the meantime, the prime minister, the Nawab of Chattari, had resigned a second and final time, following the October demonstration. A new delegation had gone to Delhi but, in the end, it signed a virtually unchanged Standstill Agreement.

A great deal has been made of the October 'coup', which is popularly regarded as the turning point, but the November reversal is equally significant: the two events together define Hyderabad's position. The November reversal shows that Hyderabad was not necessarily in the clutches of local militants. It is an oversimplification to assign all action on the Hyderabad side to the dictates of Muslim reactionary forces. The facts more readily fit the picture of a government negotiating under pressure. In the talks leading up to the October draft, the idea of accession before negotiation had not been thrashed out; in November, while it was still not thrashed out, it had become clear that such a wholesale accession posed a serious difficulty. The agreement bought time, but little hope. Hyderabad was now locked in a negotiating position from which it appeared unable to extricate itself. Pressure from India only worsened the situation.

How did things come to such a pass? To put it simply, the situation did not contain the seeds of its own resolution. First, negotiations between Hyderabad and India did not appear to even result in a meeting of minds. India saw itself as having succeeded Britain as the Paramount Power vis-à-vis Hyderabad (and all other princely states). In its view, if Hyderabad would agree to accede to India on only three subjects (external affairs, defence and communications), then everything else was negotiable. Hyderabad's position, however, was different. Upon Britain's departure, paramountcy had lapsed; Hyderabad was legally an independent state. If India was prepared to accept this, Hyderabad was ready to negotiate on everything else. To some extent, therefore, the near-agreement of October 1948 was perhaps the result of a papering-over of fundamental differences; Qasim Razvi had shown in the 'plot' incident cited earlier that popular Muslim opinion in Hyderabad was not ready for accession, thus the ease with which the façade of agreement was torn off.

Second, there seemed to be no possibility of working towards the convergence of opposing sides, which could have promoted mutual accommodation. The gap was unbridgeable between the Nizam and Delhi; between the Muslim-led ruling elite and the Hindu majority. Mountbatten felt this estrangement keenly and thought that personal contact might resolve differences. He invited the Nizam to Delhi, but the latter did not go, feeling perhaps that nothing but awkwardness would result. Those who tried to bridge the gap between the two sides were termed traitors ('ghaddars'), as if the very idea of mediation betrayed an inexcusable spirit of compromise over fundamental values and principles. Given the distance separating the two sides, perhaps the October agreement had come on too fast, before Muslim opinion could be prepared for it.

Third, there seemed to be a desperate willingness to slide down the slippery slope to chaos, as a means of initiating a process of dangerous negotiation. Did the Hyderabad ruling class manoeuvre itself into a position in which it relinquished the initiative to the Muslim militants? Otherwise, how can it be explained that the forceful Nizam, an experienced and calculating ruler, seemed to be caught as helplessly as he appeared to be in this tangled web? Was it the purpose of his tactics to get rid of an embarrassing initiative? How did Delhi both sign the Standstill Agreement and allow the state Congress to escalate its active opposition beyond civil disobedience? And was the Hyderabad administration indecisive because it was weak or weak because it was indecisive? What was the driving force behind this series of steps that added up to a large miscalculation? It is easy to lay the blame on

Muslim extremism, shaped and directed by a handful of senior civil servants. But this sounds too much like a conspiracy theory: impossible to disprove, therefore gaining a spurious plausibility.

Qasim Razvi

I met Qasim Razvi for the first time in November 1947, just before the Standstill Agreement was signed between the newly independent India and the State of Hyderabad. We met in Nizamabad, where I was the additional collector. He had arrived there unannounced; it was when he called on the collector, Farooq Baig, that I was introduced to the Majlis leader. Besides the collector and myself, the DSP and some local Razakars were also present. After tea, we gathered informally around a table for a discussion.

I had seen him before, but this was my first opportunity to talk with him in person. He was a small man, short and very thin, with sharp Arab features. A full beard added greatly to his personality. He was dressed simply but neatly. I had looked forward to meeting him, though I did not have a high opinion of him. But I knew him to be an able organizer, a man of iron will, and a very dangerous enemy. At the time, he was one of the two most important people in Hyderabad. But he looked ordinary enough at close quarters, except for his bright, piercing eyes.

I was familiar with his political views. Away from the public platform and in the company of a small group of well-informed civil servants, I wondered if he could be persuaded to acknowledge the hard realities then confronting Hyderabad.

As politely as we could, we plied him with questions. How could a Muslim minority, headed by a Muslim ruler, continue to dominate a vast and politically conscious Hindu majority in Hyderabad?

'The Nizams have ruled Hyderabad for over two hundred years in an unbroken line,' he began softly. 'The system must have some good in it if it has lasted two hundred years. Do you agree? And if it has some good, how shall we preserve the good parts?' He looked around. 'Or,' he added with an ironic smile, 'do you mean to give it all away?'

We clearly had a debater on our hands. Hyderabad was not the only difficult case, he continued. There was Kashmir, where a Hindu king ruled over an overwhelming Muslim majority.

We tried again. What did he think of Hyderabad granting responsible government and adopting the principle of majority representation?

'I see much to admire in Hindu social reform,' he declared. 'I freely admit they are more advanced educationally and more sophisticated politically, and better off economically. We rule, they own! It's a good arrangement, and they know it!' He smiled and continued:

'We Muslims rule, because we are more fit to rule!' He rapped the table with his knuckles for emphasis. While the Hindus had been subjected to centuries of alien domination, the Muslim experience of government, their martial character, convinced him of their superiority. He could foresee a time, he said, when Muslims would once again become the rulers of India. He dreamt of installing the Nizam as the ruler of Delhi, if only he would follow his advice!

Despite such talk, he could not quite mask his fear of the Nizam. He was obviously pleased with the Nizam's apparent helplessness, but he did not feel quite sure of himself. He tried to hide his unease by adopting a patronizing, blustering attitude, declaring that he would tolerate the Nizam only for the good of the people, and never let the people suffer for the ruler's sake. But soon he would be loudly protesting his loyalty to the Asif Jahi line.

Unbidden, he took up the issue of Hindu-Muslim relations again. For the poor Hindu in the countryside of provincial Hyderabad, he said, his Muslim neighbour, equally poor, equally powerless, was not the enemy. Engendering enmity resolved nothing.

'I am uncomfortable about this kind of talk, about Hindus and Muslims,' he said with emphasis, 'because it suggests that conflict between us is inevitable. Our experience in Hyderabad proves otherwise.

The incitement to violence is being introduced from outside; it does not answer the needs of the people.'

We did not want a speech on inter-communal harmony from him. We tried another tack. How could Hyderabad avoid accession to the Indian Union? Could India accept the disintegration that might result if Hyderabad stayed out?

'India is a geographical notion. Hyderabad is a political reality. Are we prepared to sacrifice the reality of Hyderabad for the idea of India?' he asked. 'What do they have to fear from an independent and friendly Hyderabad? Our government has been negotiating with them, not with Pakistan. Still they threaten us, thinking they can scare us, and by making an example of us, deter anyone else who dares to think of freedom. It is ironic that the champions of freedom in Delhi appreciate so little that same aspiration in others!'

By now he was in full flow, and we were all swept along in a flood of rhetoric. The Indian government could not afford to take on Hyderabad, he continued. India was preoccupied with Kashmir; we had our army, led by the splendid General El Edroos. And no one, he assured us, understood the Government of India better than Qasim Razvi. No one had spoken to Sardar Vallabbhai Patel the way he had during his recent visit to Delhi. From what I could understand, he had offered the Indian home minister both peace and war.

He chewed paan almost constantly, and smoked cigarettes. While speaking, he had the habit of gazing deep into one's eyes. But when he was addressed in turn, he would shift his gaze and pointedly look away. He did not interrupt as a rule, and only turned those eyes of his towards the speaker when he disagreed and wished to say something. At other times, he sat quietly and seemed to pay attention. He could lose himself in talk, and a distant look would creep over his features, as if he were in a reverie. At other times, he would throw his body into dramatic poses and jerk and wave his arms about. When his notions were challenged, he would look away, smiling and compressing his lips. From time to time, he would lift up his beard with his left hand until it covered his mouth.

It was getting dark. The gathering broke off briefly for evening prayers, most of the group joining him in worship. Then we resumed our exchange. What could we expect from a Standstill Agreement, we asked him; how would we negotiate with India, and on what points?

'Negotiate?' he said with distaste. 'I haggle at the market, certainly, when I buy mangoes or onions! But principles cannot be bought; rights cannot be traded! We have an identity that we want to preserve; we have a sense of freedom that we cherish and cannot easily give up. Is that so hard to understand? On the other hand we have interests on which we are prepared to deal: on matters of trade, for example, on taxes and custom duties and on other administrative arrangements; on such matters it is always possible to negotiate. Why do they not understand?'

After lighting a cigarette, he continued, 'We must use the time under a standstill to reason with them, but always from a position of strength. A position of strength is something they have no difficulty in understanding. That is why the Razakars are necessary! We have a strong case in law; we have inalienable rights; we have powerful allies! We must put our trust in Allah, and show that we are prepared to resist!'

I came back from the meeting frustrated rather than inspired. Qasim Razvi's personality was certainly arresting, but not his philosophy. He had been civil to us at the meeting, but there had been no true exchange of ideas; he had directed an unstoppable barrage of words at us, but there had been no dialogue. I thought he was mistaken on the viability of Muslim rule in Hyderabad. It was absurd to extol Muslim superiority or to denigrate the Hindu majority. He was unrealistic in the assessment of Hyderabad's military might, or his own diplomatic skills vis-à-vis the pragmatic Sardar Patel, who was not one to be swayed by emotional appeals to legal or historical precedents. The views that he had shared with us that day certainly existed in Hyderabad's Muslim society of the time, but they represented its lowest common denominator. If these ideas represented some sort of extremist ideology for public consumption, it was disappointing that he had not shared with us his own assessment. Could they possibly represent his deepest, innermost thoughts? Or was it just his initial bid, at the beginning of the year-long Standstill Agreement, aimed at negotiating the best terms possible for Hyderabad, by starting high?

At the moment, he seemed more inclined to resist than to concede. Could such a strategy work?

It seemed bizarre that this little man, both absurd and frightening, should be able to make his way to a position of mastery over Hyderabad. I was by no means alone in seeing through the pretensions of the Ittehad leader. Barring a few extremists, the majority in the civil service were highly skeptical of his leadership qualities and had reservations about his influence on the administration. But we existed on a different plane, and had no taste for politics.

ꕥ

Qasim Razvi was a small-time lawyer from Latur in Osmanabad district, a town known as a commercial centre for cotton, and linked to the rest of the world by the Barsi Light Railway. He graduated in law from Aligarh and, after a short apprenticeship with the late Mohammad Ali Fazil in Hyderabad, settled down in Latur. The town had attracted him for a variety of reasons: It was economically vibrant as the commercial hub of the region; and he had contacts there, established through his father-in-law, Abdul Hai, ex-DSP, who used to be the inspector of police there. It offered other possibilities too, as Latur was not known for its adherence to law and order. As a wide, open town, it held an attraction for those who liked fishing in troubled waters. A notorious gangster, Ishaq, had also made his home there.

My impression of Qasim Razvi was far from edifying. I was therefore surprised at the earlier reference made to him as 'Siddique-e-Deccan', after a dramatic and well-publicized offer of all his property to the cause of the Majlis. I had thought it blasphemous to compare him with Hazrat Abu Bakar Siddique, the first Caliph of Islam, and to recognize with such public acclaim the act of a man who, according to reports that were current about him, had amassed a fortune in shady dealings. I once spoke to Nawab Bahadur Yar Jung about this when he visited Nanded in 1943. The Nawab had assured me that Qasim Razvi had changed after joining the Majlis. I noted that he said Qasim Razvi had changed; he did not deny his past.

When Bahadur Yar Jung died suddenly and prematurely in 1944, it did not take Qasim Razvi long to emerge as a contender for the leadership of the Majlis. He was the most determined of the Muslim politicians in Hyderabad. I have not forgotten one occasion when (in order to outflank Maulvi Abul Hasan Syed Ali, the Majlis leader) Qasim Razvi suggested responsible government for Hyderabad. His Muslim audience, aflame with narrow communalism, tried to hoot him down. He stood defiantly at the microphone: They could try to cast him off, he cried, but he would stick to them like a leech! He had a powerful hold on the Muslims of Hyderabad, and he knew it. Maulvi Abul Hasan Syed Ali was followed by Mowlana Mazher Ali Kamil; then, Qasim Razvi assumed the leadership of the Majlis-e-Ittehad-Ul-Muslimeen.

However, his ascendancy cannot be seen as some sort of exercise of the will to power; the explanation is more complicated. He did not possess the charisma of a Bahadur Yar Jung; it was not a superior quality of the mind or spirit, nor a record of service to the cause of his people or that of Islam. He had none of the loftier credentials for leadership. What he had was tenacity and grit, and great good timing: he was essentially a politician.

Even that does not quite explain his rise. I think he was the man of the moment, who in some indefinable way touched the dream-life of the Muslims of Hyderabad. At a time of uncertainty and change, he had managed to tap into their psyche. It was his blustering talk – all promises and threats and ridicule – that the ordinary Muslim citizens of Hyderabad wanted to hear, no matter how disconnected from reality it might be. In return, they supported him, while accepting, even delighting, in his shortcomings. A popular comment at the time summed it up: 'What if Qasim Razvi is an inexperienced leader, untested in the affairs of state? What if he turns out to be a scoundrel? These are no times for a saint!' To blame Qasim Razvi for the tragedy of Hyderabad, therefore, is to miss the point: he did not lead Hyderabad astray; the people chose him for the job, fully aware of his political inclinations and his shortcomings, as the individual most likely to reflect their hopes and fears. Now, thrust to the top, he was about to dictate the shape of the government.

ഌര

The Standstill Agreement witnessed the departure of the Nawab of Chattari, and Sir Mehdi Yar Jung assumed the office of prime minister for a short while (1 November to 28 November 1947). Qasim Razvi actually wanted Gulam Mohammed, finance minister of Pakistan (and formerly finance secretary in Hyderabad) to be the president of the council, but he could not be spared by Mohammad Ali Jinnah. Therefore, he suggested three names to the Nizam: General El Edroos, commander-in-chief of the army; Nawab Deen Yar Jung Bahadur, director general of police; and Mir Laiq Ali, a prominent industrialist of Hyderabad. The Nizam selected Laiq Ali because, among other things, he was not the holder of a key post in the government, like the other two nominees. Laiq Ali had good contacts with the Hindu business community, and was not affiliated to any political party. Qasim Razvi was happy with this choice. The Razakar leader was now the maker of ministries.

Laiq Ali, a civil engineer by training, had enjoyed a successful career as an industrialist. He had contacts with M.A. Jinnah; as a matter of fact, Jinnah wanted him in Pakistan. He was, however, spared to Hyderabad for one year. Laiq Ali was never known as a politician and did not have any great experience in administration. But people thought that he would bring his sound common sense and business acumen to his new job and strike a favourable bargain under the Standstill Agreement. He was certainly more acceptable to the Majlis and other Muslim leaders than anyone else at the time. As a popular industrialist he had a good many Hindu friends in big business and outside it. The brain behind Laiq Ali's political activities was supposed to be Nawab Moin Nawaz Jung, a senior civil servant, who had worked all his life in the finance department of the government of Hyderabad, serving under men such as Sir Akbar Hydari and Gulam Mohammed. The two also had a family connection: Moin Nawaz Jung was married to Laiq Ali's sister. Following the Standstill Agreement, Moin Nawaz Jung worked on his public image, but with indifferent results. He was certainly industrious, with a solid grounding in finance. He was also an able advocate of Hyderabad's case. There was no doubting his administrative and diplomatic skills, but he continued to be regarded as something of a political lightweight.

On assuming office, Laiq Ali made a balanced and moderate speech that was broadcast over Deccan Radio. He expressed the hope that the Government of India would be able to appreciate Hyderabad's point of view; that having a sovereign state of Hyderabad as an ally would prove to be infinitely better than making the state accede under pressure; that with due regard to the special circumstances in existence in the state, it should be possible to present a modified constitution that would be acceptable to most of the people of Hyderabad. Laiq Ali did not say anything that was very new or very startling, but his was a new voice speaking in a conciliatory tone. Therefore, for a while, things seemed to be moving in the right direction.

After my meeting with Qasim Razvi in Nizamabad, I had grown despondent about the future of Hyderabad. But now with Laiq Ali at the helm of affairs, we hoped things would get moving in the right direction. He began well by releasing the Congress political prisoners. A lot also depended on the selection of his ministry. Some time passed before the new council of ministers was announced, in December 1947.

My opinion of the new ministers may be of interest.

1. Pingal Venkat Rama Reddy was nominated by HEH. He was to be the vice-president of the council of ministers. A man with vast experience in zamindari affairs, but by now in failing health. He belonged to a fast-vanishing generation, out of touch with the times and unsuited to hold the office of deputy prime minister, for which a vigorous constitution and bold leadership was required – qualities he could neither muster nor develop at this late stage of his life. He was mild of manner and unlikely to assert himself; it was said that even junior officers in his service could get round him. But he was undeniably a decent and upright man.
2. B.S. Venkat Rao, minister of education, was the representative of the depressed classes. He knew little and did less. I did not like him for his obvious eagerness for power, which doomed him to exploitation.
3. G. Ramachar (representative of the Congress Right, assigned the Commerce and Industries portfolio) was an elderly Congressman

who desired an amicable settlement of the Hyderabad question. His importance lay more in his party affiliation than in his own person. But the connection with his party had grown rather tenuous. He therefore did not seem destined to play a very important role in the new government. He was soon replaced by P.V. Joshi, a businessman of some influence, both in the state and the world beyond. But Joshi had no administrative experience, nor experience outside the limits of his profession. Times were hard and, in my estimation, the job would prove too much for him.

4. Mulkarajan Appa, representative of a religious group, the Lingayats, was assigned the Public Health portfolio. From his prim and upright deportment it was difficult to guess that he in fact possessed an open, inquisitive mind. He could have grown into his job, given the time. But there was no time. In this whirlpool, I felt that his little boat would most likely flounder.
5. Mohammed Abdul Rahim (Railway and Communications) was something of an enigma. He was supposed to be the best of the four Majlis members, but that remained to be seen. One thing I can say of him: he had caused many a headache in the past.
6. Abdul Raoof was supposed to be the second best of the Majlis lot, but he seemed incapable of rising to the occasion. I thought he spent more time and energy on trying to look dignified and projecting an impressive image, than on preparing for the task of office as minister for public works.
7. 'Who is Ikramullah?' was the question on everyone's lips. Those few who knew him did not hold him in high esteem: a man of small stature in every sense of the word. But he was said to have great influence over Qasim Razvi. That might have helped in advancing his political career, but how would preferment translate into statesmanship? Mohammed Ikramullah was conferred the planning and development portfolio.
8. Then there was Yamin Zubairi, the fourth Majlis member who was assigned the portfolio of local government and labour. He had a very bad reputation, and his inclusion reflected poorly on Laiq Ali and his ministry. When I was a judge in the city courts, I had actually turned Yamin Zubairi out of my house once, together

with Rais (editor of *Waqt*), when they had tried to prevail on me in an act of injustice. That incident, though, had obviously taught him a lesson, and thereafter I found him quite straightforward in his dealings with me. He too could be made to improve – but our council of ministers could hardly function as a reformatory.

There were some civil servants included in the cabinet. Here is my impression of them:

9. Nawab Fazal Nawaz Jung (Revenue) was a capable and learned man with a strong inclination towards cooperation. He was certainly a constructive force. To his efforts goes the credit of organizing the Supply Department of Hyderabad. But he lacked wide administrative experience.
10. Abdul Hameed Khan was a very fine type, a thorough gentleman, honest and even pious; most suited for the ecclesiastical department. He was a complete misfit, however, in the council of ministers, especially as minister of police and customs.
11. Raj Mohan Lal had spent all his life in the judiciary and was now awarded the judicial portfolio. He was a fine type, generous of disposition and broad minded in outlook. But he too was not in a position to provide effective leadership or to substantially influence the direction of events.
12. Nawab Moin Nawaz Jung remained a close associate of the prime minister. He was appointed minister of finance and external relations.

The new cabinet was not inspiring, to say the least. It was put together in order to represent different interests, and it was doubtful if it could act as a coherent team. It was difficult to see what vision of the future it could offer, or what promise of deliverance it could hold out. Still, Laiq Ali inspired confidence. I thought he would either steer us through or resign; I did not think we would have to wait very long to find out.

I was sorry to note that the council had been deprived of the services of several brilliant and open-minded men. They were pushed aside as traitors, or other insinuations were made about them. Of these persons I knew a few, and I can say that each one of them was better than most of the new ministers put together. But we were given to understand that they were often consulted by Laiq Ali. That at least was gratifying.

Clearly a lot depended on Laiq Ali's untried leadership skills. One question in particular troubled my mind: would Laiq Ali be a match for Qasim Razvi? I had my doubts. Would he at least be able to guide him? Again, it was doubtful that Qasim Razvi would ever accept advice of any sort, from any quarter. And which Qasim Razvi were we talking about anyway? The hopeless romantic, who dreamt of the Asif Jahi flag fluttering from the ramparts of the Red Fort in Delhi, or the rabid patriot who thought that only Muslims were fit to rule, or the vengeful politician who brooked no opposition? These thoughts accompanied me as I went about my work in Nizamabad. I took a field trip in the region of Nizam Sagar. A few days outside the office, among the simple villagers, in the company of my family, attending to a variety of agricultural and health projects, proved somewhat refreshing.

Collector of Osmanabad

Not long after the Laiq Ali ministry was announced, I met the revenue minister, Fazal Nawaz Jung, and asked him for the collectorship of one of the more difficult districts. I was due for a promotion at this time.

Fazal Nawaz Jung seemed pleased with my spirit. But he would not commit himself until I had obtained the approval of the IG of police, Nawab Deen Yar Jung Bahadur, my father-in-law. At that time, Nawab Deen Yar Jung was reckoned to be one of the most powerful men in Hyderabad.

When I chose to talk to my father-in-law about this, he was getting ready for his morning audience with the Nizam at King Kothi. As I stood outside his dressing room, I could tell by the tone of his voice that he was not pleased.

He was one of those people, highly intelligent and quick-witted, who are also laconic: you expect a longer reply but get instead a terse response, that gives you the uneasy feeling that the speaker is several steps ahead in his reasoning. It was a struggle to keep up.

I did not have to go, he said from inside, I could be usefully employed in Hyderabad. I decided to be equally direct. I said I wished to find employment outside his immediate influence. 'Strange,' he said, emerging from his dressing room, 'most people want safe havens these days.' He reminded me that I could easily obtain a deputy secretaryship in Hyderabad. In fact, the chief secretary, Syed Ahmed Razvi, had suggested a new post, created, I knew, with me in mind. It would put me in charge of border security, but I would be based in Hyderabad, near my father-in-law. I remained adamant. In the end, he agreed to let me have my way, and left for the palace.

From then on, things moved smoothly. With the IGP cooperating, Fazal Nawaz Jung was at his charming best. I could have my pick of the choicest trouble-spots. The selection soon narrowed down to two districts. When the minister pointed out that he was considering Mir Moazzam Hussain for Nalgonda, I had no hesitation in accepting Osmanabad.

Both my wife Zehra and I had been happy with my posting in Nizamabad. I liked the work, and we both enjoyed the quiet domesticity that it afforded us. After a day's work, we would go for walks in the countryside surrounding our modest home, across green fields, stopping to exchange greetings with the farm workers, who soon became our friends. I remember one day as we passed him by, an old farmer working in his field stood up and, shading his eyes with his hand, watched a plane, a Dakota of the Deccan Airways, wing its way across the sky. 'I see these planes, flying like birds. But there is one thing I do not understand,' he shook his head in puzzlement. 'When it gets smaller, what happens to the people inside?'

There was much to cherish about Nizamabad. Osmanabad, on the other hand, was not a family duty-station, given the law and order situation there. I could sense my wife's reluctance over the transfer; and she could sense my eagerness for it. Gracefully, she let me have my way, and moved to her parents' home, Aziz Bagh, in Hyderabad.

The happiest moments of my life, even as I write this in jail, are those spent in recollection of my work in Osmanabad, from my first day there, to that last and fateful day, Monday, 13 September 1948 when, for all practical purposes, I ceased to be a servant of the Government of Hyderabad.

Why did I go looking for trouble? I was thirty-three; I had learnt to stand on my own feet at an early age. I had passed the highly competitive Hyderabad Civil Service Exam in 1937, and was launched on a promising career. Like all good officers I was not averse to risk, and was looking for an opportunity to prove myself. I admired and respected Deen Yar Jung, but wanted to be known as something more than his son-in-law. I also believed that I could do a better job in Osmanabad than most others who could be sent there. Qasim Razvi had always tried to remain on good terms with Deen Yar Jung. I hoped to make him cooperate with me in keeping the Razakars in Osmanabad under control. I saw nothing wrong in using connections this way (but it is quite another matter to rely on them for obtaining preferment). On 5 January 1948, I took charge of Osmanabad district.

ꕥ

The district of Osmanabad, lying to the northwest of Hyderabad, was a hotch-potch of Diwani, Sarfekhas, Paigah and Jagir Elaqahs. Added to this pattern were the Indian enclaves of varying sizes and strategic importance. Barsi, a huge Indian enclave practically touched Osmanabad town and extended up to Tuljapur in the east, Yermala in the north and Nanaj in the south, cutting off Perenda and Kallam Taluks from Osmanabad at Yedsi. With the road blocked at Yedsi, the northwestern areas of Kallam and Perenda and the whole strip of land lying between Sendri and Nanaj would not remain within easy reach. On the main borders were Akalcot and Sholapur in the south; Maoha and Karmala Taluk in the west; and Jamked bordering on Perenda and practically touching the Bhum area in the northwest. It is not surprising that I felt hemmed in at Osmanabad.

My predecessor in Osmanabad, Farhatullah, was not present at the district headquarters to hand over charge to me. He had left under a cloud, suspected of collusion in Congress activities in the district. In fact, I was even asked to look into the matter.

But almost the first thing on the agenda was a meeting with the district magistrate of Sholapur, S.A. Ghatge. My briefing so far had concentrated heavily on the disruptive activities of the border camps, established just across from Osmanabad in the Sholapur district of Bombay. This was to be the main topic of discussion with S.A. Ghatge. Our meeting took place at Tamalwadi, 12 miles from Osmanabad on 6 January 1948. Ghatge was accompanied by the DSP of Sholapur, Superintendant Pant.[1]

As I started to brief them about the camps, Ghatge interrupted me, 'What border camps?' he asked blandly. I explained. There had been sixty-one cases of attacks in Osmanabad, launched from across the border. Innocent villagers, passers-by and customs officers were the target, along with damage inflicted on customs posts. A list of these raids prepared by the DSP Osmanabad, Abul Hasan, was provided to Ghatge.

However, Ghatge remained unconvinced. There were no such camps, he asserted; I had been misinformed. The terrorists were in fact discontented elements from our side who were fighting their own government; the Sholapur authorities could be of no assistance in the matter. Ghatge would not accept that they were taking shelter in his jurisdiction and operating from there.

I offered to go with him and identify the camps. The DSP Osmanabad too was eager to assist us. But Ghatge would only suggest that we consolidate our respective positions, preserve internal security, and devise ways of protecting ourselves from external aggression. This amounted to saying, 'You look after your shop, and I'll look after mine.' I was offering to cooperate, and he was clearly temporizing. I therefore thought I would be more specific, and proceeded to make three suggestions: joint control of some strategic positions; the pooling of resources to check border activities; and a joint tour of border areas. He became evasive at this; he would have to consult the provincial government before he would agree to the first two proposals, he said, and of course he was too busy to go on any joint tour of the border areas. Politely, all my suggestions were turned down.

On his part, the district magistrate wanted a lorry that had been taken by a group of Muslim fanatics, the Deendars. The return of the lorry was arranged and the district magistrate informed. There were some minor complaints about the behaviour of customs staff towards the cartmen of the Indian enclaves. These matters were also attended to. There were no other serious complaints made from his side. It seems surprising in retrospect that the Razakars were not mentioned in our conversation. In fact, they remained out of the picture until much later.

After the meeting, I decided to give the question of border raids high priority. If I was not going to obtain cooperation from my counterparts in Bombay, the law and order situation was in danger of deteriorating further. I immediately undertook an intensive tour of border villages, first around Barsi and then along the remaining frontiers of the district.

During my tour, I tried to establish close contact with the locals. I have always enjoyed this type of interaction and I quickly acquired a genuine feeling of affection and admiration for the people I met in the outlying areas of the district. Contact with them energized me, and enabled me to spend long hours each day, travelling, meeting local officers and citizens, gathering information and forming impressions.

It was clear almost immediately that the raids were a cause of concern among the inhabitants, also affecting the morale of the local administration. There seemed to be a general loss of nerve in the district. The administrative structure was beginning to totter. Corruption was rampant. Razakars, Deendars, Arabs and Pathan irregulars were taking advantage of these conditions whenever they could. Police high-handedness or 'zulum' is a regular feature of village life, but now life was rapidly becoming intolerable for the majority of the people in the district. A sense of ceaseless menace pervaded the atmosphere. Communal feeling was rapidly reaching flash point. These conditions were attracting undesirable groups from elsewhere in Hyderabad. Clearly, something had to be done.

Rapidly, different parts of a coherent strategy fell into place. First, I dealt with the most obvious internal threat to our Hindu population. A batch of fanatical Muslims, calling themselves the Deendars, had moved into Osmanabad some time before my arrival there. The local authorities had thought of using them as a deterrent force against border raids. The district magistrate of Sholapur had complained of their activities. The lorry mentioned by Ghatge actually belonged to a toddy contractor from Sholapur and had been forcibly taken by them. I decided that the Deendars should be removed from the district at once. They did not have a large following as yet; they could be expelled without much effort and it would discourage other groups bent on mischief. More important, it would begin to restore confidence among the Hindus.

The Hindu population of the district was very demoralized. It had got to the point where Hindus were even harassed by little Muslim children. Perhaps their greatest fear at this time was of retaliation from the border camps, which would escalate the petty persecution into something worse. The local Hindus were unanimous in their condemnation of the camps. They were especially bitter about the leaders who had slipped away to Sholapur and, by their activities, were making life miserable for other Hindus who had stayed back in the district. Getting rid of the Deendars was the first priority.

As the second part of my strategy, I decided to restore to the people the arms that had been indiscriminately confiscated from them before I took charge, so that they could once again protect themselves from armed raids. The idea was to promote deterrence and build morale, rather than provoke an upswing in the conflict.

The worst thing for a demoralized people is the feeling of helplessness that comes from becoming the passive objects of attack. In such circumstances, any sort of activity is better than doing nothing. To overcome this feeling of helplessness, we decided to establish 'Civil Centres'. This was the third part of the strategy. Local people were encouraged to get together and be vigilant and prepared to repel attacks. The district administration also actively helped in setting up the centres and advising local people to come together for mutual assurance and self-defence. They were given basic training in constructing defensive earthworks, setting up a system of nightly watches, and issued with lathis (wooden staves), among other things. These were purely defensive measures, more effective in building morale than turning these folk into fighting machines. Similarly, most of the firearms restored to the villagers were old pieces, including antique flintlocks. We took care that they went to reliable people, who were encouraged to join the civil centres, which they did readily.

The fourth part of my strategy grew out of the first three decisions: it was to take away the initiative from the raiders. I needed an acceptable way of hitting back. It occurred to me that I could confiscate the property of known lawbreakers. For the moment, I held back from taking this step, but it was becoming clear that I needed to dramatically deny the initiative to the raiders. Confiscation would show, in a very open and public fashion, that there was a price to pay for mischief. This strategy – when it was eventually put into effect – worked surprisingly well: almost too well, as it turned out.

I had already come home after an extensive tour of the interior and border villages when reports came in of an attack on a police station at Chakur in the Paigah area. Searches were carried out in several villages for the arms that were taken away by the raiders. Killari was one of the villages searched. We had just returned to the rest house in Umerga when an informant conveyed to me that the circle inspector, the inspector of police, a jamedar and several constables were responsible for a recent incident involving loot. They were also responsible for aiding the escape of one of the persons involved in the Chakur case, after taking bribes. This had happed on the eve of the Killari search, on 20 January 1948. I seized the chance. I made preliminary inquiries: there was sufficient evidence to move against the policemen. I issued orders of suspension and initiated a formal inquiry. This action demonstrated that I was being even-handed in my actions, and not in any way protecting the administration when it was in the wrong. As I have mentioned before, the administrative structures badly needed a strong dose of discipline. This was the fifth part of my strategy. The sixth and final part of my strategy was to keep the Razakars in check. In my first weeks in Osmanabad I had no occasion to put those ideas into practice. And I did not yet see, in those early days, what a menace the Pathan irregulars were turning out to be.

This is how I began my life in Osmanabad.

Note

1. The name of the DSP accompanying Mr Ghatge is recorded in M. Hyder's diary as Mugwo; it is possible that DSP Pant was replaced by DSP Mugwo.

Border Camps

With the approach of independence, the Hyderabad State Congress decided to step up agitation against the Hyderabad government in order to expedite union with India. Starting with Satyagraha, this movement gradually became violent. Its leaders left the state in order to carry out the struggle from the other side of the border. It was not clear at the time how the Congress leadership in Delhi reconciled this initiative with the Standstill Agreement, whose provisions excluded hostile action by either side while the agreement was in effect. Here it is not proposed to give a comprehensive review of this unexpected development in the history of the Indian National Congress but only present my personal account of it, and of its effects in the district of Osmanabad.

I attribute this lurch into violence to the fact that the Hyderabad State Congress was utterly frustrated in its efforts to play a constructive role within the Hyderabad state, though it could claim to enjoy the support of a clear majority of the population. It was, in my view, due to errors on both sides. On one hand, the shortsighted Hyderabad leadership failed to educate people of the political realities of post-independence India, banned the State Congress Party for great periods of time, and was keener to persecute it than to understand it. On the other hand, the State Congress itself was inept, poorly-led for the most part, prone to mistakes and ill-judged decisions, such as non-participation in the 1946 Hyderabad state elections, and had an unfortunate tendency to forge alliances with extremist parties. These weaknesses fed upon each other, and contributed to the decision to lead a campaign of violence and terror. However, my purpose here is not to go into the causes, but to present a first-hand account of what I know of this campaign.

The State Congress Party and its allies, having gone into exile, established a series of clandestine encampments along the borders of the Hyderabad state in order to harass its civil administration and terrorize the population of its border districts. The objective was to paralyze the administration, provoke a popular uprising against it, and in turn hasten the annexation of the Hyderabad state. Despite inflicting much damage, it was unable to provoke a general insurrection in Hyderabad, and the administration functioned effectively until the last day. In my own case, I left my headquarters after the Indian Army started shelling around it and after the Indian Army, not any one else, had cut off all lines of communication and almost all lines of retreat. I was able to carry out all my duties as the administrative head of Osmanabad district to the last day.

It is important to note that not all border camps were run by Congress volunteers. Only the ones working under the direct supervision of the Congress president of Osmanabad, Phool Chand Gandhi, could be called Congress camps. There were others, mainly belonging to the Kisan Mazdoor Group that owed no allegiance to Phool Chand Gandhi or the Congress party. These were either independent or under the nominal supervision of Narasinga Rao Vakil, and the actual supervision of his notorious lieutenant, Datoba Bhosla Matola.

I will now identify a few important border camps and try to recall from memory the names of some of the more important volunteers in each of them. Some of these workers have now attained positions of eminence in Hyderabad public life.

First, here are a few of the more important camps working under the direct supervision of the Congress president of Osmanabad. It is interesting to observe that some important workers were common to several camps.

CAMP	WORKERS
1. Chincholi camp	1. Raghavender Rao Dewan
	2. Chander Shekar

	3. Sesh Rao Vakil
	4. Captain Joshi
	5. Nosaji Ishwanta
2. Gond Gaon Camp	1. Baba Saheb Paranjpe
	2. Ram Bhao Chilwandikar
	3. Manohar Tapray
	4. Malkhrey
3. Chara Camp	Under camp No 1
4. Kowd- Gaon Camp	Under camp No 2

Chincholi and Gond Gaon were the major camps in the area, with a large following of 700 and 500 volunteers, respectively.

5. Wagholi Camp	1. Rajender Desmukh
	2. Vasant Rao Desmukh[1]
6. Darphal camp	Vithal Rao Patel of Jan Gaon
7. Khandvi camp	Raghavender Rao Dewan
8. Yedsi camp	Vishunath Appa Sholapuri
	Vishunath Thailu of Dhoki

CAMPS IN AKALKOT AREA

9. Wagdheri camp	Vishamber Rao Haralker
10. Musti camp	Nana Rao Vakil
	Bali Ram Patel of Lohara
	Shri Navas Ahankari
11. Kaisar Jaivalga	Vishamber Rao Hiralker
	Shri Rang of Wan Wadi

Besides these eleven camps, there was an important mobile camp, or group operating mainly on the Barsi Light Railway. Many people, including some very respectable businessmen, had suffered great humiliation at the hands of this mobile group, while many were ruthlessly murdered, even after parting with large sums of money.

Duleepji Bhai and Kander of Latur had to extricate themselves from the clutches of these ruffians after parting with Rs 10,000 and Rs 12,000, respectively. A certain Prithiviraj was treated similarly. These mobile groups consisted mainly of Chincholi camp workers.

The members of the Chincholi camp once raided Wadgaon in broad daylight. Chander Shekar, Sesh Rao and Raghavender Rao

Dewan led these attacks and killed three innocent villagers in Sailgaon and three customs guards on duty at Wadgaon. The same group was reported to have attacked Badgaon and Bhanasgaon and killed three men and driven away all the Muslims from the village. I was informed that at Ajnan Gaon, it was Chandra Shekar, Ram Bhas Chilwadikar, Malakhery and Manohar Tapray who brutally put to death seventeen Muslim villagers. They also killed ten men at Manegaon and seven at Masla. The Musti camp raiders were reported to have killed twenty-two Muslim villagers at Nandgaon. Even Hindu villagers who did not heed to their demands were done to death, as in the case of Manik Rao Patel of Chawrakhali and Yado of Rui, and many other Patels and Patwaris who refused to cooperate with the raiders.

I cannot possibly forget an old school teacher of Thair village who came to me terribly injured to narrate his story. He had been stabbed in the abdomen and stamped on until his guts spilled out. He arrived in Osmanabad in that state and died shortly afterwards. The perpetrators were Vasant and Rajindar of Waghli, a camp notorious for the brutality of its members. It was the Waghli camp members who attacked people of Sanga village and killed two or three Muslim villagers. The Patel of Bad-ki-Wadi still relates with horror the attack on his village by Seshrao of Nelanga, Pandhari and Vaijnath of Murud along with many others. But of all these terrorists, the men of the Chincholi, Goudgaon and Yedsi camps were the most ruthless killers. They have been responsible for the merciless slaying of hundreds of innocent people.

In recounting some of the incidents, I have already rushed ahead of the narrative. I have yet to say a few words here about the non-Congress camps.

CAMPS	WORKERS
1. Kajla camp	1. Morathi Rao Babuji Rao
	2. Yado of Kharosa
	3. Pandhari of Lanjana
2. Upla camp	Manik Rao Patwari of Warodh
3. Javla camp	Venkat Rao Patel of Lasna
4. Tadola camp	1. Hari Har Rao Patel of Shahpur
	2. Vasant Kulkarni

5. Katey Gaon camp	Vital Rao of Therkheda
6. Sendri camp	1. Udhev Rao Vakil of Irla 2. Bhao Rao Patel of Bopla 3. Nanba Patel of Irla

The Yedsi Congress camp under Vishunath Appa was later removed to Javla and there were many tiffs reported between the rival groups.

Of all these non-Congress camps, organized mainly by the Kerth Kari Kamgar Paksh or the Kisan Mazdoor Group, the Kajla and Tadola camps were by far the most important. Kajla had no less than a thousand members.

The Kisan Mazdoor Group was primarily interested in collecting money. There was only one incident when the Kajla group allegedly killed a total of seven Muslims, all in one day, in a series of attacks at Takli, Borekhed and Boregaon. Apart from this raid, there were no other reports of murder by these groups.

One member of the Kisan Mazdoor Group, Datoba Bhonsle, had become a regular menace in areas adjoining Kajla, Tadola, and even in areas far into the interior. He was responsible for looting the army and Sasora levy, and making off with Rs 7,500, the total revenue collected from Sailu, Taluka Lohara. This took place near Ausa. He organized a successful attack on the treasury at Lohara too, from which government money was taken. It was his party that raided the Chakur police station in Umerga and relieved it of all the confiscated arms of the Umerga area. His daring day-and-night raids, made with the criminal's almost psychic ability to avoid armed border villagers, made him famous. He came to be known as 'Mathula Devil on horseback'.

Datoba Bhonsle was reputed to be a strong, cruel and daring Maratha who was an excellent horseman and could run like a hare. Several traps were set for him, but he always evaded capture. Once he created a sensation in the district by kidnapping a wealthy Marwadi, Savla Das of Irla. He buried Savla Das up to his neck and only let him go after extracting a promise to pay Datoba one lakh (100,000) rupees. Savla Das himself related this to me soon after escaping Datoba's clutches. [2]

There were many more camps about which I recall the odd detail or a particular act of violence. However, it is very painful to recollect some of the atrocities. I have forgotten many by actually willing myself to do so and am waiting to forget what I remember now once I unburden my mind here. Until then, I remain a walking library of the unspeakable.

I have provided sufficient evidence, I hope, to establish the existence of the border camps and their activities. Under these circumstances, it was all I could do to keep armed Muslims from taking revenge. I can challenge all concerned to give one instance of a Hindu dying at the hands of Muslims at any of the places in Osmanabad that were so ruthlessly attacked and where Muslims were brutally murdered.

There was no retaliation and no murder except one. Shankar Sonaji, the Patwari of Osmanabad, and his servant were attacked about this time, in which the servant lost his life. For some time, the police was unable to trace the murderer because the Patwari pretended to have no clue to the identity of the culprit. It later turned out that it was one of his own servants, and the whole affair was a result of some domestic conflict.

The raiders particularly targeted village officials such as Patels and Patwaris. Many cooperated with them under duress; however, those who did not, put their lives at risk. I hope I offend no sensibilities when I assert that the officers of the district of Sholapur knew about the camps and their activities. In any case, I kept them informed of all the attacks on our villages. And as I write this, an important worker of one of the camps tells me that Sholapur officers frequently visited the camps. No wonder then that my offer to go on joint border tours was so unceremoniously turned down.

ຣ໑ເຂ

The reader might ask: 'How do you know all this to be true?' I would have certainly not written with such assurance if I had to base my account purely on official and intelligence reports, which I used to receive when I was in charge of Osmanabad. I would have hesitated if my observations were based on the lengthy correspondence with the Sholapur authorities on these matters because I cannot reproduce our exchanges here. Perhaps I would have even doubted the frightful results of border raids that I saw with my own eyes, afraid that my memory was playing tricks on me. But now I have been thrown in jail with some of the confirmed border terrorists. They not only vouchsafe the truth of what I have written here but have often whispered to me, 'We were also in it!'

There is more proof. If there had been any secrecy about the border camps while they were in operation, their existence was openly acknowledged by the leaders of the movement in a series of statements to the press just after Police Action.

These revelations were probably actuated by anxiety to prove that it was not the Indian Army alone that had liberated Hyderabad, and that their long-suffering political movement had also contributed its share to the toppling of the Nizam's state. The Indian Army's Police Action against Hyderabad was very swift. It was led by General J.N. Chaudhury, who was in the limelight thereafter as the military governor of the state. The erstwhile freedom fighters were overshadowed by his fame. They also wanted to nip in the bud the rather mischievous accusation that they had run away from Hyderabad during its darkest days only to return after the Indian Army had smoothed the way before them!

In any case, the newspapers of the post-Police Action period make very interesting reading. Here are some extracts from the leading English daily from Hyderabad (italics added).

Meezan, 4 October 1948

Light on Congress Action Committee

Hyd, October 3

'It is the Hyderabad State Congress alone that is capable of shouldering the responsibility in the State' declared Swami Ramanand Tirth, President of the State Congress, addressing a news conference held this morning at the Central Office of the State Congress in Madina Bagh, the residence of Dr G.S. Melkote.

This is the first conference of its kind after the termination of the State Congress Struggle in Hyderabad and *pressmen representing local and outside papers and news agencies were invited.*

Not a Miracle

It was the persistent, incessant and tremendous efforts and suffering undergone by the people throughout the struggle covering a period of fourteen months that paved the way.

Light on Struggle: The Last Phase

Referring to the last phase which resulted in the Police Action by the Indian Union, Swami Ramanand Tirth said that the Committee of action to whose able guidance the success of the whole movement went, was able to steer clear of various difficult situations and that was why he deliberately and intentionally kept the Committee of Action outside the State. He added that no other strategy was possible under those circumstances, as it was difficult to work in Hyderabad. It was unfortunate that there was some misrepresentation of this position and some sections of the people had not appreciated it. The strategy has proved successful looking at the results. It was a tremendous victory of the democratic forces for the whole India.

In conclusion he asked the Pressmen to give a real picture of Hyderabad people's freedom movement in future.

The Swamiji then left the Conference and Ramachander Rao, member of the Congress Action Committee and in-charge of the publicity and propaganda, explained the various features of Hyderabad freedom struggle to the pressmen.

The people were once dreaming that the Nizam would accede to the Indian Union willingly but the State Congress knew that he would not accede. *The State Congress knew fully well that a non-violent movement could not succeed in Hyderabad where they had to contend with forces mentioned above.*

Mr RamachanderRao declared that the State Congress knew fully well that a non-violent movement could not succeed in Hyderabad. He made this statement without casting aspersions on the principle of non-violence.

Throwing further light on the struggle, the Congress President said that under the advice of the Committee of Action, about 12,000 people went to jail. It was not merely a question of filling the jails, but the whole countryside became a live volcano. Then followed the struggle. *They had asked the people to defend themselves at all costs and by any means.* The programme had to be shaped in a strategy in three stages with the ultimate aim of preparing the ground for marching of the Indian Union force into the state.

The Three Phases:

Explaining the three phases of the struggle, Mr Ramachander Rao said that in the first stage they sent out 9,000 volunteers into the state to conduct non-violent struggle and to court imprisonment for a period of three months. *The second phase of the struggle was stiffened with the object of destroying artificial barriers existing between Indian Union and Hyderabad, Viz, demolition of Customs Posts and cutting off toddy trees. A series of border camps were organized, especially in Madras and Bombay, where training was imparted to workers.* On a border of 1,500 miles, there were altogether 750 Customs Posts out of which 500 were smashed.

Continuing, he said that *the third and last phase of the struggle consisted of sabotage activities and dislocation of communications.* For this work he said, 3,000 cadets were fully trained and sent everywhere in the districts. According to him, village dals also organized eleven border camps (in the state) and the *workers were supplied with arms and ammunitions.* Socialists who are members of the Hyderabad State Congress had played their part in the struggle for freedom and contributed their share equally.'

Similar reports appeared in the *Deccan Chronicle,* and even in the *Times of India.* What we have here then is a public acknowledgement by the highest officials of the Hyderabad State Congress Party, of participation in a movement dedicated to sabotage and violence, conducted against the State of Hyderabad and its people, carried out with impunity from across the border in India, at a time when Hyderabad and India were ostensibly at peace with each other, having solemnly undertaken a Standstill Agreement.

Notes

1. Vasanth Rao Desmukh, a volunteer of Wagholi Camp, was in the Osmanabad jail when I was sent there. He was old and ailing. He was a tall and broad-shouldered man with a slight stoop. He confirmed almost all the facts I have mentioned here about the various camps. After his arrest, Vasant Rao Desmukh became a nervous wreck and was prepared to do anything to secure his release. It is interesting that the new government regarded the very people we resisted as unsocial elements and had put them in jail, while prosecuting us for doing what they are doing now, namely maintaining law and order.

2. During my time in Osmanabad jail, I met Datoba. He was a solidly-built young man in his late twenties, fond of doing vigorous exercise. He used to boast of his ability to run very fast. He claimed that for short distances, he could keep up with a motorcar on the unpaved roads of Osmanabad. It was said that on many occasions he had unnerved motorists by performing this feat.

A Conference at Shah Manzil

There was a temporary lull in border activities after the assassination of Mahatma Gandhi on 31 January 1948. I took advantage of this respite to reinforce our vulnerable positions and to organize Civil Centres in the border villages.

Civil Centres were designed to help the exposed segments of our border population organize themselves against armed raids from across the border. They were meant not only to protect life and property against attacks, but also to build morale. We had some difficulty in organizing them effectively. Our arms position was far from satisfactory. We had only forty rifles in good condition in the district, sixteen .303 and twenty-four Martini Henry rifles. Sending poorly armed constables to guard border villages amounted to signing their death warrants. With great difficulty, I was able to hurry a few additional rifles to Osmanabad.

It seemed that I was just in time. When the raids resumed, these Civil Centres were made the main targets. They survived because by this time, trenches were dug at all Civil Centres and other simple precautions had been taken. It is remarkable how defensive positions can be maintained with a relatively modest force. This way, we probably saved many lives.

In the midst of renewed attacks, sometime in February 1948, a second meeting was arranged with A.S. Ghatge (the district magistrate of Sholapur) and his DSP. This too proved futile, as they would admit neither the existence nor the activities of the camps. On being pressed, they promised to hand over people we wanted in cases of murder and other extraditable offences. These promises were made but, I regret to say, never kept.

Even at this meeting there was no mention of Razakars, although we were getting unofficial reports of their activities in other districts. Though the Deendars had been driven out, the Sholapur district authorities had grievances against the minor customs and police officials, who did not behave well with the traffic to and from the enclaves. I could quite believe this; nor could I let it go unchecked, but I requested the Sholapur authorities to view it in the larger context. In not assuring them at once that our customs and police authorities would behave in future, I was motivated by two factors: Firstly, although I intended to check this kind of thing, I knew that under the circumstances it would be extremely difficult to prevent minor infractions. Secondly, I was getting tired of Ghatge's complete denial of atrocities of the freedom fighters. I wanted to give him a taste of his own medicine. I wish I could lay my hands on the correspondence that passed between us to show how things went from bad to worse, and to establish that until May or June 1948, no mention was made of the Razakars in his correspondence.

About this time, a statement from the public workers of Sholapur, expressing their satisfaction over the border situation on their side, appeared in the *Times of India.* I invited them to my district to study the border situation on this side. There was no response.

Nevertheless, our work continued. Malkarajan Appa, a member of the Laiq Ali council and resident of Osmanabad, visited the district and was greatly impressed with the efforts made by us to maintain law and order in the face of great provocation. He had gathered information about the border camps from his own sources, and I am sure, had passed it on to the government.

While I was doing my best to maintain law and order, the feeling had been growing in me that the Government of Hyderabad was not paying sufficient attention to the safety of the populations living in the border villages. As time passed, and with no settlement in sight, the feeling also grew in me that we were not quite up to defending ourselves against the armed might of India, should it ever decide to overrun us. We had a piecemeal response to the border raids, which included a role for the police, the army and the irregular forces. But how did it all come together? Did it amount to a clear strategy based on a well-articulated policy? Such thoughts were still formulating in my mind when the prime minister called a meeting at Shah Manzil.

Mir Laiq Ali, who had started well by releasing Congress workers from prison, ultimately failed to come to terms with the Congress Party. The Commerce Minister, G. Ramachar, resigned from the cabinet. People had started reverting to their ultimate loyalties, and were looking towards India or Pakistan, according to their ideologies. The Nizam remained out of the picture. Negotiations after the Standstill Agreement seemed to be getting nowhere. The rise and fall in the political barometer in Delhi had its effect on the affairs in Hyderabad, but it was the border camps, which always reacted most violently.

The conference was attended by almost the entire upper echelon of the Hyderabad government. Apart from the prime minister and the council of ministers, all government secretaries, heads of department, top officials of the army and the civil guard, and all the heads of the district were in attendance. Laiq Ali addressed this gathering in his usual quiet tone, and called for a frank exposition of administrative difficulties.

Baquer Hussain Qureshi, a district collector, made a particularly notable speech. His exposition of the difficulties experienced by the district officers seemed to impress the gathering. He elaborated on the various issues of an administrative nature that had arisen because of the unnecessary interference of the Ittehad leader in district affairs. He deprecated some of the Razakar activities and urged the government and the police department – particularly the director general of police – to put an end to it.

Many others, including Zainulabideen (another collector), addressed the gathering. Replying on behalf of the government, the director general of police, Nawab Deen Yar Jung made an admirable speech promising government help and cooperation in overcoming the specific difficulties raised. It was clear that the civil service continued to maintain a proper distance from the Razakar movement.

With the overview out of the way, the meeting quickly descended into the discussion of bureaucratic detail. Most of the complaints concerned petty administrative difficulties: this department not cooperating or that department not seeing eye-to-eye on matters of policy, and so on. I felt I was lucky in this at least. I had the healthy cooperation of all the departments in my district.

But I had come to the conference worried about one larger issue. What was the government's assessment of the border situation? How could we ensure the safety of the people there? Were we prepared to defend ourselves on the borders, even if it meant a clash with Indian forces? Was there a way to secure our borders without provoking a violent response? An insight into the government's stand on these issues was very important.

I spoke about this to Baquer Hussain Qureshi (the collector who had addressed the conference earlier) and Farooq Baig. During the break for lunch, I brought it up in my conversation with the deputy prime minister, P.V. Reddy. He seemed perplexed and rather vague. Nevertheless, he gave me sound advice, suggesting that I consult Nawab Moin Nawaz Jung (minister for finance and external affairs and a close associate of the prime minister). He said it was preferable to do this before raising my questions at the meeting.

I spoke next with Yamin Zubairi and Abdul Rahim (Ittehad members of the cabinet), before approaching Nawab Moin Nawaz Jung. Yamin Zubairi and Abdul Rahim both encouraged me to speak out and to press the government for a clarification. On his part, Nawab Moin Nawaz Jung seemed taken aback by my questions. He advised me not to raise such issues in the gathering. I could not very well understand what he meant; it was definitely a select gathering, taking place in closed session. Moreover, he wanted to know if there were others who felt like me, and why I felt as I did. I made it clear to him that I was speaking for myself and not for others, and that I felt I had a right to be aware of government policy because it had a bearing on my job.

Moin Nawaz Jung promised to consult the prime minister, and if he were agreeable, he would get a minister to satisfy my concerns. He also added that as far as he could see, Hyderabad was prepared to face any situation that might arise as a consequence of the stand that it had taken. And as regards the Nizam, he was keener than ever to do his share in maintaining the 'independent stand' that had been adopted, at most with certain modifications.

Even before the proceedings resumed after lunch, I was informed by Yamin Zubairi that Rahim had been requested by the prime minister to speak on the points raised by me.

It is an unwritten rule of all bureaucracies that subordinate officers do not raise awkward questions for their superiors, especially in public. A sound officer is one who gets on with his job and never rocks the boat. But I was not trying to act clever; these were grave matters that genuinely caused me concern, and others as well. But no one had raised them because they were afraid to do so. I would have hesitated too, if I had not been insulated somewhat by my connections. Nevertheless, I was clearly being requested not to raise those issues at the conference. I was assured at the same time that an arrangement would be made to address them.

When the meeting resumed after lunch, Rahim, the same person who had encouraged me to speak out not an hour ago now suggested the opposite: 'On the sidelines of this meeting,' he began, 'an issue has been raised that must be addressed right away. It concerns our state of readiness should our borders be encroached, should the negotiations fail, should an incursion take place.' There was nervous laughter at the way he put it, as if we had frightened ourselves by raising the spectre of unlikely fears.

'No, seriously,' he continued, 'I am glad this issue has been raised because it gives the government an opportunity to respond: do not baffle your minds with unwarranted apprehensions. The government relies on your unflinching loyalty to our beloved ruler and expects that you will stand firm, sure in the knowledge that you will receive the full support of the government...'

He carried on in this vein. Before his flood of rhetoric, my concern for the day-to-day insecurity that our people were actually experiencing on the borders was swept aside. There was no recognition of the untenable border situation, no clarification of the government's plans to defend our frontiers, or guidance on how to meet an incursion there. His address, strident and patronizing, did not carry conviction.

Rather, it seemed to me, his assurances had stirred the very fears they were meant to allay.

The sense of unease passed, and the conference moved to a close without further incident, having avoided the main issue. Our lack of preparedness was staring us in the face, but we had chosen to ignore it. I came back frustrated. I even thought of resigning from my position – but that offered no real solution. A day or two after the conference, however, I met Prime Minister Laiq Ali and was inspired with fresh confidence. I resolved to throw myself into my work with renewed dedication. .

On my way back to Osmanabad, I met Qasim Razvi at Umerga. He was returning to Hyderabad from a visit to Latur and Osmanabad. This was our second encounter. The meeting was quite accidental but it gave me a chance to raise with him an issue that was beginning to trouble me. I decided, on the spur of the moment, to be as direct as possible (perhaps I was still wound up from my frustrations at Shah Manzil).

'Sir,' I said, 'the Nizam's government has put me in charge of Osmanabad district, and I intend staying in absolute control as long as I am there. I am not going to tolerate any group that tries to disrupt law and order in my district. I have not hesitated to take action against the Razakars when they have misbehaved, and that is going to be my policy in future.'

His response surprised me.

'Well said, Talukdar Sahib! I want the Razakars to be an effective defence force: we don't have that. I want a disciplined body: we don't have that. All we have is a bad name: well, I don't want that! By God, I will hang the Razakars if they misbehave!'

He continued:

'They swear they are righteous warriors,' he shook his head sorrowfully. 'Maybe all Razakars are liars. But since I am myself a Razakar…' He smiled, pursuing the thought inwardly.

'Seriously,' he continued, 'I have staked my reputation on building up the Razakars, and I hate the false and malicious propaganda against them. But I want a clean movement, Hyder Sahib; I want to make it an all-party affair, and purge it of all unhealthy elements.'

I had nothing to do with his politics or the idea of converting the Razakar movement into an inter-communal affair. What appealed to me was his emphatic opposition to the troublemakers in his organization. Whether he meant what he said or not, I had at least made my own position clear. My spontaneous exchange with the political leader had gone much better than my careful demarche to my colleagues in government.

Reforms in Osmanabad: The Administration, the Irregulars and the Army

I am liable to give the impression that my struggle in Osmanabad was solely directed against the freedom fighters. However, this is far from true. I went to Osmanabad with a clear set of priorities: I had to first put my own house in order. I had to raise the efficiency of the civil administration, gain stricter control over the police and the irregular forces, check all anti-Hindu activities, reassure demoralized villagers, and obtain their cooperation. Only after all this was accomplished could I effectively deal with the border camp menace.

The administration showed all the signs of low morale. Some officers were corrupt; they openly took bribes and boasted of their indolence. Others indulged their assorted vices: drink, drugs, gambling and sex. Very few seemed to take pride in functioning efficiently and honestly. I took the first opportunity to turn on the pressure against the worst offenders. And not surprisingly, their resistance melted away at the first determined assault.

The early targets of the cleanup were the circle inspector of Umerga, Afsar Ali, and the inspector of police, Paigah Elaqa, together with some other corrupt police officials. Given their poor records, their dismissals were easily – but properly – obtained. Soon after that, I took action against the tahsildar of Lohara, for encouraging and indirectly participating in a case of loot. I was sorry to order criminal proceedings against him, but there was no way around it.

One unfortunate officer to fall prey to my cleanup was the tahsildar of Latur. He was an efficient worker, who was suspected of being corrupt and subject to certain other weaknesses, which actually struck me as inconsequential. But when I visited Latur, a host of people complained about him. He could not defend himself, and his immediate superior did not seem anxious to come to his rescue. I called for an open inquiry. Amir Ali Khan, a member of the revenue board, instituted the inquiry, and the tahsildar was demoted and transferred. Though I lost an otherwise efficient and experienced officer, my action in this matter seemed to shake others in the district administration out of their loose ways. The case was also significant because the officer in question was closely related to the revenue minister, Nawab Fazal Nawaz Jung, who grew in my esteem, and the esteem of the public, when he supported me against a member of his own family. Credit also goes to Abul Hassan, the district superintendent of police, without whose whole-hearted cooperation, my work would have been more difficult.

However, there were officers who were honest and decent workers, but unsuitable for my district because of their relative inexperience or nervous temperaments. Bajrang Pershad, for instance, was a young tahsildar, whose inexperience made him apprehensive of the turmoil in the district. He had become so unnerved that, in his anxiety he devised a letter in order to get away at any cost. My report about him was misunderstood, but I was able to get him transferred to a relatively safe district and no harm was done. I cautioned Bajrang Pershad as gently as I could and sent him on his way to his new posting at Jalna.

Apart from administrative services, we also had a contingent of irregulars, the Pathans. Meant to guard the border and to prevent raids, their numbers swelled gradually with the rise in border disturbances. There were only seven Pathans to start with, but eventually their number rose to a hundred and sixty. They were never let loose without supervision, but I have to admit that, ultimately, they did more harm than good. It took me some time to realize that they had become a public nuisance.

Pathans are Pashtun tribesmen from the North-West Frontier Province of Pakistan (NWFP) and adjacent parts of Afghanistan. Fierce, proud and wild, they are a breed apart. They look upon killing as a pastime. Excitable by temperament, they can be easily led into a scrap. They are bloody and cruel when aroused, and never afraid of anything or anybody. Fighting is in their blood, but discipline is alien to their nature, and keeping them out of trouble is almost impossible. For all their blue-grey clothing and made-up eyes, they can be incredibly brutal. The only way to handle them is to show them that you are just as tough as they are. It is no wonder then that I had problems controlling 160 of these volatile characters!

In Osmanabad, they refused to obey anyone but the head of the district; I had to look after them personally. This was probably a mistake, but I was not to know until much later. In any case, I had to exert myself to the utmost to keep them under control. If they misbehaved in spite of this, as I now understand they did, it was because I had my limitations. Under the supervision of anyone else in the district, they would probably have wreaked greater havoc. In any case, whenever instances of Pathan misbehaviour came to my knowledge, I took stern action.

When the village Dhakri in Osmanabad taluk was attacked by raiders and two young boys, aged seven and nine, were killed, and an old woman burnt to death, some of the Muslims retaliated by looting the homes of some of the Hindu villagers, who were suspected of secretly helping the raiders. The Pathan chief posted there failed to defend the village or protect its Hindu inhabitants from this retaliatory attack. When I came to know of this, I personally stripped him of his rifle and cartridge belt and sacked him on the spot. Considering that rifles are their obsession, disarming a Pathan fighter can have serious repercussions. The deputy director of police, Hameeduddin Rana, and the deputy director of customs, Qutubuddin, were with me on this fateful day and they were both surprised at the meekness with which the chief submitted himself to this monumental insult. There were several Pathans present; they went red in the face, but not one raised a finger.

In Parenda, there was a report of a Hindu employee of the Commercial Corporation being slapped by a Pathan. The Pathan was fined Rs 25 and the amount was handed over to the Hindu employee while the Pathan was subsequently removed from service. We were never lenient with them. Even a small affair like snatching a cake of soap from a Christian lad (reported to me by the Christian

Missionary in Osmanabad) was immediately attended to. I remember one or two instances of cattle rustling across the border. Although the cattle were probably strays, the culprits were punished and the cattle were driven back by the police. The Pathans were set in their ways, and I remember spending hours with them, trying in vain to put decent ideas into their heads.

Sitting here in jail now, I feel my greatest blunder in Osmanabad was to retain the Pathans for as long as I did. I think they had transformed themselves into clandestine gangs, Pathans with other Pathans, sometimes abetted by the police, such as the line inspector of police at Osmanabad. Working together, they succeeded in making much mischief without our knowledge. But I still feel that they were not able to do more harm because of our constant effort to manage them. If I had not taken over the responsibility of keeping them under control, they could have turned Osmanabad into a slaughterhouse. Nevertheless, the Pathans were a nuisance and it took me very long, about seven months to realize that it was absolutely useless to waste time on them. My eyes were finally opened, as I shall relate later, by Narayan Rao Vakil of Parenda.

Pathans were not the only nuisance in Osmanabad. Although there were some good men associated with them, the Razakars had a tendency to absorb the most undesirable elements of Hyderabad Muslim society, and to provide a channel for their troublemaking. The Pathans, those past masters of all mischief, found in the Razakars apt pupils, eager to emulate their actions.. Had the Pathans not been there, I feel the Razakaras would probably have done considerably less damage. But incited by border raids and convinced by their Pathan friends of the necessity of retaliation, the Razakars undoubtedly indulged in many lawless acts of violence. This is not to say that their acts were condoned by my administration. Of course, no government on earth has been able to devise means of checking sporadic acts of violence – and this is what their activity amounted to in my district.

In order to appreciate the difficulties that lay in the way of effectively dealing with the Razakars, the activities of the border camps have to be kept in mind too. As the incidence of border raids increased, it became difficult for us to find out, in many instances, who exactly was responsible for a certain act of violence. In this matter, the police were not always helpful. Often, other lawless elements found in the Razakars a convenient scapegoat for their own criminal acts: though the dividing line between criminals and Razakar louts was often rather blurred.

There was one other group of troublemakers that stood out because of its distinct ethnicity: the Arabs, who were always ready to do their share of hell-raising. Most of the Arabs in the districts were employed as guards in the District Treasury offices. There was some sort of check exercised on them, but many young Arabs came to Osmanabad from Hyderabad city, having heard of the opportunities the district could provide for lawless adventure. They were either friends or young relatives of the Arabs employed in the district. These elements were encouraged by local Razakars and inspired by the Pathans. This was probably true of all the districts to a greater or lesser degree. But in Osmanabad, the Pathans and the Deendars were certainly the most irresponsible elements who encouraged local Razakars or those among them who had a tendency to be misled. The unemployed Arab visitors and guests completed the unholy mix.

Though I was successful in banning the Deendars early on, I could not ban the Razakars. However, I made every effort to make it clear to the Razakar hierarchy, right up to Qasim Razvi, that I would not hesitate to deal sternly with them whenever they stepped out of line. Accordingly, I prosecuted Razakars when they broke the law. At various times, I put them under arrest: in Rajaisur, Latur and Osmanabad. Subsequently, they were tried and convicted. The Arabs of the State Bank of Latur and Tehsil Tuljapur were also apprehended, though in their case, the majority of arrests took place some time later. In all cases, when there was no direct evidence available, undesirable characters were held under the Defence of Hyderabad Rules, which were in operation; and I used them whenever there was a need to do so, in my judgement. The arrests are a matter of record, and the police and jail records will support what I state here. If I had received the cooperation of my counterparts across the border, we could have contained the freedom fighters too. Then, their provocation abating, we could have calmed the whole situation very effectively. But it was not to be. Incidentally, the last instance of a Razakar arrest was the case of the attempted murder of Bapu Rao Theli of Apsinga.

These explanations are not offered in the hope of establishing extenuating circumstances, but they certainly add to the complexity of the picture. The Razakar movement was the object of adverse propaganda by the Congress party, which painted it as vile and monstrous, often putting out false reports of Razakar atrocities, while remaining silent on the murderous activities of its own freedom fighters. In fact, the Razakars and the marauding freedom fighters existed in a state of adversarial symbiosis: each entity conjured up to fight the other, and likely to lose its reason for being if the other disappeared. Both were a threat to law and order. Nevertheless, the Razakars will probably go down in the history of this era as the unredeemed villains. I do not wish to contradict this judgement. And yet, how much more complicated the truth was!

ꕥ

There was one other body of men in Osmanabad – the Nizam's Army. In reality, the army was an empty shell. It was capable of coming to the aid of the civil power, and of maintaining order within the state; but it was not expected to stand up to India. To make its subordinate position clear, the British had historically garrisoned their forces inside Hyderabad. After 15 August 1947, the troops were not withdrawn, the new Indian government apparently being in no hurry to do so. There were other limitations. The army's overall size was restricted by agreement, and it had depended upon the Paramount Power for the supply and replenishment of arms and ammunition. During the Standstill Agreement, Hyderabad found it very difficult to restock its fighting forces. In short, the Hyderabad Army was neither designed, nor equipped nor trained to wage war against a modern force, let alone the great Indian Army. Now when our men were sent to the border districts, this reality hit them hard.

In my contacts with the army officers stationed in Osmanabad and elsewhere, I had the feeling that the very thought of military action of any sort unnerved our stalwarts. Perhaps the Hyderabad government's resolve to face all odds was a bluff, intended to strengthen its hand in the negotiation with India. But our forces were not privy to this pretence, and it went hard with them. I watched with interest two senior Hyderabad Army officers stationed in Osmanabad. One was the area commander who invariably succumbed to acute indigestion every time he received news of Indian Army movement in the neighbourhood. Even his subordinates made fun of him. The doctor who attended on him on one such occasion was thoroughly disgusted by his pathetic reaction to danger. On such occasions, he would curse his own high command and the Hyderabad government for sending him to the border area with such a small force of ill-equipped soldiers.

The other officer was a major in the Hyderabad Army, and by no means a novice. On one occasion, he came to me very disturbed, his face pale with fear, asking for help from the Pathan irregulars. He had just received reports of Indian Army concentration at Almi. In both cases, I made sure that Hyderabad was informed of the state of demoralization of these officers and both of them were transferred from Osmanabad.

There were, of course, able and gifted men in the army, though few and far between. One such was Lt Col Himayat Baig, a brave and intelligent officer who would have been an asset to any outfit. There were others like Lt Col Abidi and Lt Col Jafferi, who were fine officers, full of good sense and admired by their men. There were also excellent junior officers, such as Major Mohsin Ali, Major Ahmedullah, Major Qasim Hussain, Major Zakaullah and Major Dass. But the majority consisted of effete, pleasure-loving men, completely unfit for the profession of arms. They were enthusiasts after a carefree life, who had joined the army because other careers were closed to them. To be fair to them, it was not entirely their fault; they had received no real military training. And those who had any idea of modern warfare were nervous because they realized how ill-equipped the Hyderabad Army was, both in men and material.

The personality of General El Edroos, chief of the Hyderabad Armed Forces, served as a cover for the weakness of the army. The reputation of the general, his confident exterior and his apparent determination to fight, could not fail to impress anyone who met him, and most people formed their opinion of the Hyderabad Armed

Forces through their impression of the general. He was a large man with handsome features and a commanding presence. There is no doubt he inspired confidence. I had the opportunity to hear him address his area commanders once.

'Gentlemen,' he began, 'we shall not start the conflict, but when it comes we will not run away from it. We will not surrender. I don't want to hear of any soldier under your command being captured unless he is wounded. The only retreat I will tolerate is a tactical retreat, such as a withdrawal from one sector in order to attack at another. Stay and fight. I expect my officers to return to Hyderabad only to be buried there.'

He paused for effect, and continued:

'You know, I pity those poor Indian soldiers. We will make them regret picking a fight with us! Pay no attention to their superiority of numbers. Remember, the fortune of war favours the brave over the merely numerous. When the time comes, and the enemy is in sight, you will know what to do: You will hit and hit hard!'

It was splendid theatre. But did we really count on the Hyderabad Army to defend us? It would have been absurd to do so. But at that time, we thought it would never come to a fight. There was also the belief that with the secret shipments of arms from abroad we would soon be able to strengthen our military arm sufficiently to deter any thoughts of invasion. Others were convinced that Pakistan and other friendly states – but Pakistan definitely – would come to our aid in the event of an attack. Perhaps we allowed our hopes to cloud our judgement.

Nanaj and After

By June 1948, my worst fears were confirmed. It had become too risky for the Hyderabad Army to adopt a forward position in case it provoked a clash with the Indian forces, now gathering in strength around Hyderabad State. Without any assistance from the army in maintaining order, I could now only fall back on a pitiful police force supplemented by unreliable irregulars. The Hyderabad government still dithered, neither insisting that the military actively defend the border, nor properly reinforcing the civilian authority. With no clear direction from the centre, I struggled on both fronts – urging the army to keep peace, while also trying my best, with meager resources, to maintain order myself.

Ironically, by about June 1948, we had, to a great extent, gained control over the situation in Osmanabad. This is not to say that things were back to normal. But the administration's morale had been restored, and rising Muslim lawlessness checked. My campaign against border raids had gradually begun to pay off: some nerve was put back into the administration; fear of Muslim outrages against the Hindu community gradually subsided and the morale of the latter rose correspondingly. This rehabilitation effort needed to be shored up, with effective help from the armed forces. I counted on it.

Accounts of my work in Osmanabad, no doubt exaggerated, had made me something of a popular figure in Hyderabad – and number one villain on the other side of the border! I did not care for either estimate of my work. But the admiration of one party and the enmity of the other did me equal harm. My popularity in Hyderabad, especially in Razakar circles, conveyed the impression that I was a Razakar myself. The enmity I gained, especially that of Phool Chand Gandhi, the president of the Osmanabad Congress party, began to pay dividends after the 'Police Action'.

I did my best to present our administration in a good light and even made conciliatory overtures to pacify the freedom fighters across the border. At one point, I released about forty Congressmen from Osmanabad jail. Most of them were vakils (lawyers) and known to be politically active. They were entertained in my bungalow as my guests for a night and sent home the following morning. As most of them came from Umerga, which is about 60 miles from Osmanabad, they were provided with government transport and police escort for their journey home.

After undertaking to curb border activities, they promptly betrayed their promise, and were reported to be active participants in subsequent raids. Nana Rao Vakil of Umerga, for instance, organized the Masti Camp and was actively involved in planning large-scale attacks after his release. Nangaon was the target of one such well-organized and brutal raid, in which twenty-two Muslims were killed in a single day.

It was at this stage that I started confiscating the property of people involved in border camp activities. Though orders to this effect were in existence before I joined the district, their implementation was made out to be an unwarranted act of hostility on my part against members of the Congress party and other freedom fighters. They responded with all sorts of propaganda, depicting me as an inhuman monster. The retaliation went beyond the spreading of half-truths. Plots were hatched against my life and against the life of other district officers. It was common knowledge that offers had been made to do away with me. I was flattered to discover that my life was worth ten thousand rupees. The tahsildar of Tuljapur, Mr Qadri, was waylaid near Sarola, where he had gone to supervise levy collections, and made a narrow escape. Tahsildar Qadri was a loyal officer who had always been very helpful to me. He had been quite active on the borders, and, on many occasions, his devotion to duty had helped in preventing damage to life and property in Tuljapur. I was once tempted out with a false report of a raid on Dhoki. The landmine meant to kill me blew up a villager who happened to use the road before I did, killing him and his horse.

By June 1948, I had made a last futile attempt to come to terms with the authorities of Sholapur. A meeting was arranged. They came in a bad mood because of a recent incident at Aljapur. According to their reports, Razakars had attacked Aljapur. As a matter of fact, the Razakars had nothing to do with the Aljapur affair. After the incident involving arson and murder at Dhekri, the Pathans and the police posted there were attacked from Aljapur. The attack was repulsed and the raiders chased back. This was construed as an unprovoked attack on Aljapur. There was also the incident at Sarola where two or three Sholapur constables had been killed in the clash. Apart from this, there were a few minor mishaps reported from different villages.

Whatever the background to their pique, the authorities of Sholapur were just as noncooperative as ever. Special officers of the Government of India and the Government of Hyderabad were present at one such meeting. As usual, the existence of border camps was absolutely denied. I offered to go with them to Yedsi incognito, and show them the camp located there. They refused to listen to any reasonable argument and the meeting broke up as usual, on a negative note.

With the breakdown of the negotiations over the Standstill Agreement in June 1948, the nasty situation turned uglier still. Border raids increased in ferocity. Customs posts were, as usual, the main targets of attack, but there were signs that the freedom fighters were getting more ambitious. Concerted efforts were made by the camps at Gondgaon and Kowdgaon to cause major disruption in Osmanabad.

These were very trying times. A false step by me or my colleagues, or a spiteful word hinting at revenge, would have led to a major outbreak of violence in Osmanabad. I could feel the Razakars, the Pathans and the Arabs watching me for signs of faltering. I must again mention here Abul Hassan, the district superintendent of police of Osmanabad, without whose courageous and whole-hearted cooperation, I could not have succeeded in holding the district together.

These were the days when arms were coming in to us. The Razakars and the Arabs made constant demands for guns and ammunition.

But no supplies were ever issued to unauthorized persons in my district. This was not always an easy thing to do. By this time, my policy of being very severe with Razakars, Pathans and Arabs was well established. From my very first day as collector of Osmanabad, I had enforced the strictest possible discipline. As conditions worsened, with increased provocations, this stood me in good stead. For instance, Bidar, a village bordering Latur, was burning hot, while Latur was calm and quiet. The credit for keeping Latur intact goes to the young tahsildar of Latur, Mahmood Ali, without whose active cooperation it would not have been possible to save it from communal tension. Latur could easily have been a major headache for me. It was Qasim Razvi's hometown. At various times, the businessmen of Latur had offered to contribute money to the funds of the Razakar organization, but this was never encouraged. However, the secretary of the Latur Majlis was a troublemaker. I prevailed upon Ikramullah, the minister for development (PWD) and minister in charge of Osmanabad, to remove him from office. Ikramullah in turn persuaded Qasim Razvi and, subsequently, the secretary of Latur Majlis was removed. Such was the state of affairs in the district when information started coming in of quiet visits of Indian Army officers to some of the strategic posts in Osmanabad.

I personally met one such officer, Brigadier Bhatia, who was passing through Khanapur, on his way to Hyderabad. There had been a border attack at Khanapur and a customs post and a bus-stand by the railway had been burnt down. I invited Brigadier Bhatia to inspect the damages with me. We went round together, and he made notes on the incident.

These visits seemed ominous. There had been an attack on Nanaj on 5 May. I began to fear that Nanaj would increasingly come under pressure. I was convinced that there was an urgent need to closely watch the more important of our border areas, in particular, Nanaj and Sendri, as these were the two most important points of access to Barsi. I wanted these outposts guarded by our armed forces. This would not only keep us informed of the movement of the Indian Army but also help us maintain good relations with them. The district police and the Pathan irregulars were liable to make matters worse if they continued to be in charge of security in these areas. It was my duty to convey my fears to the government. When the minister of revenue, Nawab Fazal Nawaz Jung, and Abdul Hamid Khan, minister of police, visited Osmanabad district in July, I conveyed my fears to them. I told them that it was very significant that Brigadier Bhatia had managed to visit Tuljapur and Aljapur. I also expressed my dissatisfaction at the handling of affairs at Nanaj and emphasized the necessity of posting armed and disciplined forces at all points of possible friction, but especially at Nanaj. I had another opportunity of explaining the situation when I met Ikramullah, the minister in charge of Osmanabad district, as late as 22 and 23 July 1948. Even in my fortnightly report dated 23 July 1948, I laid stress on the necessity of handing over Nanaj to military control. At one point, I even wrote to General Edroos directly about this.

However, without any help coming in, I was forced to manage these important outposts with an ineffective police force, aided by the brainless Pathans. The Pathans at Nanaj could not get on with the Sikh forces of the Indian Army who had to pass through Nanaj to reach Barsi. The inevitable clash took place on 24 July 1948. The Pathans were routed and Nanaj was occupied.

It was difficult to apportion blame to any party for this incident without looking at all the facts. The Indian Army accused the Pathans of an unprovoked attack. I was not sure about this. Even if the Pathans had attacked first, I wondered how unprovoked their action could have been.

The Indian forces had gauged the importance of Nanaj. Our own outpost there, however inefficient, had kept us informed of the movements of the Indian Army. Not comfortable with being observed, it is very likely that the Indian Army had first built up a history of complaints and counter-complaints, then provoked the Pathans into launching an attack, which gave them an opportunity to counter-attack, and take over Nanaj. It was cleverly done; and now the Indian Army had come to stay.

Not until after Nanaj did I fully realize how weak our own army was. But even then, the personality of General El Edroos continued to overawe us. I met General Edroos on 25 July. He was sorry for the outcome at Nanaj. I was informed that Lt Col Weston, who was already at Osmanabad, was going to Nanaj to review the situation and that the general was awaiting his report. In the meantime, he had contacted the Southern Command and arranged to send Lt Col Himayat Baig to Nanaj to contact the Indian forces there, and await further orders.

I met Prime Minister Laiq Ali that afternoon and explained the importance of Nanaj to him. He seemed rather concerned and called General Edroos to the meeting. With the help of a map of Osmanabad, I explained the situation to the prime minister and the general. Possibilities of re-occupation of Nanaj were considered. General Edroos was willing to retake Nanaj if ordered to do so, with a two-pronged attack from the north and the south. I was somewhat taken aback. I thought Nanaj would be difficult to re-occupy, what with the Indian Army entrenched there and Sholapur close by. And I knew that our friends in the army who would have to do the actual job would not like it at all! And I was equally certain that the Indian Army would not give up the position at Nanaj having taken it with some deliberation and planning. But, somehow, we had to counteract the demoralizing effect of the Nanaj occupation.

The next idea was the occupation of Yedsi in retaliation for the loss of Nanaj. In pursuit of this idea, General Edroos was asked to stop Col Himayat Baig from proceeding to Nanaj. I was given my own orders. I was to report on the Nanaj incident and the possibility of retaking it. I was also to make my assessment of the Yedsi proposal.

On my way back to Osmanabad, I met the brigade commander, Syed Habeeb Ahmed. We agreed that the occupation of Yedsi was more important than the reoccupation of Nanaj. By this time, the message from General Edroos had reached Himayat Baig and I was informed that he was waiting for me at Tuljapur. On my way there, I met Lt Col Weston. According to him, it was the Pathans who had sparked off the fight, leading to the loss of Nanaj.

Proceeding to Tuljapur, I met Lt Col Himayat Baig. He was very pleased that he did not have to go to Nanaj. About the planned occupation of Yedsi, he maintained a discreet silence. Himayat Baig was an intelligent and thoughtful man: one of the few army officers who really seemed to know his job. Presumably, he did not want to share his doubts with me. I could only conclude that he did not agree with his commander about Yedsi, but did not like to say so. Perhaps he could not openly disagree. In any case, it was not difficult to read his thoughts, which were reflected in his face

Others in the army were not so cautious with me. It seemed that a majority of our military officers had a poor understanding of the situation facing them. Their mastery of their craft seemed shaky. They were clutching at straws. Instead of guiding junior officers, they relied on the untested opinions of civilians and seemed too ready to agree with some of the silly suggestions they were receiving. Later on, I had a long talk with the DSP Osmanabad. His feelings about our armed forces were more or less the same as mine. About the Nanaj affair the DSP naturally tried to shield his men; the Pathans, it is true, were attached to the Special Police Branch.

On a thorough sifting of all available evidence, I came to the conclusion that it was the Pathans who had fired the first shot at Nanaj. But I felt that the Indian Army had cleverly precipitated the situation and had set up the Pathans. And this is what I mentioned in my special report to the prime minister. I also asked for an interview with him at the earliest possible date, as I wished to speak to him about the plan to occupy Yedsi. I also wanted to discuss the general situation with him and to convey to him my feelings about the army and its morale.

I had serious doubts about our ability to retain Yedsi, even if we actually managed to take it. Our army was simply not capable of taking or retaining anything. When I thought of it, it seemed doubtful that they would even fight for Hyderabad. I wanted to convey all this to the prime minister, but did not manage to get an interview with him until some time had passed.

Two days after the Nanaj incident, Qasim Razvi arrived in Osmanabad from Latur. He was followed by a CID report, stating that he had removed the Latur Majlis secretary from office. This man had been suspect for some time. I had found sufficient grounds for requesting his removal and had conveyed this to the minister in-charge of Osmanabad, Ikramullah, who had obviously got in touch with Qasim Razvi.

It was reported that Qasim Razvi had advised the Razakars of Latur to behave themselves. Otherwise, he was supposed to have warned, pointing to his rifle, that they would be made his first targets! In Osmanabad too he was reported to have advised the Razakars to behave and to learn to respect the authorities.

Abul Hassan, the DSP, wanted Qasim Razvi's help in capturing some Razakars involved in the Gour murder case, where some Muslims were killed in a raid. The Razakars along with the constables of Yermala Special Police Force retaliated by killing several Hindus at Gour. The murderers had then gone into hiding and it was suspected that the president of the local Majlis was protecting them.

When Qasim Razvi came to see me the following morning, I spoke to him about this case. To my surprise, he readily agreed to render all necessary aid. Qasim Razvi had a very sharp tongue. The manner in which he spoke to the local president and ordered the delivery of the culprits to the police came as a pleasant shock to us. We had heard that he generally refused to hear anything against the Razakars. But he was very business-like that morning. As he got up to leave, he gave me a firm handshake and said, 'Squeeze them hard if they do not behave. Khuda Hafiz.'

After the occupation of Nanaj, the strip of land between Sendri and Nanaj came under the sway of the freedom fighters. A reign of terror was now unleashed in the area: Scores of villagers lost their lives in violent encounters in Manigaon, Anjagaon, Masla Chowdri and Sirpatih Pipri. I began to feel helpless. It looked as if the order for which we had worked so hard was beginning to break up. I had no one to look up to for help – we could no longer expect anything from our armed forces.

Civil Centres lying in the Sendri-Nanaj strip were soon rooted out. The beleaguered police force in that area began collecting in Sirpath Pipri. I knew they would have to be relieved. My telegram to Hyderabad asking for help went unacknowledged. Finally, I was informed that Ramachander Rao, sub-inspector of police, posted at Manigaon, his wife and children, along with sixty members of his police force, were now held hostage by armed raiders at Sirpath Pipri.

There was no time to lose; we had to organize a rescue. I had reason to believe there might be resistance against us at Sendri: I wanted the government to advise me: should we avoid a clash or face it when it came? There was no reply to my urgent messages to Hyderabad.

With all the roads blocked, it took me three days to reach Parenda. With great difficulty, the beleaguered police force was relieved and brought back to Osmanabad. Major Akbar Ali Khan, second taluqdar of Osmanabad; Mohammad Ismail, local fund engineer; Mohammad Khan, excise superintendent; and Syed Abdul Lateef, the CID inspector, were of great help to me. Besides them, Narayan Rao Vakil of Parenda and the court inspector of Parenda also provided invaluable support.

A very strange situation had now arisen. Our civil forces were being seriously harassed by the hooligans in our own jurisdiction and we were told that we could expect no help from the army! The armed forces had recently been given instructions that they were not to operate within three miles of the border. They were now refusing to help even in pure and simple cases of internal security.

I tried to impress upon the government that the army should be made to play a more effective role. My reports to the government are likely to be misconstrued if they are taken out of context and without knowledge of the circumstances in which I was forced to criticize their inactivity. But no help was forthcoming.

ꙮ

There was a shock awaiting me at Parenda. While I was there, an elderly Hindu gentleman, Narayan Rao Vakil came to see me. Quietly, but convincingly, he told me about the activities of the Pathans. On top of all their other mischief, they had started something of a protection racket among the villagers, forcibly collecting money and harassing the Hindus.

For me this was awful news, but not entirely unexpected. Narayan Rao was not willing to come out with an open complaint against the Pathans because he thought his life would be endangered. But there was no reason to doubt what he said.

There were around forty Pathans stationed in the Parenda area. I ordered them to be disarmed and disbanded on the spot. Without disclosing the source of my information, I gave the Pathans a summary of the complaints against them. I added that if this was how they would conduct themselves – and since there was no hope of reform – I refused to keep them in service.

The Pathans are simple people, with simple ideas. They struggled to make clear to me their understanding of the rules of engagement:

'Chief, we fight raiders. They run when they see us. All Muslims are brothers, Chief. We never hurt them; we protect them.'

They could not understand why they should provide equal protection to Hindus when the raiders from the border camps continued to make Muslims their main targets – murdering and uprooting them from border areas. It was futile to argue with them; they had to go.

But the Pathans refused to surrender their arms or leave Parenda. Besides the forty at Parenda, I had some fifteen Pathans with me; they made common cause. But I was not prepared to give in. At one point, it looked as if I might have to fight them with the police force. The Pathans had lived with me for six months. They knew that once my mind was made up, they could not frighten me into changing it. In the event, I am glad it did not come to a fight because they would have slaughtered us!

Finally, it got through to them that I was not going to retreat. It must have been rather painful for them. In their view, they had done nothing wrong, and yet were being asked to do the unthinkable: to part with their arms. On the other hand, they liked me and were a little in awe of me; they did not wish to fight me. We were truly at an impasse.

In the end, it was the Pathans themselves who thought of an elegant way out of it. They let me know that they would only surrender their arms to me personally. This was not without some risk but I accepted it at once. The Pathans were asked to assemble in an open area. I took up my position, facing them, alone. One by one, they came up, saluted, and handed over their arms to me. While collecting their rifles, I was aware that any one of them could simply raise his rifle and put a bullet through my head. You never knew with these people. But somehow I had appealed to their gallantry, and they had devised a rather stylish exit for themselves.

I escorted the forty disarmed Pathans to Osmanabad. On our way, we bumped into a batch of raiders, who opened fire on us. We returned fire and the raiders were driven back. But one of them was caught alive. The Pathans would have torn him limb from limb had

I not intervened. Our captive was a young boy from Kallam called Idram. He belonged to the party of Hari Har and Vasant of Tadola camp. He remained in the police lock-up until the 'Police Action'.

On my return to Osmanabad, I reflected on these events with mixed emotions. I was glad I had taken action against the Pathans at Parenda. But I began wondering if they had been behaving like this all over Osmanabad. I ordered all Pathans to be withdrawn from their different postings in the district and summoned to Osmanabad.

In the meantime, conditions were rapidly deteriorating all over Hyderabad State. The armed forces in my area did not seem willing to bear their share of responsibility for law and order. The more I learnt about the forces, the more convinced I became of their ineffectiveness. Then there were the Razakars. They had lost their various footholds on the borders and were pouring into Osmanabad, looking for trouble. The Razakars and the Arabs were constantly harassing our junior officers for rifles and sten-guns. They had come to know that I was receiving arms in large quantities, but was just sitting on them.

Upset and disheartened, I wrote a long report to the government. Here I was, risking life and limb to protect the people in my district. Against all odds, I had gradually strengthened the morale of the administration, and had improved the law and order situation. Now, the government seemed to be withdrawing its support, exposing the people on the borders to attacks, while I was expected to look on helplessly. In my submission, I protested against the inactivity of the army and the growing failure of the government to back my efforts. Therefore, on 6 August 1948, I offered my resignation. It was a calculated move, intended to emphasize the importance of the issue and the depth of my disagreement. I was not packing my bags just yet; I was prepared to carry on until my resignation was accepted and I was relieved.

There was no response from Hyderabad. In the meantime, the Pathans recalled to Osmanabad started trickling in. They were ordered to submit themselves to centralized control and to accept a greater degree of discipline in future. They refused, and were discharged from service. One by one, they began leaving the district, depositing their rifles with the police. While this was going on, our troops posted at Tamalwadi were withdrawn without my knowledge. As a consequence, Surat Gaon was attacked by the raiders on 23 August 1948.

The following day, I submitted my resignation for the second time. It was the only honourable way to indicate to my superiors the magnitude of the issue in question. By rejecting my request and persisting in their course, they had assumed exclusive responsibility for their policy and its consequences.

The Fall of Osmanabad

After sending in my resignation I left for Hyderabad. On my way, I met an army officer of middle rank. He had an easy way about him and we soon fell into a conversation. He turned out to be a great admirer of Qasim Razvi, the 'saviour of Hyderabad'. He said that he could claim the credit of having spared Qasim Razvi for Hyderabad. He was referring to the well-known incident in Latur, in which the notorious Ishaq and some others were shot and killed. Apparently, the officer had been ordered to shoot Razvi on sight. But, he said with pride, he had chosen to ignore those instructions.

My resignation at such a critical time was open to various interpretations. My minister, Nawab Fazal Nawaz Jung, put it down to a nervous breakdown; others thought I was shirking my duty. I met the prime minister and had a very frank and free discussion with him on 28 August 1948 (if I remember the date correctly). This was an opportunity to express my concerns at the highest level of government.

I explained that my resignation was meant to emphasize the depth of my disagreement with a policy of drift. I gave an account of the hostage-taking at Sirpath Pipri. No one seemed to have any concern about the worsening situation in the districts. When we were in trouble and sent desperate messages seeking help and advice, we were ignored and no help came our way. Then I spoke of the low morale of our army. 'A new phase of eyeball-to-eyeball confrontation is beginning,' I said, 'in which we cannot bank on General Edroos's reputation as a deterrent.' Finally, with the prime minister's permission, I laid out my reasons for proposing a review of the border policy.

'There are strong political and moral reasons,' I said, 'for defending our borders. Of course a vigorous assertion of our sovereignty would provoke a clash which we could not hope to win, given the poor state of our armed forces. An abdication of our sovereign functions would equally invite annexation. But a middle way is possible.' He nodded, listening.

We needed a redirection of our policy on three points, I explained: first, on securing improved coordination between the military and the civil administration in the border districts. Second, on imposing proper restraint on Razakar activities, which were as much a nuisance to our side as a provocation to India. Third, establishing effective deterrence against border raids. Without such a reinvigoration of policy, whatever gains we had made at district level were in danger of being lost.

The prime minister heard me out. 'This is a useful review,' he said. 'Such first-hand assessments by our senior officers in the field are invaluable to us here. Let me respond with a few comments.' I sat back, relieved that at least he had taken my comments in good spirit.

'I was of course aware of the Sirpath Pipri hostage situation,' he continued. 'It was a very serious incident. Sixty members of the police force taken hostage! I am concerned and surprised that there was no response from the headquarters. I know you took personal charge, and I commend you for it.'

I murmured my thanks.

'I was preoccupied at the time by the statement of the seven,' he continued, referring to a recent press statement by seven prominent personalities in Hyderabad politics, including Sir Mirza Ismael, the former prime minister of Hyderabad, advising accession and condemning Razakar activities.

'I was worried about the impact the statement would have in Pakistan. That took my attention. But, you know, I cannot agree with your assessment of our armed forces. You are in danger of underestimating our army and its chief. The army, I would say, is fifty times stronger than you seem to imagine! As the prime minister, I am privy to all their counsels. I closely follow all matters pertaining to the defence of the realm. Fifty times stronger!'

His voice had risen. I must have looked sceptical, because he continued in a calmer tone. 'Look, there will be no war, no attempt to invade us. Not until November at least. The Standstill Agreement is in force until the end of November. By that time I expect our forces to be much better-equipped, really in a position to meet any situation.'

The prime minister appeared confident of his views.

'Now let us assume,' he continued, 'that I am wrong, and there is a confrontation. Do you really think we would find ourselves isolated? Do you think we have no friends? If it came to a fight after all, Hyderabad will not find itself alone.'

He left this vague, and I, fearing that he was reluctant to talk about confidential matters of state, was content with vague hints. After that he had a few words of encouragement for me. I always had the greatest admiration for the prime minister. I felt privileged to be granted a lengthy interview with him. It is not surprising therefore that by this time I was prepared to forget about my resignation; the matter was dropped. We were discussing some unrelated matter when Moin Nawaz Jung came in with his files and I left.

That same evening, I was asked to attend the subedars' conference at Shah Manzil. Abdul Rahim, Yamin Zubairi, and Ikramullah were also present. In his address to the audience, the prime minister reviewed the political and administrative situation, and stressed the absolute necessity of keeping the Razakars under control. Failure to do this, he warned, would lead to disaster.

After the conference was over I spoke to several people. I tried to impress on them (and particularly on Messrs. Rahim and Ikramullah) the fact that I no longer believed in the strength of our armed forces (obviously, the Laiq Ali magic was beginning to wear off). They looked surprised but nobody seemed prepared to think about the consequences of this observation; no one seemed willing to do anything.

I remained in Hyderabad for a week, trying to collect a few jeeps for the use of district officers. During this time, I met many people and talked with them about our problems. No one was prepared to believe that we were absolutely nothing in terms of armed strength.

It goes without saying that I did not regard the Razakars as a fighting force at all.

The Razakars had been given undue prominence. They were nothing more than a nuisance. But a certain gangsterish aura surrounded them, which was being used to great effect by the Government of India. It seemed to me, therefore, that we should begin thinking about ways to minimize the importance of the Razakar movement. For instance, if Qasim Razvi could be prevailed upon to announce the voluntary dissolution of the Razakar organization of his own free will and as a means of testing the sincerity of the Government of India, perhaps the situation would start improving once again. Logically, this was a sound suggestion, but there was little hope of realizing it. Still, I talked about it; it was time for desperate measures. Many approved of my idea, but doubted if Qasim Razvi would agree.

I met Qasim Razvi in due course. He had more-or-less the same opinion of the Hyderabad Army as I did. To his credit, he seemed rather more disturbed about it than some of the others I had met in Hyderabad. But it was for this very reason, he said, that he was not inclined to consider the winding up of the Razakar organization. Strange as it may sound, he did not dismiss the idea entirely. He seemed inclined to consider it if it really served a purpose. But he doubted that any good could come of it at the time.

On the whole, like the prime minister, Qasim Razvi was also quite optimistic about the future of Hyderabad. He did not seem to attach any importance to the possibility of an armed invasion. He too believed that help would come in the event of an attack. He seemed to derive great satisfaction from the reports from Pakistan and the Middle East, brought to him by Taquiuddin (one of the secretaries in Hyderabad government).

My conversations with Nawab Fazal Nawaz Jung, the revenue minister, and Abdul Hameed Khan, the police minister, left me with the distinct impression that they knew very little about the state of our army. Both of them had complete faith in Laiq Ali, just as I did, and both urged me to rejoin my district and help him by continuing my work there.

I also met Pingal Venkat Rama Reddy during my stay in Hyderabad. The old gentleman seemed worried and perplexed as usual. He agreed with me on most of the matters that we discussed, but seemed rather helpless in the face of the situation. I tried to hint that he should put his foot down. As deputy prime minister, he could assert himself; he could make efforts to inform himself about the conditions in our army; he could try to find out about the rumoured 'understandings' with foreign governments, and so on. He was not inclined to do any of these things. I left for Osmanabad after about a week in Hyderabad.

By now we had begun receiving arms in relatively large quantities. Civil Guard Programmes were in full swing. Along with this, the Razakars were receiving training in the use of firearms, but not a single rifle was spared to them from our stock. Almost all the district officers had started taking a keen interest in rifle training. Additional Talukdar Kapoor and Dr Rainapurkar, the civil surgeon, were the most regular of the enthusiastic lot. The idea of rifle training for women was also tried. A batch of girls was being trained to use guns under the guidance of the wife of the Osmanabad Munsif, Mrs Yakoob Hussaini. Mrs Hussaini was committed to her work. I am afraid my enthusiasm about rifle training for women lagged far behind hers!

As I have already mentioned, most of the Pathans had left the district. The few who remained had good reports from the police. They were offered employment under the direct supervision of the army officers. Predictably enough, they declined the offer and left Osmanabad.

ഇരു

Around the end of August, we realized with something of a shock that for some time we had received no reports of border incidents. In the first week of September, information started dribbling in of army concentrations in Barsi. Tanks were also seen. We guessed that border camps had been wound up. This was soon confirmed. According to my sources, the district magistrate of Sholapur had summoned the leaders of the border camps to Sholapur on 6 September and informed them that they could cease operations, as the Government of India was itself contemplating suitable action in the near future. The organizers were asked to remain in Sholapur, but they ignored this request and returned to their camps to wait and see what action the government proposed to take.

The area commander continually received secret orders and messages from High Command and his behaviour usually betrayed the content of the messages. The civil authorities were kept in absolute darkness. About this time, a shot was fired at Kodar, which seemed to be a sign of the coming conflict. Even at this late stage, no clear instructions were received about what to do in case of an attack.

One evening, I think it was 10 September, we were at last informed by the army officers that 11 September would be the day. As Hyderabad had decided to go to the UN Security Council, the Government of India would try to over-run it before the council took the case on its agenda.

At this point, our army started making some last-minute make-believe preparations, miles inside our borders. Even at this stage, many of our army officers exhibited such ignorance of the topography of Osmanabad that I feared they would end up in the Union enclaves when they began their retreat.

News came of Nawab Moin Nawaz Jung's departure from Hyderabad to present our case at the Security Council. This too seemed rather futile. The governor general of India, Dr C. Rajagopalachari, made a last appeal to Hyderabad. It seemed obvious that the Indian government had come to the end of its patience with us.

Meanwhile, the irresponsible utterances and exhortations to the public by the Ittehad leaders in Hyderabad made our task extremely difficult in Osmanabad during our final days. I had never worked so hard in my life as I did during those last days, struggling to maintain law and order. But I did not have to struggle for long. Hyderabad had attained the required white heat and there could not be a more opportune moment for the Iron Man of India to strike.

The attack on Hyderabad began early on 13 September 1948. Indian troops, supported by tanks, poured into the Osmanabad district. Early reports brought news of the attack on Naldurg and Tuljapur, and of Indian forces sweeping past Tamalwadi and Aljapur. Almost simultaneously came the news of their advance towards Osmanabad from the Ahmi area. Nor was Osmanabad the only point of entry; Indian forces began their advance on a dozen fronts, at different strategic points on the Hyderabad border.

By 7 a.m., the Hyderabad propaganda machinery had swung into action. Deccan Radio began whipping up the emotions of the people with fiery exhortations. We in turn began receiving messages to fight 'to the last man and the last round'.

Tuljapur fell early in the day. The civilian officers there left their posts and scattered for life. The Razakars and the Arabs started coming to us in numbers, clamouring for arms. With some difficulty, they were all turned away without a gun or a single round. In consultation with the area commander, disciplined and reliable members of the Civil Guard were issued with rifles and forces.

Incredible as it may seem, one company, a single, independently operating military body of men, armed with no more than rifles, was sent out from Osmanabad town to check the advance of the Indian armoured division. Its progress was unhurried. As the tanks crawled in, closer and closer, it felt as if the invading forces were trying to avoid casualties by not taking unnecessary risks.

The commanding officer at Osmanabad, Major Mohsin Ali, was a fine officer, one of the finest I had come across. That day, Major Mohsin found himself sinking into a state of absolute helplessness. The men under his command were no better equipped than civil defence forces. Major Mohsin kept himself busy burning papers, hurrying to receive army messages and making last ditch efforts to keep up the morale of his men. He went about his business like a man under sentence of death.

One of the earliest casualties in Osmanabad town was the jail sentry. He was hit as he stood at his post in front of the jail gates. As he fell, our advance unit (sent out to resist the tanks) came running back, thoroughly frightened and panting for breath.

Major Mohsin now informed me that he had no means of resisting the advance of the tanks. His men were armed with .303 rifles and hopelessly short of ammunition. What was Hyderabad importing all these days, I wondered? What were those legendary feats of gun-running?

ꕥ

All that remained of my job now was to prepare Osmanabad for defeat. There were many people in Osmanabad that day who were in a mood for heroics. If this was the end of Hyderabad, they wanted to go down fighting – they would end it all in a glorious blood bath. There were others who were simply frightened and wanted to get arms and ammunition in order to protect themselves and their families against the inevitable chaos that follows an armed invasion. And, of course, there were still others for whom this was a heaven-sent opportunity for murder, loot and rape.

The Razakars were kept out of the show as far as possible. To make them feel important, they were asked to guard the approaches to Osmanabad from Tuljapur. But as the news of the inglorious return of our advance unit spread among them, the Arabs and the Razakars began to clamour once again for better firearms. Meanwhile, some miscreants were planning to go on the rampage. They were quietly rounded up on the pretext that they were to be briefed on a secret mission and taken into custody.

I addressed groups of people who gathered around wherever they found me. The collector of a district is more than just a high official; people turn to him in times of trouble as naturally as children to their parents. Some of these people wanted to resist the oncoming armies. I tried to reason with them that they could not hope to succeed where our army had failed, and it was no use marching to death in the face of advancing tanks. I warned them against the consequences of acts of vandalism. I exhorted them to accept defeat with good grace. In my eight months in Osmanabad, even the Razakars and the Arabs had learnt to listen to me; the others looked up to me with respect. As the day advanced, I grew increasingly apprehensive about our hot-heads. Later that day I addressed a rather anxious crowd that had gathered outside my office. I advised the people to stay calm, even in the face of grave provocation, such as the murder of local leaders, or even the officers – not excluding myself. The people listened to me with great attention. Someone asked if they should not kill, even in self-defence. I said it would be better if they would die quietly without resistance because any resistance could mean more bloodshed: 'You can die to save ten others,' I said. I had about 100 rifles, 25 sten-guns and 5,000 rounds at my headquarters. There were people in that crowd who wanted those weapons. But I managed to disperse the crowd by talking to them quietly without making any threats. They could have burst in and taken away the rifles and ammunition by force because, by that time, I was not in a position to stop them. But that did not happen. It seemed like a great victory then.

That evening, as I waited for the arrival of Indian forces, news arrived that our armed forces had fled. I went to the army camp; it was deserted. Almost all the civilian officials of the district were with me at that time. They urged me to leave as well. But I could not very well leave; my orders were to stay. A message received as late as 6 p.m. had stressed the need to fight to the last. There was no one left to fight, of course, but my orders were to stay.

I tried looking for Major Mohsin, hoping to find him but he too had left. My colleagues were getting restive. By now, the tanks had come up to the Osmanabad jail and shelling of the outskirts of Osmanabad was in progress. The Indian forces could have fired directly into the town but they probably chose to warn us first. It became clear that by ourselves, we could do nothing. If I did not move quickly, I would be cut off from the rest of the district and would have to give myself up to the advancing Indian forces. If I wanted to stay on my job, I had to leave the district headquarters. I decided to move to Murud, which was a large army garrison, and get help from there. By this time, all the major roads were already in control of the Indian forces. At about 6.45 p.m., 13 September, we started out cross-country.

We drove all night. Even in a jeep, black cotton soil is difficult to traverse in the rainy season. The following morning, at 10 a.m., 14 September 1948, we heard on All India Radio that Osmanabad had fallen. We reached Murud shortly after, at eleven. The Hyderabad forces there had no instructions to help us; they were planning a retreat and were anxiously awaiting orders to that effect. I contacted the Hyderabad Army High Command, which conveyed a message from the prime minister, asking me to return to Hyderabad. We had lost Osmanabad.

From Murud I drove to Latur, where arrangements were made to shift the treasury and the large amounts of money lying in the State Bank of Hyderabad. After that I left with other Osmanabad officers for Hyderabad.

On our way to Hyderabad, we crossed Bidar, which was in turmoil. The news of the steady advance of the Indian Army towards Hyderabad on the Sholapur–Hyderabad road had upset the whole Bidar administration. The district officers did not even know how close the Indian forces were to Bidar. According to them, Zaheerabad had already fallen.

Actually, there was no truth in that report. Relying on this piece of information, we left for Nanded. Reaching Nanded on the morning of 15 September, we found the taluqdar of the district and the DSP preparing to march to the border, with a batch of Razakars to confront the Indian Army. In a few words I conveyed to them exactly what they were likely to encounter at the border. Then we moved on towards Hyderabad. About 14 miles from Nanded, we were spotted by an Indian Air Force plane, which dived at us, intending perhaps to drop a bomb or to strafe us. But it almost crashed into a lorry proceeding in front of us and lost interest in harassing our little convoy further. We finally reached Hyderabad on the night of 15 September 1948. Arriving home, I discovered that my feet had swollen from staying upright for too long, and my shoes could only be removed by cutting the laces.

Police Action and My Arrest

As I looked around on the morning of 16 August 1948, I was surprised to see Hyderabad absolutely unmindful of the coming dangers. There were only a few people who seemed concerned about the possibility of bloodshed in the city. More anxious than most was the director general of police, Nawab Deen Yar Jung. He was busy making the most elaborate arrangements against a possible reaction to reports from the districts. A communal uprising at that time would have been a disaster of unprecedented magnitude. The after-effects of such a calamity, its impact on the rest of the subcontinent, simply cannot be imagined.

At about 9.30 p.m. on 16 September, I met the prime minister and briefed him about my last ten days in Osmanabad and my eventful return. I reminded him of what I had said so often about our armed forces. I remember suggesting that we should now concentrate our efforts on averting the possibility of Hyderabad and Secunderabad becoming a battleground in their turn.

What he said next left me flabbergasted. What had taken place so far, he said in the same old confident tone, was according to plan: our armies had carried out a tactical retreat. He hoped to break the encirclement and surround the Indian forces in turn when they came a little closer to Hyderabad. He seemed to attach little importance to the loss of the border districts.

'The few roadside places that are now occupied,' he said, 'can easily be retaken.'

It made me sad to recall that this was the way he had talked when we lost Nanaj. I asked:

'How do we plan to retake them – with what?'

'We are expecting a consignment of anti-tank guns; they should arrive at any moment,' he said, in his usual matter-of-fact, confident manner.

'Yes,' he continued, 'they should have been here a long time ago, but due to some bungling, I discovered they were still in storage at Cairo Airport. These things happen... But that's been put right. When they arrive, they will be devastating! We plan to use them against the Indian tanks when they come a little closer to Hyderabad.'

Was all this true? I had no knowledge of these things and I could hardly cross-examine the prime minister.

Next, I went to see Qasim Razvi. He had lost some of his supreme self-confidence, and was in a contemplative mood:

'Shall we be destroyed? That's up to them. Shall we be defeated? That's up to us.'

For the first time, on 16 September 1948, he conceded that perhaps in some ways the Razakar movement had been a mistake. But even in the face of defeat, he clung to his belief in his own destiny.

'Let us see what happens tomorrow,' he said.

I had reason to recall those words.

ജ

Early on the morning of Friday, 17 September, there was a call for me from Qasim Razvi. This was the first time I had spoken to him on the telephone.

'Stay indoors,' he advised me. 'Do not stir out of the house, because the inevitable will happen after Friday prayers.'

'Do you expect the Indian Army to enter the city by then?' I asked.

'No, that's not it.'

'Then what...?' I asked.

'The inevitable,' he repeated. 'Our people have been armed.'

It turned out that he had actually distributed several thousand rifles among his followers, with instructions to start a massacre of the Hindus that afternoon.

I was horrified. I told him that this was wrong and it would mean the complete devastation of Hyderabad when the Indian forces reached there. He was in no mood to listen. I begged him to make his last gesture before retiring from politics a merciful one. He did not listen to very much of this and rang off.

I rushed to Nawab Deen Yar Jung. He had already received information that Qasim Razvi was contemplating such a move. There was no time to lose. Both of us began trying to get Qasim Razvi on the phone. I remember vividly with what desperation the director general saw the minutes pass. I finally got the connection and passed the receiver to the director general.

Deen Yar Jung sensed that perhaps Qasim Razvi wanted to be dissuaded from a rash and tragic final act. And as I listened to him, I was reminded of Bacon's advice on negotiation: 'If you would work any man, you must either know his nature and so lead him; or his ends and so persuade him.'

At the beginning of the conversation, I heard Deen Yar Jung say yes, yes, yes on the phone for several minutes. He was obviously letting him talk, and listening carefully. He was soothing in his brief responses, even talking at one point about Qasim Razvi's place in history. As Qasim Razvi grew calmer, Deen Yar Jung's tone changed. He condemned the logic of distributing arms: 'Is this move in line with what you have tried to accomplish?'

He then drew him into his own preoccupations with law and order. They agreed that the Indian forces were now drawing near with irresistible force. If they could not be stopped, they (and the murderous gangs that were following in the army's wake) should at least be denied the opportunity to exact revenge.

'The military should be obliged to protect us, and not stand on one side and allow massacres to take place in the city. How can we ensure that?'

They spoke for over half-an-hour. Nawab Deen Yar Jung had spent over a quarter of a century in public service. He had great powers of persuasion. But never, I am sure, were his talents put to a more terrifying test than in that half-hour on 17 September 1948. What he accomplished then must be his greatest contribution to the people of

Hyderabad. At the end of the half-hour, Qasim Razvi agreed to ask his followers to surrender their arms.

Later in the day, there were reports of Laiq Ali and his cabinet resigning that morning (17 September), and handing over the reins of government to the Nizam. This was confirmed by a broadcast by Laiq Ali, who declared that his ministry was not able to carry on the government and that he had entrusted the affairs of the state to HEH.

By 5 p.m. on the same day, a cease-fire was effective throughout Hyderabad State. By evening it was known in Hyderabad that General Edroos had met HEH the previous day and advised him that further resistance would be futile and would only lead to heavy casualties.

HEH the Nizam himself went on the air and announced that he had accepted the resignations of the Laiq Ali ministry and had asked K.M. Munshi, Agent General of India, to propose the names of ministers who would form the new government. The Laiq Ali ministry, he declared, had failed to fulfill its mandate, and he had taken direct control of the administration.

That evening, Qasim Razvi too went on air. His voice was heard on Deccan Radio for the last time. He accepted his failure in fulfilling his promises, saying that circumstances had conspired against him. He exhorted the Muslim population to remain calm even in the face of provocation, and hoped that the traditional unity of Hindus and Muslims would be maintained at all cost, forgetting the events of the immediate past. People who heard him were unanimous that this was his finest and most statesman-like speech.

On 18 September 1948, Indian forces reached the outskirts of Hyderabad, and their commander, General Chaudhuri, spent the night in Bolarum at the residence of the Indian Agent-General, K.M. Munshi.

'Police Action' was over. On 19 September, General Edroos signed an unconditional surrender. Hyderabad had been knocked down like a ripe fruit. Qasim Razvi was arrested and handed over to the Indian Army.

There were scenes of jubilation in Hyderabad. Those who had occasion to grieve, nursed their sorrows in private. However, there were some disturbances in Secunderabad. The Hindu community, which had for long endured the persecutions of the Razakars, had reason to celebrate the fall of Hyderabad. The Indian Army had been preoccupied with fears of an anti-Hindu uprising in Hyderabad. But I do not think adequate precautions were taken in the districts against the dangers of a sudden release of the pent-up feelings of the Hindus after the fall of Hyderabad.

I have no desire to exaggerate the horrors that followed Police Action; but these tragic occurrences were largely preventable. In most places, there was chaos in the wake of the swift Indian advance. Instead of just smashing through, the victorious army could have taken greater care to either restore local administration, or set up its own military administration. It did neither. Thugs quickly filled the vacuum, drawn in from across the border, and following the armed forces into Hyderabad. The violence was not entirely random and opportunistic. Among the thugs were several thousand young men from the border camps that had just been broken up: they were trained in violence, familiar with the terrain and vengeful in spirit.

The anarchy lasted weeks. Mobs broke into prisons (as in Osmanabad) and set convicts free. There was murder, loot and arson. Razakar 'suspects' who tried to give themselves up or even those who were herded together by the army, were, in many instances, slaughtered by the thugs. Thousands of families were broken up, children separated from their parents and wives, from their husbands. Women and girls were hunted down and raped. There were many other shameful deeds perpetrated in those days; I cannot bring myself to write about them even now.

ꙮ

From the day I returned from Osmanabad, friends and relations had been urging me to leave for Pakistan. As conditions grew increasingly worrisome for me, my well wishers became more insistent. However, I refused to accept their advice. On 7 October 1948, I was put under suspension with effect from 18 September 1948. No reason was given for this action. Even the secretary, revenue department, was unaware of the reasons. These orders were received from the office of the military governor, putting a number of senior government officials under suspension, and they were simply communicated to us.

This was ominous. But even then, I refused to leave in circumstances that would imply that I had run away. I was proud of my work in Osmanabad; I wanted to see how it could be criticized. Nor did I wait passively, as if hypnotized by the rush of events. I made energetic representations, at the highest levels, in an effort to ensure that my record of work would be reviewed fairly and dispassionately. I believed I could expect justice from the new administration. In due course, I met most of the personalities that were likely to influence my case.

Of all the officers I met in this period, the IG of police, A.V. Patro, impressed me the most. I met him on 5 October 1948. At a time when people had begun to avoid us, Mr Patro spoke to me as one civil servant to another. He warned me of the dangers I was courting by choosing to stay in Hyderabad. He had been on a tour of Osmanabad. The district officers, helped by the Congress leaders there, had collected sufficient 'evidence' against me to charge me with several murders and dacoities! I too had got an inkling of the cases being fabricated against me. My explanations seemed to satisfy Mr Patro. He promised to have a thorough investigation when my case came to him. I wanted nothing more.

I also met General Chaudhuri, now military governor of Hyderabad, sometime in mid-October. I spoke to him about my suspension and related matters. The general was very polite, and promised to refer my case to the chief civil administrator.

My meeting with General Chaudhuri was arranged by General El Edroos. His popularity had declined somewhat, which was obviously a natural consequence of our precipitate defeat. We had fed our people lies about the strength of the Hyderabad Army; its sudden collapse was seen with incredulity, suspicion and resentment. That resentment focused on General Edroos. Some of his comments are still fresh in my memory. He was always made to believe that Pakistan would not stand by and see India attack Hyderabad. He believed all along that India would be deterred by this and other considerations from ever launching an armed attack on Hyderabad. He had felt that as long as India was going to keep her hands off Hyderabad, the latter might as well assume a defiant posture. Apart from that, he said, the whole affair, at least the military aspect of it, was one vast bluff: Hyderabad never wanted to fight; he knew very well we could never resist an Indian attack. He had gone along with this policy in the hope that it would strengthen our hand at the negotiating table.

I also met Nawab Zain Yar Jung, minister of development. He promised to give me a chance to explain myself to the government in the event of charges being brought against me. He too assured me that the cases against me would be thoroughly scrutinized before any action was taken.

All this time, my well wishers kept urging me to flee Hyderabad. I was surprised and pained when I heard that Abul Hassan, the DSP of Osmanabad, had left abruptly for Pakistan. There was a regular exodus of Hyderabad officials to Pakistan during those days. The exuberant self-confidence of pre-Police Action days had suddenly given way to panic and demoralization. Somehow, the thought of running away never tempted me. By January 1949, I had made up my mind to stay – even if I had to face legal prosecution on trumped-up charges. As time passed, it became certain that I would be arrested and put on trial. Now it was time to be mentally prepared for it.

At about this time, my health started to give me some cause for concern. I had picked up a case of dysentery in Osmanabad. Back in Hyderabad, I started a course of treatment under our family physician, the respected Dr Bankat Chander. I did not realize at the time, but my struggle with this debilitating affliction was just beginning.

Some time in mid-February 1949, I was summoned by the revenue secretary. He asked me a few questions about the matters that I knew were connected with the cases against me. At the end of the interview, he told me that I would have to see Col Rehman regarding an inquiry into my case. Col Rehman had been appointed by the government to make a preliminary inquiry into the charges levelled against all government officials. He was given ample powers to either dismiss an officer outright or recommend criminal prosecution against him. Many officers were served with notices to appear before him and were dismissed with or without prosecution. And some of the officers were not called at all and a decision was taken to launch an outright prosecution against them. I fell in the last category of officers who were neither called nor questioned but were put under suspension by the government and were prosecuted subsequently in courts of law.

The meeting with the revenue secretary gave me a fairly clear idea of the kind of action being contemplated against me. On my return from the meeting, I wrote to the revenue minister, asking him for a chance to explain my case to him before any action was taken. There was no reply.

My request had a basis in the administrative law of Hyderabad, which prescribes that any charge against a government officer has to be referred for investigation to a commission of inquiry. But in my case, neither had charges been furnished to me nor had there been any inquiry.

On the morning of Friday, 18 February 1949, I was informed that my arrest would probably take place that afternoon. Mentally, I was ready for it. Physically, I was suffering from chronic dysentery. And emotionally, I was disappointed that my note to the chief civil administrator had obviously had no effect, nor my interviews with the director-general of police, the military governor, the minister of development, or the revenue secretary.

ꕥ

I was arrested at two in the afternoon, on one of the charges brought against me. As far as I can recall, it was the Upla murder case, which I shall describe later. I had a hurried lunch, said my goodbyes, and left in very good spirits, accompanied by my advocate, Mahmood Ali. The CID inspector who had come to arrest me had not arranged for any conveyance. I had to borrow a car from a member of the family; I wonder if I would have been made to walk the streets otherwise.

My first priority after the arrest was to seek bail. Therefore, I asked to be taken to the house of the special magistrate, Mr Osman Jaffer, a colleague from the Hyderabad Civil Service. He was not in; no one could tell us where he could be found – which was unusual for a city magistrate, who is supposed to be available to the police and the accused at all times.

His wife, learning that I was waiting outside, sent word for me to come in. When I declined, Mrs Jaffer came to the door herself, puzzled. I explained to her that I was not there as a guest but as an accused and that it was better for me to wait outside.

We spent a long time waiting. One of my wife's uncles, Mr Asadullah, came to see what was happening, accompanied by Mr Ekbote, and left in due course. Eventually, the magistrate returned. It was by now eight in the evening. He hurried up to me:

'My dear Hyder! I cannot possibly consider your bail application. My cordial and fraternal relations with you prevent me from doing that. I am sorry. I can only direct your application to the city magistrate.'

We proceeded to the house of the city magistrate, Afzaluddin Farooqui. He was also an acquaintance of long standing. It was past nine when we reached his house. I had an attack of stomach cramps just as he came over to my car. Mr Farooqui was very concerned. He made me get down from the car and escorted me into his house. He dismissed the CID inspector, and instructed him to come to his office the next day.

His response was in remarkable contrast to that of the special magistrate, who had obviously wanted to avoid any involvement in my case. I thanked Mr Farooqui but I could not possibly take advantage of his kindness. I insisted that he should send me into court custody. Finally, Mr Farooqui agreed. I had tea with him and left for the city civil courts, to spend the night there. The police guard there, Ahmed Gafour, was very solicitous. Nevertheless, I went to bed supperless, with an upset stomach, and spent a restless night.

The next morning, on 19 February, the city magistrate transferred the bail application to Digamber Prashad, the second magistrate. I requested that my physician, Dr Bankat Chander, be sent for in order to examine me. Dr Chander, who was familiar with my medical condition, certified after examining me that I needed hospitalization.

The bail hearing was fixed for 4 p.m. I was waiting in the hall of the court when I happened to come across a lawyer whom I knew faintly. He stopped and sat with me, and we talked about my arrest. He appeared sympathetic at first, but his conversation took an unexpected turn.

'Your change of fortune has little to do with your outstanding work, Hyder Sahib. It has everything to do with your shocking criticism of a holy man, Maulawi…'

'Yes,' I replied. 'As I recall, I called him a humbug. I think I said that the average shopkeeper had greater spiritual sensibility than this holy man.'

'Don't say that, Hyder Sahib!' he said in alarm, 'you must contact the Maulawi through Azam Ali. You must seek to be restored in his favour so your misfortune may be lifted. He is an enlightened man of God!'

His suggestion annoyed me. 'Sir,' I said, 'try to live in the real world. Are you aware that Hyderabad has fallen? Have you heard that there has been wholesale slaughter in the districts? Do you know that not just the government but a way of life has been overturned? Don't you feel that our faith is being profoundly tested? And here you are babbling on about the hurt feelings of a charlatan!'

'For God's sake, Mr Hyder, the man deserves some respect.'

'So do I. You are sadly mistaken if you think you can make me eat my words in fear of that charlatan!' I replied. 'I might have lost my freedom but I am still in possession of my senses.'

Our conversation ended on that note. I must admit that I have a strong dislike for all false mullahs that prey upon the susceptibilities of the poor and the vulnerable. There is a sacred dimension to our existence that we ignore at our peril; but to exploit our highest longings in this way is utterly despicable.

My application for bail was heard and rejected. I requested to go in Revision to High Court. At the end of the proceedings, the city magistrate allowed me to remain in court custody for one more night.

On Sunday, 20 February, the application for revision, together with an application to try my cases in Hyderabad was filed. The applications were admitted and transferred to Mr Ansari's bench. I knew Mr Ansari too, having worked with him in the City Civil Courts, where I was a special judge when he was the senior judge. The case was taken up at 2 p.m., but the government pleader wanted time to study the file. Therefore it was fixed for the next day. In the meantime, the city magistrate ordered me to be transferred to the Central Jail, Hyderabad. I instructed my advocate to put in an application to the second magistrate to send me to the hospital for treatment. This application was allowed, and I was ordered to be admitted into the jail and then taken out for treatment at Osmania Hospital, provided the medical officer in jail agreed to my hospitalization.

As luck would have it, I had a severe attack of stomach cramps just when the medical officer, Dr Taher Ali, was examining me. He had no hesitation in prescribing hospitalization. Therefore, having entered jail at 4.30 p.m., I left for Osmania Hospital with a police guard at 6.30 p.m. After three nights in a noisy public ward, I was assigned a private room on 23 February 1949.

I spent the next month in Osmania Hospital. I owe a large debt of gratitude to two persons there: Dr Bankat Chander and Sister Anandam. Dr Bankat Chander was not only a very good physician, but also a very kind and warm-hearted person. Sister Anandam of the nursing staff was remarkable for her devoted and tender care of her patients.

During this period, one of my colleagues from Osmanabad was also sent to the hospital for treatment. He was Mr Mohammad Khan, the excise superintendent of Osmanabad. He had been needlessly and mischievously involved in a murder case and it seemed to get him down.

'Sir,' he said to me, 'they know that I am innocent. Then why do they persecute me?'

He was a very fine person. I think he took the false charges to heart and this was why he succumbed so suddenly two days after he was admitted to Osmania. His death was a great shock to me.

I was still ill when I was transferred to Central Jail, Hyderabad, on 16 March. From there, I was sent to Osmanabad Jail on 21 March 1949, in an open truck. Halfway there, we changed to a covered truck. I reached Osmanabad Jail on 22 March. It was a difficult journey. I cannot understand why I was transferred, unless it was to humiliate me by sending me to a jail in the district where I had until six months earlier been the head of administration. There could be no other explanation. I do not think that the officers investigating the cases against me would have been inconvenienced to any great extent if I had stayed in Hyderabad. But if it was intended to humiliate me, I think my transfer to Osmanabad had the opposite effect. I was treated with great respect, both by the district authorities and the jail staff.

I was able to keep a diary from the time of my arrest onwards. The actual events of my arrest and the day-to-day developments from that point onwards are all recorded in it.

The Charges Against Me

Since there are many misconceptions about Hyderabad, let me make it clear that the Government of Hyderabad was not in the business of inciting its district administration to acts of violence, or of tolerating them. It is not my intention, therefore, to hide behind the excuse that I was following orders. The prime minister of Hyderabad, Mir Laiq Ali, was far from advocating violence of any sort. No other minister that I came across, including the minister in charge of my district, Mr Ikramullah, ever spoke approvingly of such low acts as murder, theft or arson. Even Qasim Razvi did not preach violence or hatred in my district while I was there. Whatever he might have been to others, I always found him helpful and straightforward in his dealings with me. Otherwise, it would not have been possible for me to keep the Razakars under control, or to take action against them, as I did on several occasions.

Nor can it be claimed that the government was ignorant of my actions. The Nizam's government was fully aware of conditions prevailing on the borders and the steps I had to take in order to protect outlying communities from harm. In the course of my work, I confiscated the property of persons directly involved in criminal activities. I had people suspected of breaking the law put under arrest. I was clear in my warning to others who were suspected of disruptive activities. For instance, I was severe with lawyers who indulged in anti-state propaganda. Throughout this period, the state government remained fully informed of new developments and completely supportive of the actions that I took in meeting them.

It was not some unrecognized or illegal regime whose writ I administered. This was a government recognized by the Government of India, as clearly indicated by the Standstill Agreement of November 1947, and by subsequent negotiations. It was a government with which the two governors general of India had also made contact in their efforts to reach a settlement. The Indian and Hyderabad authorities had exchanged senior officials or agents-general, who represented the two entities in Delhi and Hyderabad respectively. The status of the government that I served, therefore, was not in doubt.

There was no doubt either about the deliberate and systematic attempt to break the will of the civil administration in the border districts of Hyderabad through acts of violence and disruption, led by the State Congress and its partners, operating from border camps, made worse by Razakar attempts to 'defend' Hyderabad. This posed a serious double threat to the maintenance of law and order, which required firm and even-handed action on the part of the Hyderabad district administration. Instead of recognizing my efforts in this regard, the new government had moved to punish me. They demonstrated little of that spirit of magnanimity that victors are supposed to show.

The government took some time to decide if it was going to proceed against the civil servants of the former administration. At the time of my arrest, I had no idea of the charges against me, apart from some hints received in the course of my representations to senior government officials immediately after the fall of Hyderabad. It was not even clear for months thereafter whether any specific charges would be brought against me. It was just before the trials began, in April 1950, that the charges were finally presented. I was not accused of the usual white-collar crimes commonly associated with civil servants, such as corruption and embezzlement, but with numerous indictments for conspiracy, murder, arson and loot. Needless to say, they were all trumped-up charges of various degrees of absurdity. Moreover, the complaints had not arisen spontaneously from an aggrieved citizenry, but were actively generated by a government that was by now predisposed to establishing my guilt.

Initially, there were seven cases filed against me, as follows:

1. Dacoity in Killari: Committed on 20 January 1948 , reported on 10 March 1949;
2. Murder in Chilwadi: Committed on 20 March 1948, reported on 22 February 1949;
3. Dacoity accompanied by mischief and hurt in Dhekri: Committed on 26 April 1948, reported on 22 February 1949;
4. Murder of 12 cartmen in Upla: Committed on 29 April 1948, reported on 24 January 1949;
5. Murder of 2 persons in Int: Committed on 6 May 1948, reported on 26 January 1949;
6. Dacoity in Apsingha: Committed on 22 to 24 June, reported on 4 February 1949;
7. Murder of 4 persons in Apsingha: Committed on 24 June 1948, reported on 27 March 1949.

I recorded my first impression of the charges soon after I received them, based on preliminary inquiries, and long before the cases came to trial. Eventually, these seven cases were broken into 24 specific indictments.

Dacoity in Killari

In January 1948, barely two weeks after taking over in Osmanabad, I found myself in Killari, following up on an attack on a police station at Chakur in the Paigah area. Searches were carried out in several villages for the arms that were taken away by the raiders. Killari was one of the villages searched. This case is based on the allegation that I had actually conducted gang robbery there. The date of the supposed dacoity, as mentioned in the chargesheet, was 20 January 1948. My tour diary must have been used to match my movements with appropriate crimes. The case was reported in March 1949, fourteen months after the alleged event, seven months after the surrender of Hyderabad, and about three weeks after my arrest. Anyone familiar with the judicial system in India knows that a delayed first information report (FIR) is viewed with great suspicion, particularly when no reason cogent enough to carry judicial weight is assigned to the delay.

The witnesses could not explain why they did not report the crime earlier, at least immediately after Police Action. Later, during cross-examination, it became clear that none of the complainants had registered the case on their own. Instead, some of the local leaders and the police had approached the villagers and pressed them to lodge the complaints.

There were nine complainants who asserted that the dacoity was committed in their respective houses, presumably during the Killari search. Besides me, the circle inspector, the inspector of police of Umerga, the levy inspector of Osmanabad and several Razakars were accused of the crime. The name of the DSP of Osmanabad, Abul Hassan who was actually with me at the time of the Killari search, however, did not appear in the list of accused, probably because he had left for Pakistan.

There were other obvious weaknesses in the case. If dacoity was the prime motive of the Chakur searches, the other four or five villages that were searched at the same time should also have been plundered. However, there were no complaints received from other villages. More significantly, immediately after my return from Killari, I had put both the circle inspector and the sub-inspector of police of Umerga, under suspension for their alleged involvement in a recent incident involving loot, that is, for aiding the escape of one of the Chakur raiders and for receiving bribes (as I have mentioned in chapter 3). These two police officers remained under suspension until 13 September 1949, and the inquiry was in progress at the time the Hyderabad government fell. The constables who were involved along with these officers had been immediately terminated from service by the DSP. Would anyone take such drastic steps against his own accomplices?

The weaknesses of the case were evident to the investigating officer, who seemed disgusted by what he had to do. He knew that the cases were made up, but he was not in a position to reject them. His predecessor, an assistant superintendent of police, had earlier reported that the entire case seemed to be a pure fabrication, whereupon he was transferred. The case was then handed over to the current inspector of police, who took care to carry out the wishes of the political leaders to have the case registered. But he himself told me, when he met me in jail in connection with this and other cases, that under ordinary circumstances, the complainants would have been prosecuted for wasting police time.

In my cross examination, I had asked this inspector whether he had made any effort to recover any of the goods that were allegedly looted in the village. He confessed that no such effort was ever made.

Murder in Chilwadi

The second case registered against me was that of a murder committed in Chilwadi on 20 March 1948. This was only reported on 22 February 1949, eleven months after the actual killing, seven months after Police Action, and a few days after my arrest. It was alleged that Mohammed Khan, excise superintendent of Osmanabad, accompanied me to Chilwadi, and shot dead a villager, Nanad Narsu.

This allegation made no sense. Mohammed Khan was a gentle giant, with a good service record stretching back twenty years. I knew him well as he was devoted to me. I could not believe that he would ever behave in this manner. The accusations were designed to upset him. I met him in Osmania hospital soon after my arrest. He died there soon afterwards, a broken man.

The first time I visited Chilwadi was when a raid was carried out on the village. I clearly recall that the raiders had attacked some Muslims, and set their houses on fire. The perpetrator of these acts was believed to be Ram Rao of Chilwadi, the person in charge of the Gondgaon Camp. I also recall Chilwadi from another incident, when I had intervened to restore to the villagers the domestic articles stolen by some Pathans and Arabs.

According to the FIR, I was present at the time of the murder; indeed I was identified as the co-accused. If I was there, I am sure that the DSP and other police officers must also have been present. But curiously, they have not been charged. The report was filed in a manner that made it appear that Mohammed Khan alone was involved in it. Therefore, with poor Mohammed Khan's demise, it soon became apparent that the case would be dropped. In due course it was, on the advice of the investigating officer.

Dacoity in Dhekri

This was another case of dacoity reported from Dhekri. Along with Mohammad Khan and me, about 150 Razakars were also charged. Besides dacoity, I am accused of looting, causing mischief by fire with an intent to destroy houses, and causing hurt while committing robbery.

Apparently the crime was committed on 26 April 1948, but it was reported ten months later, on 22 February 1949, six months after Police Action and four days after my arrest.

I had been to Dhekri; I have mentioned the incident that had drawn me there in an earlier chapter. Dhekri was attacked by border raiders. Two young boys had been murdered, and a woman brutally burnt to death. The Pathan chief in charge of security was punished for failing to protect the village, and for not controlling the situation that arose there after the attack. The enraged relatives of the victims had looted the homes of two or three persons whom they suspected of inviting the raiders. But no house was set on fire. The looters were not Razakars. They did what they did in a fit of anger. They were made to return all the looted property. The injured parties (those persons who were suspected of conniving with the border raiders and were looted) were given generous compensation in the form of fairly large sums of money.

This incident had been turned on its head in an attempt to implicate me and the late Mohammed Khan. Luckily for us, there were two senior officers in our company on the day we visited Dhekri – the deputy director of police and the deputy director of customs. They were both impressed by the prompt action taken in the case. I do not understand why these two officers were not mentioned as the co-accused. Nor was the DSP Osmanabad mentioned at all, either as an accused or as one who was present at the scene of the crime. Although, according to the report, there were about 150 Razakars involved in the crime as well, not one Razakar was arrested.

The FIR stated that I accompanied Mohammad Khan, thus making him the main accused. As my subordinate, he must have accompanied me. I think the prosecution wanted him to be involved in two cases as the principal accused: one case of murder and the other of dacoity, according to some plan. It was clear that the local parties who had encouraged the concoction of these cases were not interested in involving other officers. With Mohammad Khan's demise, I anticipate that this case too will be withdrawn, like the Chilwadi murder case. The practice of withdrawing cases after making them up is sufficient to make any unbiased observer suspicious.

Murder of twelve cartmen from Upla

In the fourth case, I was charged with the murder of twelve cartmen from Upla. According to the FIR, I had them arrested on their way to Barsi from Upla on 29 April 1948. No date of the subsequent murder was given, nor was any place mentioned as the actual scene of the crime. The report also stated that at the time of their arrest I was accompanied by several Pathans, some officers, and members of my personal staff.

The case was reported to the police on 24 January 1949 – ten months after the date of the capture of my alleged victims and three weeks before my arrest. And if I remember correctly, it was this case for which I was arrested in Hyderabad and eventually taken to Osmanabad to stand trial.

I had no knowledge of this case, that is, I had no knowledge of the murder of the cartmen until I was charged with the crime. I faintly recall the collector of Sholapur making a reference to the arrest of some cartmen in one of his letters to me. I had no records available in jail and determined to check them later. On 29 April 1948, I had actually visited the village of Gadh because of an attack carried out by the raiders from across the border. A woman named Malan Bee had been injured in the hand and I had brought her back to Osmanabad for treatment, along with her husband and brother (or son). But nothing was reported to me about this murder at the time.

Malan Bee, her husband and her brother sat in the trailer attached to my jeep. Ahmed Khan, the peon, and Ghulam Rasool, the driver, also rode in the trailer. I sat in the jeep with the officers accompanying me. The officers were Abul Hassan, DSP Osmanabad; Hameeduddin Rana, deputy director of police; Qutubuddin, deputy director of customs; Mohammad Khan, and some others. There were no Pathans with me.

Mohammad Khan and Zaman Khan (line inspector) figure in the case as the co-accused. Of these two, Mohammad Khan died in Osmania Hospital soon after my arrest,, and Zaman Khan was allowed to migrate to Pakistan. He was in Hyderabad for several months after the fall of Hyderabad, as was the DSP, Abdul Hassan. They used to visit me often to consult me about the future – whether to stay and face the charges or flee to Pakistan. I had told them that I would stay, as I had nothing to fear. They were afraid of being unnecessarily harassed. After a couple of months, they quietly left for Pakistan without being apprehended. I think it is strange that the authorities let the accused in a murder case escape from under their noses.

Everything appears to have been an afterthought, a frame-up, with fact and fantasy being hurriedly stitched together to make a plausible story. Since my personal staff and the Pathans were actually mentioned in this case (though not by name) one would have thought they would also be apprehended. I should imagine it would not have been difficult to get hold of some of them: I could myself have given their names! If the personal staff and officers were not listed as co-accused in this case, it is possible that they had agreed to appear as witnesses for the prosecution; but I doubt it. It is more likely that these people were dropped from the case altogether, because it is not the intention of the police and the interested parties to harass them. As I understand it, the inordinate delay in bringing the case to trial, or filing a *chalan* (the document presenting the facts of the case and listing the accused and the witnesses) was caused by the police's hunt for witnesses. What was the need for 'witnesses' when I had so many men and officers with me?

I later learnt the real story behind the Upla affair in jail from Ishwanta, son of Ganapati, an inmate of the Osmanabad jail. According to Ishwanta, some cartmen were actually arrested by the customs Pathans and taken to Osmanabad. They were all young boys of fourteen and fifteen. Ishwanta's own son, Prabho, was one of them. No one seems to know what happened to them after they were taken to Osmanabad. After the Police Action, their relatives learnt that the cartmen were all in the Gulbarga jail. The families of the boys then contributed Rs 25 each and sent Shankar Sirpati and Amrosi

Sahib Rao in a futile attempt to look for them, and came back empty-handed. After their return, the families of the villagers and Shankar Sirpati consulted a person named Manik, who contacted the leaders in Osmanabad. Finally, it was decided to lodge a complaint against the taluqdar. This is how I was implicated, on a mere presumption, and accused of an unsolved murder. If it was known (as alleged by the prosecution) that the villagers had been murdered, why were the families kept in the dark, and allowed to launch a search? Why had the witnesses, who were later produced, not informed the parents that their children had been murdered?

Ishwanta's account of the affair sounded convincing. Bapu, another inmate of the jail, who hailed from Upla, also corroborated the story.

Still, I wonder if the customs superintendent of Osmanabad knew about this crime. Perhaps the customs Pathans had actually done it, because of which the customs superintendent became nervous and fled to Pakistan. The Pathans were employed in the customs department as well as in the police force. Neither the customs superintendent nor the DSP had ever reported this case to me. They could have thrown some light on this later, but as mentioned earlier, they had both left for Pakistan.

It was difficult to understand why it was necessary to 'discover' witnesses and bring them from Upla and Surat Gaon, when I already had several people with me on the day of the crime, and who could have easily be brought against me if the allegations were true. The investigating officer had told me that he was forced to do what he was asked, and that he had no discretion in the matter. He later told me that the cases had been prepared by the civil administrator, and were given to him for fulfilling certain legal formalities before presenting them to the special court. He even shed a couple of tears and said that if he had an income of even fifty rupees, he would have thrown up his job. He assured me that he would try to find a way to inform his senior officers that all these cases were fabricated. These were the words of a very junior officer. But similar feelings of unease and doubt existed in higher circles as well. After my arrest, the then DSP of Osmanabad, Mr Bedekar, told me on 26 April 1949, that he was neither satisfied with the evidence nor convinced of the truth of the cases against me. I said it was strange that I should remain in prison when the DSP had such serious doubts about the cases against me.

'Sir,' he replied, 'it is government policy to prosecute you. You will be held until that policy changes.'

I had no answer to that.

Three months after my arrest, there was an identification parade in Osmanabad jail in connection with this case. As the identification line formed up, I suggested to Jaswant Rao, the magistrate, that I should be kept separate from the others in the line-up as I thought it would not be difficult to pick me out from the other prisoners, who were in a very shabby condition, in tattered clothes, dishevelled, unshaven, etc. And so I remained in my room.

Both my suggestion and its acceptance by the magistrate were highly irregular. But the whole thing was a farce in any case. Actually, I had first suggested to him that he should get a few properly dressed persons of my description and put them up for identification with me. Because he could not manage that, apart from including the tehsildar of Tuljapur, Mr Quadri, he was definitely feeling inadequate and agreed to any suggestion that came from me.

The purpose of the identification parade was to give the witnesses a chance to identify me. But predictably enough, the first witness pointed to the tahsildar, Mr Qadri, who was nearest to my description in the line-up. In spite of the prompting of the magistrate, the witness pointed to the tahsildar three times and claimed that he was the taluqdar of Osmanabad. The magistrate shook his head in disgust and asked him to look inside my room. Taking the hint, the witness came to my room and after some hesitation said, 'He is the taluqdar.' But he was still not quite sure. Many persons witnessed this scene, and I hoped they would remember it at the right time. The next witness knew exactly where to look because the police had told him. The behaviour of this witness also betrayed him. He came directly to my room without even bothering to look at the identification line and pointed in my direction. All this was outrageous and farcical but I could not do anything about it.

When I was asked to sign the identification parade report prepared by the magistrate, I took the magistrate's permission to comment on the report before signing it. My note about the proceedings went on record and the magistrate took no exception to it. Perhaps he felt a little better in his conscience for having allowed me to vent my grievance.

Finally, there is one more significant aspect of this case. The FIR clearly alleged that I had joined Qasim Razvi and the Razakars in a conspiracy to terrorize both the government of Hyderabad and the government of India. It was in furtherance of this policy of terrifying both governments that I had the villagers of Upla murdered by my subordinates and the Pathans. But if I had 'conspired' with Qasim Razvi, why was he not listed as an accused? Why had the police failed to name the date and place of this conspiracy? Surely the police could not get away with being so vague.

I could not understand how the murder of innocent and insignificant villagers could terrify any government, much less the government of India. I doubted if the Indian authorities had any inkling about this murder. The agent of the Government of India in Hyderabad, K.M. Munshi, always took great care to notify us through our government of all cases of ill-treatment, and even of cases of mismanagement. It was strange that a mass murder of this kind was not brought to his notice. Even the district magistrate of Sholapur, who had been in constant correspondence with me, was obviously not aware of the murders at the time. I recall that he had only mentioned the arrest of the cartmen, not their murder.

Double Murder in Int

This case, the fifth on the list, concerned a double murder committed in Int on 6 May 1948. It was reported on 26 January 1949 – nine months after the incident and five months after the Indian takeover of Hyderabad. The accused in this case, as in the Upla case, were Zaman Khan, Mohammad Khan and myself. It was alleged that I had ordered Kishen Teke and his wife shot in my presence at Int, and had their bodies burnt. The Pathans and the Razakars were believed to have done the actual killing, at my instance. But I was the only one accused as of 25 August 1949.

There was one difference between the Upla and the Int case. While I did not have any details of the Upla case, I was well acquainted with the details of the Int case. These are the facts as I knew them:

Int was once attacked by raiders. I went there accompanied by the DSP, the excise superintendent, the line inspector and some members of the police force. I had with me my peshi clerk, Abdul Ghani, and a peon named Ahmed Khan. My driver, Ghulam Rasool was also with me. I reached Int a day or two after the attack, and stayed there for just a couple of hours. The DSP had, however, instructed a small party of the police force to stay back in order to distribute the salary of the force posted on the borders near Int. A couple of days after our return, the party under Zaman Khan returned from Int and informed the DSP, who was with me at the time that Kishen Teke and his wife had been killed. He explained that he wanted to search Kishen Teke's house as he had learnt that he was in possession of some unlicensed arms. When he went to search his house, Kishen Teke fired at his party with a revolver. 'We returned fire in self-defence,' he said, 'killing Kishen Teke.' Teke's wife, who happened to be standing behind her husband, was also killed in the exchange.

I remember I had not quite liked this story; something made me suspicious. I thought of going over to Int myself, for further investigation, but I could not do so because of continuous border raids. Sometime later, the DSP informed me that he had instituted an inquiry and that he was satisfied that the police party had indeed fired in self-defence. These were the facts of the Int case as I knew them. If there was murder committed, it was a member of the police party who did it. But the DSP was satisfied and, in any case, a report had been made to the authorities. The deputy director of police and the director of police who were on tour were satisfied with the explanation of the DSP and the case was closed. It was strange that after all this, I was accused of these murders. It seemed stranger still that the DSP did not figure anywhere in the case at all. It was mentioned in the charge that I not only had Kishen Teke and his wife murdered, but also had their bodies burnt – I suppose this was meant to add insult to injury.

It would have been very simple indeed to establish the truth of the matter. I was sure that the actual facts could be established by visiting Int. Also, the facts as I had presented them could be checked against what the people who accompanied me to Int remember of the case. If the police were really after the truth, there could be no difficulty in finding it. Most of the persons who accompanied me to Int were still available. I obviously had no control over them any longer, but I still believed they would bear me out.

I believe Kishen Teke's son, Raghunath Teke, was there in jail just before I was shifted to Osmanabad jail. Apparently, he had once approached Mohammed Khan with a proposal to compromise the case. I believe he said that he would produce no evidence about the murder of his own parents if he were paid a substantial sum of money. I once had a similar experience when another inmate of the Osmanabad jail, Ganpath Lokandy of Int, promised to withhold evidence in the Int case if I gave him Rs 500. I said I would not even give him five rupees.

As in the Upla case, an imputation was made that the Int murders were committed in furtherance of the policy of terrorizing the governments of India and Hyderabad, and that a conspiracy was entered into in order to wage war against the two governments. My arguments in the Upla murder case with regard to this imputation apply with equal force in this case too.

Dacoity in Apsingha

This was a unique case of continuous dacoity lasting three days, from 22 to 24 June 1948, committed at Apsingha. It was reported, however, on 4 February 1949, nearly eight months after it took place, five months after the Police Action and fifteen days before my arrest.

There were seven complainants who submitted that dacoity had been committed in their houses at my behest by Mr Quadri, the tahsildar of Tuljapur, by the Razakars, and some poor peasants belonging to the 'Dhed' and 'Mang' castes.

In actual fact, Apsingha had come under attack by the raiders. A good many people had already run away from Apsingha to Barsi and Sholapur, and after the attack many more left, leaving their houses and kothas unprotected. The tahsildar of Tuljapur was ordered to remove the tin roofs from the kothas as well as the good grain stored in them and transport it all to Tuljapur. This was done, and he duly completed the panchnama. By no stretch of the imagination can this be described as dacoity. The complainants who say that they left their houses because they were afraid of the Razakars surely could not have left their valuables in their houses for the tahsildar to plunder.

I had of course been to Apsingha. The DSP had accompanied me, and his police force had been left behind to help the tahsildar. But neither the DSP, nor any of his men seemed to have any significance in the eyes of the investigating officer; no police officer was arrested for this alleged crime.

This was the only case where an attempt was made to involve local inhabitants – the Dheds and the Mangs in this instance. Some of them were also arrested. They told me that they were originally asked if they would depose against the tahsildar and on refusal they were also implicated in the case as co-accused. The complaint against me was that I had ordered this dacoity.

This was the third case of dacoity where I appeared as an accused. However, no effort was ever made by the investigating officers to recover any property from any of the accused in the case. The tahsildar was not even interrogated regarding the looted property. The importance of non-recovery of property from the accused cannot be over-stressed in a case of dacoity. I should like to add a word here about the tahsildar of Tuljapur. I have mentioned earlier how action was taken against two tahsildars of my district, namely, the tahsildar of Latur and the tahsildar of Lohara. It was about the time of the Apsingha affair that I ordered prosecution against the tahsildar of Lohara for alleged participation in a case of loot. If the tahsildar of Tuljapur had also indulged in loot (at Apsingha) I would have taken similar steps against him.

The investigating officer who was entrusted with these cases of dacoity had been in the district for a long time and was well acquainted with the situation. He also knew me personally and my reputation in Osmanabad to be acutely embarrassed by his new task. Though he had to do what he was asked, he had the grace to offer me his apologies!

I was informed later that property belonging to one of the complainants, Deena Nath Sekrey, was recovered from Bhagwan Dangey, Sidran Lokay, Gana Guru and Gundae Guru. Apparently, these four had been in police custody for fifteen days, but this development was hushed up by the police for fear that it might have an adverse effect on the cases against us. This information was subsequently confirmed by a more reliable source.

Murder in Apsingha

The seventh case against me concerned the murder of four men in Apsingha. The murders were said to have been committed on 24 June 1948, one or two days after the Apsingha dacoity began. Obviously, I did nothing but go around committing murders and violent robberies! This case was reported on 27 March 1949 – nine months after the alleged crime took place and a month and a half after my arrest.

The facts of the case were these: Apsingha village and the police outpost located there were both made the object of a raid from the border camps. Hearing of this, the tahsildar of Tuljapur, Mr Qadri, immediately proceeded to Apsingha, with a police escort. He was still making inquiries when a Razakar fired at Babu Rao, alleging that he had sheltered the raiders in his house on the night preceding the attack. Babu Rao escaped unhurt but the bullet hit the health inspector of Tuljapur, Abdul Gafoor, and killed him on the spot. Vakil Ahmed, the Razakar who had fired the fatal shot, was immediately put under arrest. When I visited the village later, I felt that the place was still not safe for Babu Rao. He was an old man of about eighty. I shared my apprehensions with the DSP, who ordered him to be taken to Osmanabad, saying that he would also like to investigate whether the report that Babu Rao had given shelter to the raiders was true.

Babu Rao did not travel with us to Osmanabad. It is pure fabrication that I brought Babu Rao and some others with me. As a matter of fact, I did not even know about the others who were taken along with Babu Rao. Those travelling with me that day were the DSP of Osmanabad, some members of the police force, the peon Ahmed Khan and the driver Ghulam Rasool. A day or two later, the DSP told me that he had let Babu Rao go home and that was the last I heard of the affair.

According to the report, five persons were taken to Osmanabad, along with Babu Rao. They were Vir Lakshmi, Iwarsad, Prabhakar, Ganga Ram and Shiv Murthi. If it is to be believed that I had four of these six murdered, there must be sufficient reason for letting Ganga Ram and Shiv Murthi go. Why were these two spared? There was no explanation, nor any theory advanced by the police to account for my discrimination in murdering some and sparing others.

As far as I could remember, I had visited Apsingha on 22 June 1948. The date of the murder is given as 24 June. I presume that for two days these men were in police custody – but no police officer was mentioned as an accused.

No witness to the actual murder was ever produced in court. In spite of the allegations against the Pathans by a solitary witness, there was no mention of a single Pathan as an accused. Only I stand accused – and along with me the Razakar Vakil Ahmed, who shot and killed Abdul Gafoor by mistake. He was arrested on 22 June 1948, the day of the fatal shooting.

There was something else that struck me as odd about this case. One of the complainants, Deena Nath, was the son of Babu Rao, one of the alleged victims. This Mr Deena Nath was also a complainant in the Apsingha dacoity. He reported the robbery on 4 February 1949, but he neglected to inform the authorities about the murder of his own father until two months later, on 27 March 1949! The incongruity did not end there. No relative of the other three victims ever came forward to report the alleged murders. It seemed that despite all efforts to uncover something really damaging, all that could be found or concocted against us were these ridiculous and weak charges. After June 1948, they could not even find the most flimsy evidence upon which to build a case against me – although the period after June has been described as the darkest in the recent history of Hyderabad.

Trials in Court

There was a lapse of fourteen months between my arrest in February 1949 and the commencement of my trial in April 1950. During this time, I was not even produced before a magistrate. No reason was given for the delay but it was obviously caused by the police needing time to prepare and file their cases. I endured this situation as best I could. My illness had brought my weight down to less than a hundred pounds. On my way to Osmanabad jail in the back of a truck, I resolved to get better. It struck me that I could not afford to rely on medical help; it was something that could be denied me. I would rely on myself instead. Rather dramatically, I threw out all the medicines I was carrying. Later, I relented and went back on Entero Vioform.

Once settled in the jail, I started a regimen of regular exercise and proper diet. Gradually, my health improved. But it still took three months before the episodes of stomach cramps and bloody diarrhea disappeared altogether. I had been keeping a diary since my arrest; I continued with it and began thinking of writing a proper account of my work in Osmanabad.

I was treated well in Osmanabad jail. I was sent there, as I have stated before, with the intention of humiliating me. But the jail authorities received me with courtesy, going to great lengths to make me as comfortable as possible. I had a cell to myself, and was allowed books and writing material. I could receive visitors, get food from outside, and even get my clothes washed. I could mingle freely with other prisoners and jail staff. The exercise sessions, for example, were always a pleasant social affair. On 12 May 1949, instructions were received regarding the treatment of various classes of detainees. I was to be treated as a Class 'A' prisoner. I was already being treated well, but now I was formally entitled to these perquisites.

Since I was far from home, my family made arrangements for supporting me locally. My general assistant in Osmanabad, the person who acted as my link to the outside world, was a remarkable man, Maulana, who had worked for different members of the family of my in-laws. Now, at this low point in my life, he was assigned to look after me. Barely literate, endlessly resourceful, sharp and energetic, he soon understood and expanded his terms of reference. Apart from assisting in simple domestic arrangements, which included supervising a cook that we had engaged locally, he took care of messages, letters, petitions, and files. He was excellent at tracing potential witnesses. Very soon, he was familiar with all the cases filed against me, and became a sort of paralegal assistant. Without him, things would have been a lot more difficult for me.

But Maulana also needed supervision. He was subject to the occasional wild impulse and not easy to manage, especially from behind bars. But no one could have served me better. It was one of those relationships where the servant gives more than the master has either the right to expect or the ability to reward, putting the latter forever in his debt.

ꕥ

While my personal arrangements were as good as they could be, considering that I was locked up in jail, the legal side of my affairs was a disaster. Good lawyers were not willing to come to Osmanabad, or indicated that they would charge very high fees, which I could not afford. In mid-April, a lawyer was sent over from Hyderabad. He was charging us fifty rupees a day, and doing nothing more than collecting FIRs. I knew this lawyer, Kazi Abdul Qayum Khan; he was lazy and ineffective. I asked Maulana to pay him fifty rupees and send him packing. I applied to the court of Kallam to send the FIRs directly to me. I then considered engaging a local lawyer, Mr Narsing Rao. But I learnt that the Bar Association of Osmanabad had decided not to take any cases of officers charged with criminal offences.

On 11 May 1949, Barrister Akbar Ali Khan (a veteran of the Hyderabad State Congress Party), came on a mission to Osmanabad, and made it a point to visit me. We talked about my cases. I explained to him that I did not want my family to take on the financial burden of engaging a lawyer; I was prepared to defend myself. Mr Akbar Ali Khan, who knew my family well, undertook to convey my views and to discourage my family from making expensive commitments. I am sure he conveyed the message faithfully but some time later another lawyer, Hyder Raza Zaidi, was engaged. He did not prove very useful either, and I had to make an effort to dismiss him. In the end, the court appointed a legal advisor. He too remained ignorant of the details of my case, partly out of disinterest and partly because he could not lay his hands on the relevant documentation; he had no files on my case.

Soon after my transfer to the jail in Osmanabad, the civil administrator of the town, Mr Baitmangalkar, came to see me. He was sympathetic.

'Extraordinary!' he exclaimed. 'I am surprised to find you under arrest, Mr Hyder, and astonished that you have been lodged in Osmanabad jail, in your own district!'

A little later during our conversation, he added, 'Please understand that I had nothing to do with your arrest. I simply passed on the reports that reached me, without comment. I was unaware of what followed.'

'Now,' he continued, anticipating me, 'this whole sorry affair must be looked into, of course. But since I am under orders of transfer, it would serve no useful purpose to explain the cases to me. My successor will look into the matter.'

I learnt subsequently that Mr Baitmangalkar's transfer was taking him to Bidar, to serve on the Tribunal set up there. His successor in Osmanabad, M.G. Pimputkar, I.C.S., arrived in due course, and came to see me in jail on 27 July 1949. He was a personable officer, considerably younger than his predecessor. He explained that he could not help me at all, as it had all been wrapped up by Mr Baitmangalkar.

'I can't see what I can do at this stage, Mr Hyder,' he said, evenly. 'I could hardly undo what has been done, even assuming that mistakes were made. Sorry!'

In this way, each passed the responsibility for taking action on the other, and seemed to think no more of it. Not for the first time since the fall of Hyderabad, I noticed an erosion of the courtesy owed by one government colleague to another. The Indian civil servants that I had recently encountered, from Ghatge, the collector of Sholapur, to Patro, the new police chief in Hyderabad, to Messers Baitmangalkar and Pimputkar – my successors in Osmanabad – were all able and honourable men, trying to behave decently, but held back, to a greater or lesser degree, by some common, shared prejudice against the previous regime.

For some time, I had been thinking of writing an account of my work in Osmanabad. On 28 July 1949, I actually made a start, in an exercise book, without benefit of any reference material. By the end of August, I had filled seven notebooks, ending with a summary of the cases against me. The exercise was quite helpful in keeping the details of those tumultuous days of my collectorship well-ordered in my mind.

All this time, from April 1949, there were rumours that the Special Tribunal was about to start its work. At this stage I did not even know what I was to be charged with, and whether the government really intended to proceed with the cases or would drop them. On 10 May 1949, I met Mr Jetley, the IG of police, during one of his visits to the jail. He said that he was only aware of one charge against me, that of the desecration of a Hindu temple (which was a complete surprise to me). He encouraged me to write to him, which I did. He wrote back later that month, saying that it was now his impression, having looked into the matter, that the government intended to proceed, and the (unspecified) charges against me would not be dropped.

Still, the rumours of imminent release persisted, alternating with rumours of the arrival of the Special Tribunal. Like an unseen enemy, the tribunal assumed an ominous character that seemed to terrify everybody. It was clear that few witnesses would be bold enough to stand up for me in such a body.

Time passed. The hopes of an early release gave way to the grim realization that we were in for a long haul; and that however absurd the charges, we were to be engaged in a fight for our lives. My trial finally began in April 1950. On 30 May 1950, I was transferred to Gulbarga jail. By now I was managing my own defence, hoping that the court would appreciate my spirit of cooperation, and help me. Having some training as magistrate, I could appreciate my own shortcomings as a criminal lawyer.

A kindly judge can make a great deal of difference in the conduct of a case. I, unfortunately, did not enjoy the court's favour. From the beginning, the special judge, Rai Vasudeo Pershad, was unhelpful. My first appearance in his court set the tone for the future.

'I see you are dressed in a suit, Mr Hyder,' he said, addressing me in open court, 'soon you will be in convict garb.'

I could have put up with sarcasm and jibes; judges often display a quirky sense of humour. But Vasudeo Pershad basically did not see any need to help me, and interpreted the law accordingly. I encountered the greatest difficulty in obtaining documentary evidence essential to my defence, or in summoning witnesses, or in ensuring a fair interpretation of the rules of procedure. I knew that the government had in its possession records that, if produced in court, would make short work of the cases against me. But when I asked for them, I got various unhelpful responses. The most egregious example of such obstructionism came from the chief secretary of the Hyderabad government, in response to my request (made through the Special Judge) to look at the evidence the police had allegedly gathered against me. In any criminal case, the prosecution shares the evidence with the accused. But in this instance, the government refused. The chief secretary's letter is worth quoting in full:

GOVERNMENT OF HYDERABAD
No.401/GAD/C/50. Dated 25 October 1950
From
L.C. Jain, I.C.S. Chief Secretary to Government.
To,

The Special Judge, Gulburga & Osmanabad.
Subject: - Government through CID Vs. Mohd. Hyder,
Talukdar Suit no. 22/8 of 1950.

Sir,

Reference your letter No. 1215, dated 16-8-1950 and subsequent reminders, I am directed to state that as the documents called for by you in your letter under reply are of a strictly confidential nature and it would be prejudicial to the interests of Government to disclose them, this office regrets its inability to produce these documents before the Court. The documents relate to unpublished affairs of the State and the production of the same before the Court has not been permitted by Government. In view of these circumstances this office claims the privilege of the non-production of the documents in question provided for in Sections 126 of the Hyderabad Evidence Act and Section 87 (c) of the Hyderabad Criminal Procedure Code.

Yours faithfully,
Sd/-
L.C. Jain
CHIEF SECRETARY

How was I to refute evidence that I had not seen?

The special judge accepted the government's view, and did not insist on producing the police file. Later on, when the Int murder case went to the High Court on appeal, the judge vigorously disagreed with the government's view. But he too passed the opportunity to call for the file.

There were other examples of obstructionism. I will cite a few here, starting with the Upla case, which alleged that I had twelve young cartmen arrested and murdered. As this case got under way, it was learnt that Mr Ghatge, the district magistrate of Sholapur, had already investigated the case and had made a detailed report to the Government of Bombay. The cartmen, it might be recalled, had crossed over from Indian enclaves into Osmanabad district, and had been arrested, but had then disappeared, presumably murdered. When the papers relating to the investigation were sent for by the court, the government again claimed privilege, stating that the records were of a confidential nature, relating to unpublished affairs of state. This was another blow, as I had hoped that the details of the investigation would exonerate me. Again, the judge was not inclined to challenge the government's ruling of confidentiality.

But others were. Upon learning that information vital in a criminal case against me was being withheld, Mr Ghatge came to the special judge's court, bearing the file in question. He handed the 53-page document to the court, declaring that it contained information relevant to the case being tried, and left. It was a dramatic intervention. Ghatge, who had been so unbending when he faced me across the border as the district magistrate of Sholapur, was now showing uncommon decency by coming to my aid in this way. He had been an adversary but not an enemy.

The court, however, took its cue from the public prosecutor, who noted: 'Mr Ghatge has left the file for the examination of the court. It is a government file containing confidential papers. Without obtaining the permission of the authorities copies cannot be given.'

My request for copies was denied. This was the second time the court had let the government get away with the 'the privilege of non-production'.

As I had feared, the tribunal intimidated my witnesses. I was supposed to have arrested the twelve cartmen during my tour of Gadh. I had been accompanied by two senior officials during my trip there, Mr Hameeduddin Rana, deputy director of police, and Mr Qutbuddin, deputy commissioner of customs. I felt that it could help my defence if they could give a true account of my movements in Gadh. But at the preliminary hearing, Mr Qutbuddin took me to one side.

'You are in trouble, Mr Hyder,' he whispered to me. 'Leave me out of it.'

'Just tell the truth,' I urged.

'I am sorry, Mr Hyder. I have a family to think of.'

'How would you like it,' I said, 'if you were in trouble and I refused...'

He lowered his gaze. 'I would understand,' he murmured.

And I could understand his reluctance. Fear renders us indifferent to each other's fate.

The manner in which Qutbuddin gave his evidence subsequently made it necessary to call for the tour notes of these two officers. This was, in any case, a perfectly reasonable request.

The police replied that Rana's notes were not available, as the police office covering the region had been abolished, and the records destroyed. I pointed out that even if the regional office had been abolished, the tour notes could still be found in the offices of the director of police and the director general of police, as it was an established practice for deputy directors and superintendents to forward their field reports to their senior officers. I observed that neither had their offices been abolished, nor had the records been destroyed.

The jail superintendent wrote back repeating that the regional office had closed and the documents did not exist. 'When a definite reply has been received,' he noted loftily, 'no useful purpose will be served in writing to them again.' The special judge agreed, noting: 'Need not be sent for. The party is to be informed accordingly.'

In the meantime, the Treasury Office, Gulbarga, which was requested to obtain TA bills for the two officers (needed to establish that they had travelled with me to Gadh), added the following insult: 'I am to say that the copies of such irrelevant papers cannot be given without requisition by the competent Court.'

Nor was it easy to summon witnesses. It will be recalled that there had been an identity parade three months after my arrest. In the course of those farcical proceedings, Tahsildar Syed Mohammed Qadri was identified by one of the witnesses as the collector of Osmanabad. I wanted Qadri to appear as a defence witness, to testify that the witnesses could not identify me.

The special judge scored out his name from the list of defence witnesses. When I wrote explaining why I wanted Qadri to appear, the special judge made this annotation:

'Besides many difficulties, money is to be spent summoning this witness – the application is rejected.

Sd/-Judge.'

I wrote back:

'I beg to state that the witness is in Gulbarga Jail as a prisoner under trial. He has been present in this court along with me. I am at a loss to know what the difficulty is in producing him as a defence witness.'

Despite this type of difficulty, I was acquitted of the Upla murder charge by the special court. But I was convicted of kidnapping the cartmen, which was not the charge originally framed against me. Subsequently, the high court set aside that sentence too.

Other cases came up one by one in the special court, and in each case, rules of procedure and evidence were flouted at will. In the Killari case (actually nine cases of arson and loot), the officer investigating the crime, Abdul Khader, assistant superintendent of police (ASP), Criminal Investigation Division, was not produced, although he was present in the court on several occasions. The report of the investigation itself was not made available. Although it was alleged that gold and cash had been looted, none of it was recovered. And the police never questioned me, the defendant, about the case. Despite these extraordinary defects, the special court sentenced me to 18 months in prison. Later, the sentence was quashed in appeal.

In the Apsingha murder case, it turned out that one of my alleged victims had lived on for months after I was supposed to have killed him, passing away eventually of natural causes. Human bones were produced by one witness, while the other stated on oath that he had had the bodies cremated. There were mix-ups regarding dates as well: government permission was accorded to proceed against me in relation to an occurrence of 24 April 1948; whereas the actual murder was said to have been committed on 24 June 1948. And so on. This murder charge failed. The other Apsingha case relating to loot in the village of Apsingha (actually twelve cases of loot) ended in acquittal. The nine cases of loot in Killari were dismissed by the Supreme Court.

I was also charged originally with conspiracy, with attempting to terrorize both the governments of India and Hyderabad, and for associating with Qasim Razvi and the Razakars. No case was ever brought against me for these alleged crimes.

Finally, in the Int double murder, I was convicted by the Special Court and sentenced to death, and the case went in appeal to the

High Court. The decision of the High Court is summarized later in this chapter. The full text is provided as an annex, and is worth reading, because it is a compelling account of the High Court judge's view of that case, and of the defects, as he saw them, in the decision of the Special Court to condemn me. If anyone thinks that I have been critical of the special judge, they should read the judge's comments!

In prison you hear everything. On the night of my sentencing in the Int case, someone whispered to me about a disturbance in the gypsy camp on the outskirts of the town. Apparently, Judge Vasudeo Pershad, rather the worse for wear, had chased a gypsy woman into her tent, importuning her, and had been thrown out by the men in the encampment. My first thought was, 'I am not the only victim of this sentence; it has cost Vasudeo Pershad something too.' But soon all such charitable musings vanished, as I got busy in transferring to that special part of the prison that is reserved for inmates condemned to death. Thereafter, I lived in a condemned prisoner cell or 'death cell' for over a year.

Gradually, however, things improved for me. But Vasudeo Pershad fell on hard times. After all this was over, some time in the late 1950s, when I was sitting one day with Nawab Deen Yar Jung, my father-in-law, in Aziz Bagh, his house in Hyderabad, Maulana rushed up, in a state of high excitement.

'Vasudeo Pershad is here, Vasudeo Pershad.... He wants to see you. Just say the word and I will take him by the scruff of his neck and throw him out, the Haramzada. Just say the word...'

I turned to my father-in-law. 'It seems we have a visitor!'

Deen Yar Jung addressed Maulana, 'Tell him we are unable to see him. You are not to touch him.'

We never heard from him again.

Poor Vasudeo Pershad. In the end I felt sorry for him. He had obviously been under pressure to find me guilty. He didn't realize until too late that it would cost him too, not only weighing on his conscience but also eventually destroying his professional reputation as well when my cases went in appeal to the High Court.

ജ്ഞ

In 1951, when the High Court started reviewing my appeals, I was transferred first to the Secunderabad jail, and then to Hyderabad Central Jail, Chanchalguda. Once in Hyderabad, it was possible to see my family regularly. Our pleasantest meetings were in the grounds of the Hyderabad High Court. The High Court, a stately building in the Indo-Saracen style, is situated on the banks of the river Musi. I would arrive in a police truck. If there was time, my handcuffs would be removed and I would be allowed to walk across to our blue Packard, parked under the trees in the beautiful grounds of the court. I would sit in the back of the car with my wife; my sons in the front seat. We would chat about coming home. I would joke with my two young sons, and hold my wife's hand. My daughter, born four months after my arrest, was too young to visit me. I only saw her on my release, when she was almost three.

This was the beginning of a more hopeful period. The judgement that was eventually delivered was a major breakthrough. It is notable on several counts. It was the first time that I had been adequately represented in court. My counsel was the distinguished British advocate Brian Mackenna (later Justice Sir Brian Mackenna), who had been retained originally as part of Qasim Razvi's defence team. But as he became acquainted with the cases against me, Mackenna offered his services, gratis. His offer was readily accepted. Mackenna was motivated by a sense of fair play; I badly needed competent legal representation. I had gone through a difficult time before the Special Tribunal.

The case that had come up in appeal concerned the murder of Kishen Teke and his wife in Int. I was supposed to have ordered the Pathans to open fire on them because they would not haul down a flag they had hoisted over their house. I had said in my defence that although I had been to Int that day, I was not there at the time of their death (which occurred some time after I left Int), nor had I played any part in it. Upon learning of the incident at the time, I had ordered a formal inquiry through proper police channels. But the special court had found me guilty of murder and sentenced me to death. On appeal, the case came before Justice Vithal Rao Deshpande of the Hyderabad High Court.

His judgement is notable for the strictures passed on the special judge for his handling of the case, on legal points, and for his brisk treatment of the evidence offered by the prosecution witnesses. Given that judges are usually circumspect in their comments on fellow judges, and allowing for the understated language that they employ, the criticism is actually quite devastating. It condemns, among other things, the procedures followed by the special court, sharply disagrees with the special judge's interpretation of the rules of evidence, and sternly notes his failure to be of greater assistance to the defendant in summoning documents essential to his case.

Justice Deshpande makes the following comments on the legal points:

- The accused was not examined as per provisions of the Criminal Procedure Code;
- The accused was examined in the wrong order;
- The accused was not provided with the statements of witnesses;
- The Court failed to attach weight to the written statements of the accused;
- The Special Judge was wrong in supporting the Government's claim of privilege.

After dealing with the legal points of the case, the judge reviewed its substance. One by one, he picked out the inconsistencies in the statement of the prosecution witnesses (PW 1, 2, etc), effectively destroying the prosecution's case.

The TA Bill of PW 2 shows that he was not at the scene of the crime:

This finding shakes the evidence of the next witness (PW 3):

A key statement of PW 3 was not produced.

PW 4 was not an eyewitness to the incident, and did not mention the name of the accused to the Investigating Officer.

PW 7 could not identify the accused.

PW 8, Rukmani Bai contradicted herself about the presence of the accused at the scene of the crime.

PW 9, a police head constable, was asked to investigate the murder at Int by Hyder (Collector of Osmanabad at the time); his First Information Report is different from his evidence in the case against Hyder. He must, therefore, have knowingly filed a false First Information Report.

These are the essential points of the judgement. In a measured, unhurried way, the judgement proceeds to an unambiguous finding in favour of the defendant. This point is worth noting, as later the government tried to argue that I was cleared by the courts on a technicality, the Special Tribunal being declared ultra vires by the High Court. In the case presented here, the High Court ruled in my favour after a full review of the merits of the case, overturning and quashing the sentence of the lower court.

(For the full text of this judgement see Appendix, Ex. P. 27.)

I File a Writ

On 6 February 1952, all remaining charges against me were dropped. On 29 February 1952, I was released on bail, which was put up by Hakeem Moizuddin, founder of Zinda Tilismaat, a family friend. I had been in prison for three years and eleven days.

By the time of my release, the government's case against me was falling apart. The High Court had declared the Special Court unconstitutional, and I had either won my cases in that discredited body or on appeal to the High Court of Hyderabad. Although it was open to the government to ask for a retrial of all the cases that it had lost in the Special Court, it did not take up that option. Nor did it persist with its appeals to the Supreme Court of India in the cases that it had lost in the High Court. Now probably realizing that the Supreme Court might be even harsher in its strictures than the High Court had been, the government withdrew its appeals. The Supreme Court closed the cases against me in June 1954.

One question remained: What was to be done with me? I was still under suspension. After two more years of waiting, the government issued orders in 1956, removing me from service. The order informed me that henceforth I would be paid a 'compassionate allowance' equal to half the pension I would have drawn had I retired prematurely on medical grounds on 18 September 1948, the day of my suspension from service. This amounted to Rs 58 per month (or 19 US dollars at the prevailing rate of exchange). My salary and allowances as collector of Osmanabad had been Rs 1600.

Normally, a civil servant cannot be dismissed out of hand, without giving him an opportunity to defend himself or issuing him a 'show cause notice', thereby affording him the possibility of challenging his dismissal. But the government invoked a special proviso in the Constitution of India, which states that a civil servant may be so removed if the security of the state were involved (Proviso (c) to clause (2) of Article 311 of the Constitution). By resorting to this proviso, it was sending out a clear message: innocent or guilty, it did not want me.

It seemed to me that this would be a difficult position for the government to maintain. I was suspended on 18 September 1948 because, the government had said there were certain charges of a criminal nature against me. Subsequently, I had been cleared of those charges, either by the Special Court or on appeal to the High Court of Hyderabad, and the government had itself withdrawn its appeals to the Supreme Court. Therefore, if the charges could not be made to stick, should my suspension not be lifted as well? To get round this awkward development, the order removing me suggested that I had not actually been tried in the courts, that the cases were merely withdrawn by the government, and that I had been set free on a technicality. This was neither true nor very helpful to the government's case, because if the courts could not prove me guilty, then the presumption of innocence should work in my favour. Under the circumstances, my dismissal was tantamount to removing an innocent man.

To overcome that obstacle, the government had now invoked the special proviso in the constitution, which gives the executive the power to remove a civil servant if the security of the state would otherwise be compromised. But here too, there were weaknesses in the government's case.

Civil service rules require that wrongdoing must be ascertained first through a preliminary inquiry. For this purpose, the petitioner should be allowed an opportunity to prove, by examination of witnesses, that he is not guilty of the charges. If at that stage, the provisional conclusion is reached that he is in fact guilty, then Proviso (c) gives the executive the right to deny the petitioner any further opportunity to defend himself if, in doing so, the security of the state is compromised. In my case, there had been no preliminary inquiry. Therefore, the conditions for applying Proviso (c) had not been met. Subsequently, I had undergone a much more thorough investigation, namely, trial in court, on no less than twenty-four charges. Even that rigorous examination had failed to establish my guilt. Without first establishing my guilt, either through a preliminary inquiry or through the courts, the government could not invoke Proviso (c).

But the government order to remove me seemed to argue that I had not actually been exonerated by the courts, therefore I was guilty; and because I was guilty, I posed a security risk. Nowhere was it explained why I posed a security risk. It was very muddled thinking. But muddled or not, it effectively denied me the right – yet again – to examine the government's case against me, or ask for the confidential files that it had refused to produce all along.

It remained to be seen whether the courts would stand up to the government and ask why I was still to be regarded a security risk, after the courts had thoroughly scrutinized my actions. Much would depend on the court's willingness to take on the executive branch in this way. Still, I felt I had a strong case. In 1957, I brought a writ against the government, requesting that my dismissal be overturned.

Five documents are presented here. The first is the Petition itself, requesting the court to quash the order removing me from service, and to direct the government to reinstate me. The second document is my sworn affidavit in support of my request. The third document is the government's reply or counter-affidavit, which appears in Chapter 13; the fourth document is my response to the counter-affidavit (Chapter 14); and the fifth document is the court's decision on my Writ Petition, (Chapter 15).

The entire case is reproduced here, in Chapters 12-15. Comments, added sparingly and impartially, are meant to help the reader through the legal arguments.

(Document One: Petition)

IN THE HIGH COURT OF JUDICATURE
OF ANDHRA PRADESH
AT HYDERABAD
Writ Petition No: 148 of 1957.
(Under Article 226 of the Constitution)

MOHAMMED HYDER
Vs.
THE STATE OF ANDHRA PRADESH

Advocates for Petitioner

1. S. Malkonda Reddy
2. Anwarullah Pasha

IN THE HIGH COURT OF JUDICATURE
OF ANDHRA PRADESH
AT HYDERABAD
Special Original Jurisdiction
(Under Article 226 of the Constitution)
Writ Petition No. 148 of 1957

Mohammed Hyder .... Petitioner
VERSUS
The State of Andhra Pradesh)
Represented by the Chief)
Secretary to the Government,) Respondent.
General Administration Dept.,)
Hyderabad – Deccan.)

1. The address for service of all notices and processes on the Petitioner is that of his counsel Shri S. Malkonda Reddy and Anwarulla Pasha, Advocate's Association, High Court of Andhra Pradesh, Hyderabad.
2. The address for service of all notices and process on the Respondent is as given above.

3. For the reasons stated in the accompanying affidavit the Petitioner prays that this Honorable Court may be pleased to issue a Writ of Certiorari or any other appropriate writ, order or direction calling for the records relating to the order of the Government of Hyderabad No. 300-GAD-1SRC-CSP-56 General Administration Department, dated 13.10.1956 and quash the same;

   (b) to issue a Writ of Mandamus or any other appropriate writ, order or direction to re-instate the Petitioner into office with back emoluments from 18.9.1948 and

   (c) for costs of the petition and such other reliefs as may be appropriate in the circumstances of the case.

Dated at Hyderabad
7th Day of March, 1957
COUNSEL FOR PETITIONER.

ജഢ

(Document Two: Affidavit)

IN THE HIGH COURT OF JUDICATURE OF
ANDHRA PRADESH
AT HYDERABAD
Special Original Jurisdiction
(Under Article 226 of the Constitution)
Writ Petition No. 148 of 1957

Mohammed Hyder .... Petitioner

VERSUS

The State of Andhra Pradesh)
Represented by the Chief)
Secretary to the Government,) Respondent
General Administration Dept.,)
Hyderabad – Deccan.)

Affidavit of Mohammed Hyder

I, Mohammed Hyder, son of Mohammed Ghouse, aged about 40 years, Muslim, residing at Hyderabad, do hereby solemnly and sincerely state as follows: -

1. I am the Petitioner in the above Petition and I am well acquainted with the facts of the case.
2. I belong to a respectable Muslim family of Hyderabad. In 1936 I passed the B.A. Examination of Osmania University with distinction. Thereafter, I appeared for the H.C.S. competitive examination and being successful was admitted to the Hyderabad Civil Service in 1937. After two years of training in British India, I was appointed as a Munsif-Magistrate in the regular Judicial Service in Hyderabad State in 1940. After serving in other capacities I was appointed Collector of the border District of Osmanabad, in January 1948.
3. At that time there was conflict between two major political parties in Hyderabad, the Razakars and the State Congress involving violence, murder, loot and arson. The Petitioner in obedience to the directions of the Government in Power, had to put down the lawless activities of both these groups and in the course of his administration as Collector in charge of law and order, he had incurred the bitter enmity of one Mr Phool Chand Gandhi, who was then the leader of the State Congress in the District, and other members of his party.
4. In September 1948, immediately after the Police Action in Hyderabad the Military Governor took charge of the Administration, and under the orders of the Military Governor the Petitioner was placed under suspension with effect from 18.9.1948. Neither any charges were furnished to the Petitioner nor was there any inquiry as prescribed by the law then prevailing in Hyderabad under which any charge against a Government Officer had to be referred for investigation to a Commission of Inquiry.
5. On 18.2.1949 about six months after the Police Action the Petitioner was put under arrest and prosecutions were launched against him before a court specially constituted for the purpose called the 'Special Judge's Court', in about 24 cases of murder,

dacoity, arson etc., alleged to have been committed by him in the course of the discharge of his official duties as Collector.

6. The charges against the petitioner were fabricated at the instance of the persons against whom the petitioner in the discharge of his official duties had to take action while he was the Collector. The trials commenced in 1950. The Government claimed privilege in respect of several official documents which were summoned by the petitioner and which would have unequivocally proved the innocence of the Petitioner. The prosecution put all sorts of obstacles to a fair trial of the petitioner. The trial judge acquitted him in several cases but convicted him in two murder cases and 9 dacoity cases. He was sentenced to death in one murder case and to various terms of imprisonment in the rest. He was then confined to a condemned cell, and he had to undergo harrowing agony for over a year as a condemned prisoner. On appeal to the High Court of Hyderabad, he was acquitted in all the cases and the convictions and sentences were reversed. The State, however, preferred appeals to the Supreme Court; but obviously finding these appeals had no chance of success, withdrew the same and the Supreme Court passed orders dismissing all the appeals.

7. The result was that the petitioner was able to establish his innocence on all the charges against him, after a long and protracted period of agony and harassment. Not satisfied with the criminal prosecutions referred to above, the petitioner's private accounts were frozen under the Nullification of Transfers Regulation No. IV of 1358 F. He was then directed to face an inquiry by the Board of Revenue of the State relating to the disposal of the monies held by him as Collector of Osmanabad prior to Police Action. The petitioner was able to satisfy the Board that he was not guilty of any misappropriation. Thereafter his accounts were defreezed, thereby exonerating him of all the charges.

8. Nevertheless, the petitioner continued under suspension and in spite of his acquittal on all the criminal charges, the Government would do nothing to right the wrong they had done to him or to restore him to office. But after a long lapse of time, on 13.10.1956 a few days prior to the formation of the state of Andhra

Pradesh, the then Government of Hyderabad passed an Order Ref. No. 300-GAD-I-SRC.-CSP-56, General Administration Department, dated 13.10.1956, removing the petitioner from service without notice, without holding an inquiry, without giving any opportunity to defend himself and without respecting the judgements of the duly constituted courts exonerating him from all the criminal charges.

9. The full text of the Order is given hereunder:

   (a) 'Shri Mohammed Hyder, a Member of the Hyderabad Civil Service, who was serving as Talukdar, Osmanabad, was placed under suspension with effect from 18 September 1948 in view of some serious allegations of a criminal nature against him. Sanction to prosecute him in Courts of Law was given but in view of the general policy of Government in respect of such prosecutions the cases against him were withdrawn from the Supreme Court.'

   (b) 'The case against him has been fully examined. The Rajpramukh in exercise of the powers conferred on him by the Proviso (c) to clause (2) of Article 311 of the Constitution has satisfied himself that in the interests of the security of the state, it is not expedient to give Shri Mohammed Hyder an opportunity as required under Sub-Clause (2) of Article 311 of the Constitution.'

   (c) 'After considering all the facts, the Rajpramukh is pleased to decide that Shri Mohammed Hyder be removed from service with effect from 18th September 1948; and on purely compassionate grounds and as an act of clemency, Shri Mohammed Hyder be paid a compassionate allowance for life equal to 50 per cent of the pension that he would have drawn had he been retired on medical certificate on 18 September 1948. The compassionate allowance will be paid only from the date of this Order.

   'For the period from 18 September 1948 to the date of this Order Shri. Mohammed Hyder will receive from Government of Hyderabad only the subsistence allowance which he had been in receipt of. With effect from the date of this Order the subsistence allowance will stop and a compassionate allowance as mentioned in para (3) above will be paid.' The original order is filed herewith and marked Ex. P. I.

10. The Petitioner submits that the Order of the Government of Hyderabad is illegal, malafide and totally without jurisdiction and that resort to Article 311(2) (c) is only a colorable exercise of power and an abuse of legal authority, in view of the fact that the petitioner had been acquitted in all the criminal cases filed against him and that even in the departmental inquiry by the Revenue Board for alleged embezzlement of Government monies, the petitioner had been exonerated.

11. The Order shows as stated earlier that the action taken in suspending the petitioner from 18.9.1948 was in view of some serious allegations of a criminal nature against him. When this is so, the acquittal by Criminal Courts must have been taken to be conclusive and the petitioner should have been deemed innocent of all the charges framed against him. It is not open to the Government to go behind the acquittals entered by the highest courts of the land and then resort to removal or dismissal from service on grounds of security of state.

12. The recital in the Order suggesting that there was no trial of the charges against him by the Criminal Courts and that the cases have been withdrawn by the Government is absolutely incorrect and contrary to truth. As stated earlier as many as 24 cases had been trumped up against the petitioner. Several cases ended in acquittals in the trial Court and the rest in the High Court. The averment to the contrary in the Order is really a suppresio veri and suggestio falsi. The misleading averment has been made apparently with a view to furnish grounds for invoking Article 311(2) (c).

13. Nowhere does the Order state that the petitioner has been found guilty of any of the allegations or that the Rajpramukh was satisfied that the petitioner was guilty of any charges entailing his removal from service. It is not open to the Rajpramukh to remove or dismiss a person from Service unless he is satisfied that he has been guilty of the charges against him. Satisfaction regarding the

expediency of not giving an opportunity to show cause against the action proposed against him does not entitle the Rajpramukh to remove a person without arriving at a finding that he has been guilty of the charges against him.

14. Article 311(2) (c) was thought of, only after a long lapse of eight years after placing the Petitioner under suspension, when the Government found that the petitioner has been acquitted on all the criminal charges framed against him and had emerged without taint both from the criminal courts and also from the departmental inquiry by the Revenue Board. As stated earlier the petitioner is a victim of deep-seated hatred and vengeance of those against whom he had to take action when he was the Collector of Osmanabad. The criminal cases and the departmental inquiry had given him an opportunity to clear himself of all the charges. Finding that the grant of such an opportunity by an open inquiry or an open trial had only enabled the petitioner to prove his innocence, the Government have now thought of resorting to Article 311(2) Proviso (c) to deny him an opportunity to show cause against the action proposed lest, in case such an opportunity is given, the Government will be compelled to exonerate him. The petitioner submits that there are no charges left for investigation and that the application of Article 311(2) (c) is only a device to get rid of the petitioner from the State Service, having failed in their attempts to get him convicted by ordinary legal process through courts of Law. The petitioner submits that resort to Article 311(2) (c) is an abuse of statutory power, motivated by improper purpose and actuated by malice.
15. It is obvious from the recitals in the order that the Rajpramukh has been induced to pass the said Order on account of suppressio veri and suggestio falsi, by making him believe that the prosecutions against the petitioner have been withdrawn, that, therefore, no trial had been held, no acquittal entered, and that he had not been thus cleared of all the charges. The petitioner submits that no order obtained by fraud can be allowed to stand and that the entire order is vitiated on that account.

16. The removal from service was with effect from 18.9.1948. The Constitution came into force only on 26.1.1950. Article 311(2) Proviso (c) was not in force on 18.9.1948. On 18.9.1948, the petitioner had a vested right not be removed or dismissed from service except under and according to the then existing law of Hyderabad which required that the charge should be investigated by a commission after giving the petitioner an opportunity to defend himself. A true translation of the relevant provisions of Act, No. III of 1314 Fasli and the rules framed there under are annexed to this Affidavit, marked as Ex. P.2 and 'P'3 respectively and may be read as part of this Affidavit. As can be seen from a perusal of those rules there was no provision in the law of Hyderabad similar to that enacted in Article 311(2) Proviso (c). The petitioner, therefore, submits that the dismissal as from 18.9.1948 without conforming to the then existing law of Hyderabad, but in conformity with Article 311 of the Constitution which was not in force at that time is void, illegal and without jurisdiction. The Constitution is not retrospective or retroactive in operation.
17. Assuming without admitting that Article 311(2) (c) could be invoked, it would be seen that Proviso (c) is a proviso only to Article 311(2) which states that no civil servant shall be dismissed or removed until he has been given a reasonable opportunity of showing cause against the action proposed to be taken in regard to him. It is only such an opportunity that could be denied on the satisfaction of the Rajpramukh under Article 311(2) Proviso (c). Under the Hyderabad Civil Service (Classification Control and Appeal) Rules enacted under Article 309 (annexed hereto and marked 'P'.4) the petitioner is entitled to an oral enquiry if any charge is framed against him. He is then entitled to show by examination of witnesses that he is not guilty of the charges, and it is only after the provisional conclusion is arrived at, that he is guilty of the charges, that the next stage arises when he has to be given a reasonable opportunity of showing cause against the action proposed to be taken in regard to him. If he is found not guilty, the second stage is not reached and does not arise, and the application

of Proviso (c) would not arise. In other words, clause (2) and Proviso (c) have no application to the first stage of the inquiry which the petitioner is entitled to under statutory rules. Against the petitioner no charges were framed, no explanation obtained, no oral inquiry held and no provisional findings arrived at. In these circumstances, the petitioner submits that resort to Proviso (c) without compliance with the Civil Services (Classification Control and Appeal) Rules, and without arriving at a provisional conclusion of 'guilty' is illegal and without jurisdiction.

18. The Hyderabad Civil Services (classification Control and Appeal) Rules GAD Notification No. 75/GAD-SRC 6/49 dated 17.3.1952 (which have been published in the Hyderabad Gazette, dated 3.4.1952 at pages 77 to 117 of Part I S.C.) are intended to apply to all civil servants. In willfully denying to the petitioner the protection of these Rules, the petitioner has been denied equality before the law and equal protection of law under Article 14 of the Constitution.

19. Article 311 applies to the removal or dismissal of a Government Servant by way of punishment on disciplinary proceedings. The essential requisite is that the Government servant should be found guilty of the charges against him and it is only in that event that the Proviso (c) in Article 311(2) becomes applicable. When the Order does not disclose that the petitioner has been found guilty of any of the charges against him, the question of removal as a punishment does not arise and the State Government has no jurisdiction to invoke Proviso (c) and dismiss him from service.

20. Assuming without admitting that the retention of the petitioner in Public Service was prejudicial to National Security, the petitioner submits that under the rules framed under Article 309 of the Constitution of India called 'The Hyderabad Civil Services (safeguarding of National Security) Rules 1954' a true copy of which is annexed hereto and marked Ex. P.5, the competent authority should have by notice in writing informed the petitioner of the action proposed to be taken in regard to him and given him an opportunity to make to the Rajpramukh representation in writing against the action. The petitioner was

not given any such notice. He had, therefore, no opportunity to make any representations to the Rajpramukh against the action proposed to be taken against him. Under Rules 4(a) of the said Rules, it is obligatory on the Rajpramukh to give the petitioner such an opportunity and under Rule 4(b) the Rajpramukh shall take into consideration the representation if any so made by him, before passing final orders. The absence of such a notice and the denial of an opportunity to make representation to the Rajpramukh being flagrant violations of the rules framed under the Constitution, make the order illegal, void and without jurisdiction.

21. The security of the State depends on conditions and circumstances which vary from day to day. The petitioner was suspended in September 1948. He was exonerated from all charges in 1954. There is not the slightest suggestion that either in 1948 or 1954 the interest of the security of the state would have led the Rajpramukh to deny the opportunity to the petitioner to show cause against his dismissal. There is no suggestion that on the material dates the security of the State would have been affected by the grant of such an opportunity. And the security of the State in October 1956 is not the relevant factor to be taken into consideration for invoking the proviso, particularly when the dismissal in this case is not prospective but retrospective.

22. The petitioner submits that the reference to the security of the State in the said Order is the mechanical recital of an empty formula made merely for the purpose of avoiding an open inquiry knowing fully well that such an inquiry would enable the petitioner to clear himself of all the charges against him. The antecedent efforts of the government to deprive the petitioner of his life and liberty by trumping up various charges against him including murder, arson and dacoity having become unsuccessful, the petitioner has now been subjected to the present device, in order to oust him from his office, to evade the provisions of Article 311(2). It may be mentioned that the compassionate allowance now proposed to be given to him ex-gratia is about Rs

50 when the pay he was drawing as Collector was Rs 1,100 and allowances amounting to Rs 500.

23. The long lapse of time in finding some legal provisions to circumvent the inquiry and dismiss the petitioner is itself suggestive of the motive behind the resort to the Provisions to Article 311(2). If the grant of an opportunity to show cause was not expedient in the interests of the State, there was no reason either why the power should not have been exercised in 1950 at the earliest. The resort to the proviso has not been made in good faith.
24. Under the Hyderabad Civil Service Regulation in force in 1948 (a true Copy of the relevant articles 141 and 142 is annexed hereto and marked Ex.'P'6.) when a civil servant is placed under suspension pending inquiry into original charges and the charges end in acquittal, the civil servant is bound to be restored to office with back pay and allowances. The petitioner, therefore, submits that it is incumbent on the Government in view of the acquittals to reinstate the petitioner to office with all back emoluments due to him from 18.9.1948.
25. The petitioner, is therefore, constrained to approach this Honorable Court:-
    (a) for the issuance of a Writ of Certiorari or any other appropriate Writ. Order of direction calling for the records relating to the Order of the Government of Hyderabad No. 300-GAD/1/SRC-CSP-56, General Administration Department, dated 13.10.1956 and quash the same:
    (b) for the issuance of a Writ of Mandamus or any other appropriate writ, order or direction to reinstate the petitioner into office with back emoluments from 18.9.1948; and
    (c) for costs of the petition and such other reliefs as may be appropriate in the circumstances of the case.

Solemnly affirmed at Hyderabad)(
This 7th day of March, 1957, and Mohd. Hyder,)(
signed his name in my presence)(

Before me.

The Government's Counter-Affidavit

Introduction

This introduction briefly explains how a counter-affidavit works, without going into the details of the case. My own response to the points made here is discussed in the following chapter.

The purpose of a counter-affidavit is to rebut. The government's response goes over my affidavit line by line, covering all points, and conceding nothing. A court is hardly ever a debating chamber where the validity of the opponent's best points may be graciously allowed. The reader has to keep this in mind in going over the government's response. A weak case is argued here with vigour, even to the point of turning the facts inside-out.

Thus the government asserts that there was 'no conflict as such between Razakars and the State Congress' and maintains that I was 'acting on the initiative of the Ittehad, and prosecuting members of the other party only' (para 4).

It urges that my rights as a civil servant could be curtailed: '... in view of prosecution in Court of Law, there was no necessity of departmental enquiry by a commission of enquiry' (para 5).

It asserts that the government claimed privilege sparingly: '... only in respect of two files (...) as they were confidential in nature. The rest of the papers and documents were made available to the petitioner' (para 6).

It argues that I could still be considered guilty, as I had never been proven innocent: 'I submit it is totally incorrect that the petitioner has established his innocence' (para 5). In our system of justice, the accused is presumed innocent until proven guilty, not the other way round.

It explains how the government arrives at this conclusion:

'On appeal, the Hon'ble High Court did not dispose of the cases against him on merits but the conviction as well as acquittals were set aside on the technical grounds that the constitution of Special Judge's Court was ultra vires the constitution' (para 6).

The Special Courts had indeed been declared ultra vires by the High Court, but later, on appeal, the Supreme Court held the constitution of the special courts was intra vires the constitution. Therefore, 'The conviction by the Special Judge is proof positive against him' (para 21).

In any case, it contends, the government was satisfied of my guilt:

'It was only after the detailed examination of the petitioner's case and after personally satisfying himself, that the services of the petitioner were terminated by the Rajpramukh under Article 311(2)(c).' (para 15)

Finally, the affidavit declares that the Rajpramukh had a 'subjective' impression of my guilt, and that he was 'personally' satisfied that I was guilty as charged. Actually, the constitutional proviso allows the dismissal of an employee who poses a security risk; this is different from the issue of guilt or innocence that is being raised here. In any case, the statement is somewhat ironic, as the Rajpramukh (or Governor of Hyderabad) happened to be the Nizam himself, who had gone out of his way, in 1955, to personally recruit me in his service (as Secretary of his trust foundation), where I remained until his death in 1967.

ജ്യ

(Document Three: Counter-Affidavit)

IN THE HIGH COURT OF JUDICATURE OF ANDHRA PRADESH AT HYDERABAD

WRIT PETITION NO. 148/57

MOHD. HYDER Versus THE STATE OF ANDHRA PRADESH

Counter-Affidavit on behalf of the Respondent

I, Girdhar Raj Saxena s/o Mahboob Raj aged about 43 years, residing at Hyderabad, do hereby solemnly and sincerely affirm and state as follows:-

1. I am the Assistant Secretary to the Government of Andhra Pradesh and I am well acquainted with the facts of the case.
2. I have read the affidavit filed in support of the petition and I state that it discloses no valid and substantial grounds for the grant of any of the reliefs prayed for.
3. Paras I and 2 require no comments.
4. In reply to para 3, I submit that there was no conflict as such between the Razakars and the State Congress. The Ittehadul Muslimin being imbued and inspired by the political ideology of an independent sovereign State for Hyderabad it was perpetrating all sorts of violence, such as murder, loot and arson through the Razakars and the petitioner was working hand in glove with them. It is incorrect that the petitioner in obedience to the direction of the Government in power had to put down the lawless activities of both these groups. As a matter of fact he was acting on the initiative of Ittehadul Muslimin and in every possible way prosecuting the members of the other party only. It is equally incorrect that in the course of his administration as Collector in charge of Law and Order he incurred the enmity of one Mr Phoolchand Gandhi and other members of his party. No such allegation had ever been made at any time previously in any of his representations to the Government either oral or written or even before the Special Judge's Court before whom he was tried for several offences of murder, loot and advocacy of strong action against Indian Union.
5. In reply to paras 4 and 5, I submit that the petitioner was placed under suspension under orders of the Military Government with effect from 18.9.1948. The Inspector-General of Police was addressed to inquire and report with regard to charges leveled against him. On his report that there were eyewitnesses to the charges leveled against him and the charges could be proved, sanction was accorded for his prosecution and prosecution was launched against him before the Special Judge's Court which was

especially constituted under the Special Tribunal's Regulations in respect of about 24 cases of murder, dacoity, arson etc. I submit that under the circumstances there was no necessity of furnishing the charges to the petitioner, before or at the time of his suspension. I further submit that in view of prosecution before a Court of Law, there was no necessity of any departmental enquiry by a Commission of Enquiry.

6. In reply to para (6) I submit that the contention of the petitioner that the charges against him were fabricated at the instance of persons against whom he had to take action in the discharge of his official duties is not correct. No such contention was raised before the Special Judge's Court nor any evidence adduced to that effect. I submit that the Government claimed privilege only in respect of two files connected with the Uppala Murder case as they were confidential in nature. The rest of the papers and documents were made available to the petitioner. It is equally untrue that the prosecution put obstacles to the fair trial of the petitioner. He was given full opportunity to prove his innocence before the Court. The Special Judge sentenced the petitioner to death on a charge of murder of Kishen Teke and his wife Goda Bai committed on 6.5.1948 in the village Int. On some other charges leveled against him he was sentenced to various terms of rigorous imprisonment or fine or both. On appeal the Hon'ble High Court did not dispose off the cases against him on merits but the conviction as well as acquittals were set aside on the technical ground that the Constitution of Special Judge's Court was ultra-vires the Constitution. Against the said Judgement an appeal was preferred to the Supreme Court but the same was withdrawn on certain political considerations. It may be mentioned that the Hyderabad Special Tribunal Regulation No. 5 of 1358 F., under which the Special Judge's Court was constituted was held intra virus the Constitution by the Supreme Court in the case of Syed Qasim Razvi Vs The Government of Hyderabad (A.I.R 1953 S.C.156).

7. In reply to para 7, I submit that it is totally incorrect that the petitioner has established his innocence of all the charges

leveled against him. The further contention that the petitioner satisfied the Board of Revenue that he was not guilty of any misappropriation of Government money is also not correct. The decision to absolve him was taken because of the relevant cash books, vouchers, and files having been lost or destroyed during the Police Action.

8. In reply to para 8, I submit that the contentions are without substance and totally untenable. As already submitted the Hon'ble High Court did not pronounce any judgement on merits. I further submit that the petitioner was dismissed from service under the order of the Rajpramukh under Article 311(2) (c) and as such it was not necessary to conduct any enquiry, or afford any opportunity for defence to the petitioner.

9. Para 9 is a verbatim reproduction of the dismissal orders and needs no comment.

10. The contentions raised in para 10 are legally untenable. The order of the Government is neither illegal nor malafide nor without jurisdiction. I further submit that the contention that resorting to Article 311(2) (c) is a colourable exercise of power and an abuse of legal authority is equally untenable. The powers under Article 311(2) (c) were properly exercised. The doctrine of colourable exercise of powers is not applicable in such cases.

11. In reply to para 11, I submit that there was no acquittal of the petitioner by the High Court in the sense that he was absolved of all charges against him. The operative portion of the majority judgements reads as follows:-

'I would, therefore, allow the appeals of the accused and dismiss the revision petitions. The regulation being void, any judgement of acquittal by the Special Judge would also be unlawful and must be set aside. Consequently, the State appeals were also allowed..................... In the circumstances the proceedings, convictions, sentences and orders of acquittal are set aside. The accused persons are entitled to be tried in accordance with Law, they may be continued to be bound over pending such further proceedings as the State Government may be advised.'

Under the circumstances I submit that the Government was perfectly competent to consider whether such an individual could be safely retained in service.

12. In reply to para 12, I submit that the contentions are totally incorrect. A reading of the above extract from the judgement of the Hon'ble Court would clearly show that the petitioner himself is guilty of suppresio veri and suggestio falsi. No misleading averments were ever made with a view to furnish grounds for invoking Article 311(2) (c).
13. I submit that the contentions in para 13 are totally misconceived and legally untenable. Article 311(2) (c) does not make it necessary to state that the Rajpramukh is satisfied about the guilt of the person concerned. It was only after such satisfaction that action has been taken. I further submit that the satisfaction of the Rajpramukh under Article 311(2) (c) is a subjective satisfaction which cannot be made a subject of controversy before the Hon'ble Court.
14. In reply to para 14, I submit that the prosecution against the petitioner was launched in 1950, and the judgement of the High Court was delivered on 21.7.1952. The appeal that was filed against the said judgement was pending before the Supreme Court. The Government later decided that the appeals against the said judgements pending before the Supreme Court should not be pressed for political reasons. The cases regarding the future service of the petitioner along with other officers were considered by the Government. The petitioner was given an opportunity to make any personal representation, he wished to make by letter No. 713/716/GAD-a/54, dated 10-3-1954 and he was also interviewed accordingly. After due consideration the Government decided that the petitioner should be removed from service from the date of suspension after obtaining an order from the Rajpramukh under Article 311(2) (c) and he should be paid as a matter of grace 50 per cent of the proportionate pension in respect of service until the date of suspension. Finally, orders of dismissal were passed on 13.10.1956 under Article 311(2) (c) of the Constitution. The other allegations made in para 14 are unfounded and are denied.

15. The contentions in Para 15 are not correct. The order of removal of the petitioner from service was not obtained from the Rajpramukh by suggesting any false facts or suppressing the true facts. It was only after the detailed examination of the petitioner's case and after personally satisfying himself, that the services of the petitioner were terminated by the Rajpramukh under Article 311(2) (c).
16. The contentions of the petitioner in Para 16 without substance. The dismissal orders were passed after the Constitution came into force and under the circumstances Article 311(2) (c) could be rightly resorted to. The fact that the orders were given retrospective effect did not mean that the law in force on 18.9.1948 should have been applied. I further submit that the provisions of Act No. III of 1314 F., are not applicable to the instant case.
17. In reply to paras 17 and 18, I submit that the contentions of the petitioner are not legally tenable. Proviso (c) to Article 311(2) contemplates that an opportunity by way of oral enquiry or showing cause against the action proposed to be taken need not be given. The proviso is a proviso to Clause (2), which postulates two opportunities to a civil servant sought to be dismissed, removed or reduced in rank. The contention that the proviso has no application to the first stage of enquiry is not correct. I further submit that Proviso (c) to Article 311(2) has been incorporated in Rule 23(3) of the Hyderabad Civil Service Classification, Control and Appeal Rules, 1955 and under the circumstances there has been no violation of any statutory rules and the petitioner has not been denied equality before law or equal protection of the laws.
18. The contentions in Para 19 have already been replied to supra. I further submit that it was only after due satisfaction about the guilt of the petitioner that Article 311(2) (c) was invoked. As already submitted he was convicted by the Special Judge for many offences and though the said judgement was set aside by the High Court on technical grounds, it was not advisable to

retain the services of the petitioner in the circumstances of the case.

19. In reply to Para 20, I submit that the Hyderabad Civil Service (Safeguarding of National Security Rules, 1954) have no application to the case of the petitioner. The said rules have no retrospective application.
20. In reply to Para 21, I submit that it is not correct that the petitioner was exonerated from all the charges in 1954. The Judgement of the High Court is self-speaking on the point. I further submit that the materials date for satisfaction of the Rajpramukh under Article 311(2) (c) is the date when the order was passed. The satisfaction being a subjective satisfaction, it cannot be canvassed in any court of law.
21. In reply to Para 22, I submit that the contentions are without substance and incorrect. The reference to the Security of State, in the said order, is not the mechanical recital of an empty formula made merely for the purpose of avoiding an open enquiry. There was perfect justification for invoking Article 311(2) (c) under the circumstances of the case. It is equally incorrect that the Government trumped up various charges against the petitioner including murder, arson and dacoity. The conviction by the Special Judge is proof positive against him. It is equally incorrect to say that the Government was unsuccessful in getting him convicted and that is why it resorted to Article 311(2) as a device in order to oust the petitioner from his office. The allowance of Rs 58/- and not Rs 50/- as alleged has been granted to him ex-gratia, though as a matter of fact he was not entitled to the same.
22. In reply to Para 23, I submit that the allegations are quite incorrect and are denied. The resort to the proviso was made in all good faith. The reasons why the final order was passed in 1956 and not earlier have been explained in detail in Para (14).
23. I submit that the contentions in Para 24 are misconceived. As already explained the charges did not end in the acquittal of the petitioner and as such there was no obligation on the part of the Government to restore the petitioner to office with back pay and

allowances, under Articles 141 and 142 of the Hyderabad Civil Service Regulations that were in force in 1948. I further submit that the said articles are not applicable to the instant case in as much as the dismissal orders were passed in 1956.

Under the circumstances I submit that the petition is legally untenable and deserves to be dismissed with costs.

Solemnly and sincerely affirmed this the 30th day of December, 1957 and signed his name in my presence.

DEPONENT

BEFORE ME

Sd/
(E. Venkat Ramaiah)
Registrar,
Revenue Department, Hyderabad

My Reply to the Government's Counter-Affidavit

In my reply, the assertions made in the government's counter-affidavit are vigorously rebutted, point-by-point.

On whether or not there was a conflict between the Razakars and the State Congress: 'It is not clear what exactly is intended to be conveyed by the statement of the Respondents that "there was no conflict as such between Razakars and the State Congress". Either there was conflict or no conflict. To say "there was no conflict as such" is to seek refuge in evasion, contrary to facts.'

On whether or not Civil Service Rules were violated by the failure to hold a departmental inquiry: 'Para 5 of the Respondents Affidavit is a clear admission of the violation of the service rules, insofar as it is admitted that there was no enquiry preliminary to the prosecution of the petitioner, that no charges were framed against the petitioner and that no departmental enquiry was held as prescribed by the law then prevailing in Hyderabad, as any charge against a government officer had to be referred for investigation to a Commission of Enquiry.'

'To state that the government claimed privilege sparingly is an admission that privilege was nevertheless claimed. The petitioner submits that no record of evidence pertaining to a criminal case can be claimed as "unpublished affairs of the state" and treated as confidential.'

'In fact the State was suppressing the fact that there was no police case. According to the respondents, the IG of police had reported that there were eye-witnesses to the charges leveled against the petitioner, but when these records were asked for, the then chief secretary to government had, through his letter No. 401/GAD/C/50, dated 25 October 1950 thought fit to state:

"... The documents relate to the unpublished affairs of the State and the production of the same before the Court has not been permitted by Government. In view of these circumstances this office claims the privilege of the non-production of the documents in question provided for in Section 126 of the Hyderabad Evidence Act and Section 87 (c) of the Hyderabad Criminal Procedure Code."

If there was such a report, and the subsequent prosecution was not 'malafide', it is not understood why the Government should have claimed privilege. The petitioner submits that no such report could possibly be produced by the Government even today.

In the Upla case, in which the petitioner was charged with the murder of nine cart men, the court denied the petitioner access to the report prepared by Ghatge, fearing that it would exonerate the petitioner. Ghatge had personally delivered the file to the court.

On the consequences of the Special Tribunals Act being declared unconstitutional: 'It is perfectly true that this Hon'ble Court allowed all the appeals of the accused as well as that of the Government on the ground that the Special Tribunals Act was ultra Vires and that the accused persons be tried in accordance with law and that they might be continued to be bound over pending such proceedings as the State Government may be advised; but the State Government did not prosecute them under the ordinary law of the land and in those circumstances the fact that they did not prosecute the accused again cannot be availed of to charge the accused with the commission of those crimes. When the State was given the rights to prosecute and it did not prosecute the accused, the only inference is that the State was satisfied that the accused were not guilty of the offences for which they were charged.'

On the charge of embezzlement: 'It is not clear how the petitioner could be directed to explain in detail the items outstanding against him, as shown by the audit notes, to the Board of Revenue on I May 1952, when the relevant cash books, vouchers, files etc., were said to have been lost or destroyed during the Police Action. No explanation could have been called for in the absence of any record involving the petitioner. Anyway, if the petitioner had not satisfied the Board of Revenue, the Board of Revenue would not have been given the petitioner a clean bill and defreezed the petitioner's account, which clearly meant exoneration from all charges. The denial of this fact by the Respondents is clearly wrong.'

There is one point in the argument that requires comment. I end up over-stressing Phool Chand Gandhi's enmity as one of the causes of my troubles.[1] It would be more accurate to say that he was the immediate cause, while the political climate in Hyderabad was the permissive cause, supporting Phool Chand Gandhi's vindictiveness. After all, other senior officials also got into trouble, such as Habib Muhammad (subedar or commissioner, Warangal), District Collectors Moazzam Hussain of Nalgonda, or Baquer Hussain Qureshi of Warangal, without benefit of Phool Chand's malice. But note the parallels in their histories. Like me, they were arrested, charged with criminal acts, suffered prolonged incarceration, and were eventually released, the government failing to make any charge stick.[2]

Greater stress must be put on the permissive cause: Why was the policy of prosecuting civil servants adopted by the government? For Delhi, Hyderabad's separatist tendencies represented a serious threat to India's integration, a threat it was determined to quash at almost any cost, and as quickly as possible, before its example incited breakaway tendencies in other parts of India, and before Hyderabad's recalcitrance gained support or solidified into independent status. Hence the border camps, and hence the military invasion. Subsequently, India's reaction (some would call it over-reaction) had to be justified: a reason had to be found for having tolerated the border camps, for sanctioning the military invasion, and for ignoring the mass killings that followed the Police Action. Therefore it was convenient to show that there had been murderous civil servants on the rampage in the districts. For anyone who knew him, of course, it is laughable to imagine the gentle, cultured Moazzam Hussain on the rampage, or for that matter any of the other senior civil servants subsequently trapped in the web of false allegations spun around them.

Having started on the policy of implicating senior civil servants, the government could not afford to have the courts pull down its elaborate structure of suborned witnesses, false charges, and protracted incarceration. The charade had to be played through to the end. Hence the resort to the strongest tools in the government's arsenal: special tribunals, privilege and reason of state.

ഇര

(Document Four: Reply to the Government's Counter-Affidavit)

IN THE HIGH COURT OF JUDICATURE OF ANDHRA PRADESH AT HYDERABAD
Writ Petition No. 148 of 1957
MOHD. HYDER Vs. STATE OF ANDHRA PRADESH

Reply to the Counter-Affidavit filed by the Respondents.

I, Mohd. Hyder s/o. Mohd. Ghouse, aged about 41 years, residing in Hyderabad do hereby solemnly and sincerely state as follows:-

1. I have read the Counter-Affidavit filed by the Respondents and Para (1) thereof, requires no comment.
2. The allegation by the Respondents that the affidavit filed in support of the petition by this petitioner discloses no valid and substantial grounds for the grant of any of the reliefs prayed for is denied as explained in paras below.
3. Para (3) requires no comments.
4. In reply to para (4) it is submitted that at the end of the war there was great agitation for political changes in India. In the year 1947, the Cabinet Mission had come and had declared that the pramountcy that had till then lain in the hands of British had lapsed and that any Indian Prince was free to join any state or was free to remain independent. The Subjects of the State of Hyderabad were divided into two parties. One party comprising largely of the Muslims of the State was known as

the 'Razakars' whereas the other party was the Hyderabad State Congress. The Razakars had aimed at keeping the Hyderabad State an independent state, while the aim of the State Congress was to make Hyderabad a part of the Indian Union. Both parties had built up their organizations and were carrying on vehement propaganda in favour of their own viewpoints. The State Congress under Phool Chand Gandhi had organized border camps and had taken to violence which created problems not only to the creed of the Indian National Congress but also to the administration of the District. The State Congress and the Razakar Organizations were in open and at times in violent conflict with each other. It is not clear what exactly is intended to be conveyed by the statement of the Respondents that 'there was no conflict as such between Razakars and the State Congress'. Either there was conflict or no conflict. To say 'there was no conflict as such' is to seek refuge in evasion, contrary to facts.

A rough view of the state of affairs may be gathered from what Swami Ramanand Tirth, the President of the State Congress himself and Madhapati Ramachander Rao, a member of the Congress Committee of Action had admitted in a statement to the press at that time (4 October 1948). This public record of proceedings of the Press Conference published in all the local dailies of Hyderabad under the caption 'Uncompromising and relentless opposition to autocratic Government' is sufficient to counter the denial by the government. A copy of the relevant portion of the *Deccan Chronicle*, dated 4 October 1948 giving details of this press conference is enclosed for ready reference.

Swami Ramanand Tirth commenting on the sudden collapse within five days of the much boasted might of Razakar's Raj in Hyderabad said:

'That there are many who considered the military operation to have wrought a miracle. He declared that it was not a miracle but was "the incessant, persistent and tremendous efforts and sufferings of the people of the State during their struggle for their rights for the past so many years" that has brought about the change.'

'In assessing the achievements of the Congress struggle he wanted the people and the press to remember that it had to steer clear of many troubles and overcome difficult situations, daily changing, ever increasing, within the State. That was the reason, he said, why the Committee of Action, to whose able guidance the success of the movement was due, had to locate itself outside the State. Their action has won laurels today. This strategy proved successful as could be seen from the results.'

Madhapati Ramchander Rao while addressing the conference had said:

'They carried the campaign in three stages. They fought a non-violent battle through Satyagraha, over nine thousand entered the jails and the struggle lasted for three months.'

'The second stage was to smash up the artificial barriers created by the State and 750 Customs Posts were the targets, over 500 of them were smashed and nothing impressed more the people in the villages than the visible disintegration of the might of the great "Islamic State".

'Even as they were going on with the struggle from the borders the final stage was entered into which meant a systematic sabotage and dislocation of communications thus paving the way for "anarchic and chaotic conditions wherein no law and order prevailed". The three phases culminated with the entering of the Indian Units into Hyderabad State.'

There were thus many border incidents resulting in loot, arson and murder. The task of administration and maintenance of peace in a border district of which the petitioner was in charge at the time was a very difficult one.

The petitioner denies the charges of 'working hand-in-glove with the Razakars' and acting on the initiative of Ittehadul Muslimin and in every possible way prosecuting the members of the other party only'.

Similar allegation had been made by the then government in the memorandum of charges sent by the chief secretary to the IG of police 'Memorandum No. 78-OSD, dated 10 January 1949' (copy enclosed for ready reference) but failed to substantiate this charge marked 'A' in the said memorandum. The respondents may, therefore, be ordered by this Hon'ble Court to produce the petitioner's weekly reports to government from January 1948 to September 1948, as collector of the district, wherein it will be seen that the petitioner in order to maintain law and order had held in custody many a Razakar and Rohillas from Osmanabad, Latur, Paraenda and Rajaisur and from various other places in the district. From one of such reports, dated 20 Isfandar, 1357 F., (true translation enclosed for ready reference) it will be seen that the petitioner had taken action against the secretary of the Ittehadul Muslimin of Latur, and had him removed from that position for his nefarious activities. Similarly, the petitioner had also taken requisite action against Phool Chand Gandhi and his party for their lawless activities on the borders. The properties of Phool Chand Gandhi situated in Osmanabad were confiscated and his business closed down. Members of his party who were reputed to work hand-in-glove with him were either put under arrest or their properties confiscated. These facts can be gathered from the weekly reports to government submitted by the petitioner. All these activities of the petitioner were misconstrued as acts of personal enmity when the party of Phool Chand Gandhi came into power after the Police Action. The petitioner had made a number of representations to the Revenue Secretary, the Civil Administrator and the IG of police (copies of these representations enclosed), bringing in these facts as best as he could, for by then Phool Chand Gandhi had become a force to be reckoned with, and was later made a minister in the government. A copy of one such representation to the Revenue Secretary, dated 8 October 1948 and his note on this representation is self-explanatory.

The allegation that no representations were made by the petitioner in this regard is, therefore, not correct.

5. Para 5 of the Respondents Affidavit is a clear admission of the violation of the Civil Service Rules, insofar as it is admitted that there was no enquiry preliminary to the prosecution of the petitioner and that no charges were framed against the petitioner and that no departmental enquiry was held as prescribed by the law then prevailing in Hyderabad, as any charge against a Government officer had to be referred for investigation to a Commission of Enquiry.

According to the Respondents, the IG of police had reported that there were eye-witnesses to the charges levelled against the petitioner, but when these records were asked for, the then Chief Secretary to Government had, through his letter No. 401/GAD/C/50, dated 25 October 1950 (copy enclosed) thought fit to state:

'... The documents relate to the unpublished affairs of the State and the production of the same before the Court has not been permitted by Government. In view of these circumstances this office claims the privilege of the non-production of the documents in question provided for in Section 126 of the Hyderabad Evidence Act and Section 87 (c) of the Hyderabad Criminal Procedure Code.'

If there was such a report, and the subsequent prosecution was not 'malafide' it is not understood why the government should have claimed privilege. The petitioner submits that no such report could possibly be produced by the government even today.

6. In reply to para 6 it is submitted:-

   (i) that relevant records were withheld with a view to secure convictions against a responsible government officer;

   (ii) refuge was sought under certain provisions of law by claiming privilege malafide;

   (iii) the original report of the investigating officer was not made available nor was he produced in court which clearly hampered justice and put obstacles in the way of a fair trial.

These facts may be proved if the files of all the cases are sent for and looked into by this Hon'ble Court. The petitioner had filed affidavits and submitted petitions bringing these facts to the notice of the Special Judge but without any result. True translations of two representations of 11 September in cases 9/2 and 22/2 of 1950 and two other representations, dated 15 and 25 September 1950 respectively go to show that it is not correct to say that the petitioner had never contended that the charges were false and that there were no obstacles placed in the way of administration of justice. A reference may here by made to:

(1) The endorsement of the Treasury Officer on the application of the petitioner, dated 29 October 1950 in case No. 9/2 of 1950.

(2) The letter No. 1340, dated 26 August 1950 addressed to the Director of Accounts and Audit, in Case No. 22/2 of 1950.

(3) The letter No. 102/7-C-58 F., dated 20/21 September 1950 from the Superintendent of Police, Crime Branch, C.I.D., in case No. 22/2 of 1950.

(4) Letter No. 929, dated 13/14 March 1951 from Collector, Osmanabad, in Case No. 22/2 of 1950; and to

(5) Letter No. 1517, dated 15 March 1951 from the District Superintendent of Police, to the Registrar, High Court, in Case No. 22/2 of 1950.

From these, it is clear that every effort was made to establish the charges against the petitioner by withholding documents which could be made available and which would have helped the cause of justice.

The petitioner reiterates that the charges against him were fabricated at the instance of persons against whom he had to take action in the discharge of his official duties.

The Respondents admit 'that the Government claimed privilege only in respect of two files connected with the Upla Murder Case as they were confidential in nature.'

As is stated below, a charge (in the Upla Murder Case) was levelled against the petitioner for the murder of (9) men from the village Upla but from the record of evidence in the Special Court it was clear that an enquiry into this murder of (9) men was instituted by the Collector of Sholapur and that he had made a detailed report to the Government of Bombay in this regard. When this record of enquiry into this case was called for by the Special Court trying the petitioner, the Government had claimed privilege stating that records were of confidential nature and relate to unpublished affairs of the State. The petitioner submits that no record of evidence pertaining to a criminal case can be claimed as 'unpublished affairs of the State' and treated as confidential. The privilege claimed by the Government, was therefore, malafide. Particularly, when the Collector of Sholapur, S.A. Ghatge had, for the sake of justice, brought the file to the Court and had categorically stated that the file contained relevant documents and statements of witnesses and had left it in Court as mentioned in letter No. A-9227, dated 30 August 1950 from the District Magistrate, Sholapur and the petitioner had made it clear to the Court that the file was of real importance as per his application, dated 11 September, 1950 in Case No. 9/2 of 1950. The endorsement of the Special Judge on this petition is self-explanatory and amply justifies the contention of the petitioner.

The Respondent's statement that in the Yeet Murder Case no decision was taken by the High Court on its merits is incorrect. This case was decided on its merits and that the petitioner was acquitted by Justice V.R. Deshpande on 4 December 1951; a copy of this judgement is enclosed for ready reference wherein the Hon'ble Judge said:

'In view of my finding there is no need for me to discuss the contention that the Special Judge's judgement was unconstitutional. In the result the appeal of the accused is allowed and the appeal of the Government dismissed.'

In view of this judgement it is absolutely inaccurate to make the statement on oath:

'On appeal the Hon'ble High Court did not dispose of the cases against him on merits, but the conviction as well as acquittals were set aside on the technical grounds that the constitution of the Special Judge's Court was ultra virus the Constitution.'

7. It is not clear how the petitioner could be directed to explain in detail the items outstanding against him, as shown by the audit notes, to the Board of Revenue on 1 May 1952, when the relevant cash books, vouchers, files etc., were said to have been lost or destroyed during Police Action. No explanation could have been called for in the absence of any record involving the petitioner. Anyway, if the petitioner had not satisfied the Board of Revenue, the Board of Revenue would not have been given the

petitioner a clean bill and defreezed the petitioner's account, which clearly meant exoneration from all charges. The denial of this fact by the Respondents is clearly wrong.

8. As stated above it is again wrong to say that the High Court did not pronounce any judgement in the Yeet Murder Case on merits. Copy of this judgement on merits is enclosed.

   As already submitted, the petitioner was acquitted by the High Court in the only murder case in which he was sentenced to death by the Special Judge, i.e., in the Yeet Murder Case.

   It is admitted by the Respondents that the petitioner was dismissed from service under Article 311(2) (c). It is said that it was not necessary to conduct any enquiry or afford any opportunity for defence to the petitioner. The Respondents interpretation of Article 311(2) (c) of the Constitution is incorrect.

9. Para 9 needs no comment.

10. The petitioner denies the averment in Para 10 of the counter and reiterates that resort to Article 311(2) (c) was a colourable exercise of power and an abuse of legal authority.

11. It is perfectly true that this Hon'ble Court allowed all the appeals of the accused as well as that of the Government on the ground that the Special Tribunals Act was ultra Vires and that the accused persons be tried in accordance with law and that they might be continued to be bound over pending such proceedings as the State Government may be advised; but the State Government did not prosecute them under the ordinary law of the land and in those circumstances the fact that they did not prosecute the accused again cannot be availed of to charge the accused with the commission of those crimes. When the State was given the rights to prosecute and it did not prosecute the accused, the only inference is that the State was satisfied that the accused were not guilty of the offences for which they were charged.

    The Petitioner submits that the last sentence in Para 11 of the Counter Affidavit reveals that resort to Article 311(2) (c) was colourable and a mere pretence. If the fact is that the commission of the Criminal Offences was a motive for the Government's consideration whether the individual involved therein could be safely retained in service, it is clear that it was not the security of the State that motivated the removal of the petitioner from service. The Government found that the petitioner could not be successfully prosecuted. If his misconduct was the commission of such criminal offences he should have been given an opportunity to show cause against his removal and if he had been given a reasonable opportunity the Government knew that he would be able to refute them successfully. The Government, therefore, invoked the provisions of Article 311(2)(c) to get rid of him.

I submit that the last sentence of Para 11 gives a clue to the real reason of his dismissal on the alleged ground of security of State.

12. The allegations in Para 12 are misleading.

Immediately after the Police Action, an effort was made by interested parties to involve the petitioner in some criminal charges. It would be clear from the perusal of the records withheld by the Government that in no case was there a complaint made against the petitioner by any of the complainants, who were later produced in Court by the prosecution. In every case the interested political parties (not the complainants) obviously moved the then Government and the government thereupon prepared a self-contained note of allegations (Memorandum No. 78-OSD, dated 10 January 1949), which was made over to the IG of police by the Office of the Chief Secretary. On instructions from the Office of the IG of police, the police had approached the complainants and an effort was made to involve the petitioner in some criminal charge or the other.

It is, therefore, obvious that the statement recorded by the police could not be made available for fear of certain disclosures adverse to the State.

The charges leveled against the petitioner in the aforesaid memorandum may be briefly dealt with:

Charge (a) deals with active participation in the Razakar and Ittehad Muslimin movements by the petitioner, but this charge was neither alleged nor established in a Court of Law by the Government as stated in para (4) supra.

Charge (b) dealt with the 'Yeet Murder Case', wherein as stated supra (para 6), the petitioner has been acquitted by the Hon'ble Court.

Charge (c) deals with the murder of twelve cartmen of Upla. The petitioner has been acquitted of the murder charge by the Special Court and was convicted of the charge of kidnapping under section 301, Hyderabad Penal Code for which no charges were framed against the petitioner. It was in this case that the Government had claimed privilege for the file of the Office of the Collector of Sholapur as detailed in para (6).

This conviction, however, came up before the High Court, where, as stated in para (11), the High Court was pleased to quash the sentence of the Special Judge, which in effect amounted to an acquittal. The Government then went in appeal to the Supreme Court but later as per the letter from the Secretary to Government, Home Department No. SPI/IP/39-51 dated 6 February 1952 instructions were issued to the IG of police to withdraw all the appeals and they were withdrawn.

Charge (d) of the self-contained note pertains to the looting and arson in village Killari. Nine cases of loot and arson were brought against the petitioner and the petitioner was wrongly sentenced by the Special Court to undergo imprisonment for a period of one and a half years. Apart from the patent defects which went to the very root of the case it may be noted that the original investigating officer's report in regard to these cases, was not produced in spite of its being called for and that he himself was not examined as a witness despite the petitioner's efforts to get him as a witness and his being present in court on several occasions. This fact was brought to the notice of the court through this petitioner's petition, dated 22 April 1950 in Case No. 8/2 of 1950. This conviction was also quashed by the High Court as explained above. The appeal by the Government against this order was finally dismissed as withdrawn on 25 June 1954, by the Supreme Court. (Copy of Supreme Court order is enclosed for ready reference).

Complainants in this case alleged that cash and gold worth several lakhs was looted by the petitioner but the police did not even question the petitioner about this cash and gold much less recover it. The original investigating officer, Abdul Khader, ASP, CID, was not produced and in spite of an affidavit by the petitioner his original report in regard to this case was not called for, still the petitioner was convicted by the Special Judge.

Charge (e) contained two charges, one of murder and the other that of the twelve cases of loot in village Apsinga.

The murder charge failed and the petitioner was discharged by the Special Court for it was established that the case was absolutely a false one; one of the murdered persons was cited as a witness and was alive for a long time after his alleged murder by the petitioner. No action was, however, taken either by the judge or the then Government to correct the sad state of affairs. A copy of the said judgement in case No. 10/2 of 1950 is filed for ready reference.

All the other twelve cases of loot and dacoity in village Apsinga ended in acquittal, for they were patently mischievous and showed how the police was out to get the petitioner involved in cases of dacoity and loot.

Thus of the 24 charges, the petitioner was acquitted of 14 charges, i.e., 12 Apsinga dacoity cases and one murder at Apsinga village and of the Upla murder case by the Trial Court, alone. Of the 10 remaining cases the petitioner was acquitted of Yeet murder case by the High Court on merits as explained above.

There remained only 9 cases of loot in Kellari which in fact was a single case pertaining to a particular date and time and which was split up into three groups which were finally dismissed by the Supreme Court.

The Upla murder case as already stated ended in acquittal by the Special Court but the petitioner was convicted for kidnapping which conviction was again set aside as already explained.

It is, therefore, clear that the averment to the contrary in the order was a case of suppresio veri and suggestio falsi made apparently with a view to furnish grounds for invoking Article 311(2) (c).

13. It is submitted that satisfaction regarding the expediency of not giving an opportunity to show cause against the action proposed to be taken is a condition precedent to the issuance of an order under Article 311(2) (c). Any other interpretation of this constitutional provision is misconceived.
14. It is true that the petitioner was called to a Special Committee of the Cabinet on 12 March 1954 but was orally interviewed and questioned with regard to the case that had already been decided by Court of Law, and incidentally on the petitioner's relationship to some persons in Hyderabad. No reference whatsoever was made during the interview to the action proposed to be taken against the petitioner and no reasonable opportunity of explanation against the action to be so taken was given which was against the spirit of Article 311(2) (c), and the cases decided under this Article.

    Consequently, the so-called opportunity to make any personal representation failed to comply with the constitutional provisions. The interview granted was a sad attempt at furnishing grounds to the Government for invoking Article 311(2) (c).
15. Petitioner submits that it is not correct to state that no opportunity need be given to the petitioner to show cause when action is taken under Article 311(2) (c). There is absolutely no reason given as to how the security of the State is involved in my continuing in service.
16. Para (16) is incorrect.
17. Since the order of dismissal has taken effect from 18 September 1948, it could have only been passed according to the then existing laws of Hyderabad. The present order it is submitted is illegal and unconstitutional.
18. Para (17) is equally incorrect.
19. The requisites for invoking the provision of Article 311(2) (c) have to be separately complied with. A failure to comply with the same is a failure which vitiated the entire order.
20. The legal position as explained in the petitioner's affidavit Para (20) still stands good and Para (19) of the Respondent's affidavit does not minimize the importance of the legal proposition enumerated therein.

21. Para 20 of the Respondent's affidavit is a bare denial of Para (22) of the petitioner's affidavit. It is unnecessary to repeat what the petitioner has stated already in his affidavit.
22. The petitioner submits that in the light of the above facts of acquittal and in view of the fact that the Government of Hyderabad regards the petitioner as entitled to pension; the petitioner is entitled to re-instatement and to receive his full salary for all these years of suspension and incarceration.

ꕥ

Notes

[1] Phool Chand Gandhi eventually became minister of education in the state government of Hyderabad; his poor performance in that post was memorialized in an Urdu couplet, with a play on his name Phool Chand, which could be understood to mean 'few flowers'. The verse mocked his incumbency at education, claiming it had produced 'many thorns and few flowers':

'*Chaman aisa aiga kis ko pasand,*

Hon kaantey ziada jahan phool chand'

[2] Editor's note: Here is Moazzam Hussain's account of what happened to him:

'Most of the officers who were under suspicion by the new regime left for Pakistan. Arrangements were made for me, as it was clear I was going to be arrested. But my father said, "Face the firing squad. I will disinherit and disown you if you run away from your post." So I stayed, and after a farcical trial full of paid witnesses, I was sentenced to death. I could see the noose from my cell. Later that year the sentence was reduced to life imprisonment. Three years after that, following an appeal in the High Court, I was honourably acquitted.' See, William Dalrymple, "Under the Char Minar" Google site under "Moazzam Hussain" 2005)

Final Judgement

This is an odd judgement, narrowly interpreting the law, with no regard to the looming issues of justice and fair play.

The judgement focuses on two questions: One, were provisions of the Constitution being applied with retroactive effect, in order to remove me? The court finds that since I was being removed in 1956, there was no premature application of the Constitution (which came into effect in 1950). Two, could I be so removed? The court finds that an employee serves at the pleasure of the government; there is no vested right to employment.

While these points of law were being settled, other more fundamental doubts remained. It was unclear why I was being removed. There was a presumption of guilt and wrongdoing, which the judgement failed to scrutinize, only stating (and that too incorrectly) that the High Court had cleared me on a technicality and not on the merits of the case. To claim that someone is guilty because their innocence is not established is to stand our system of justice on its head.

The court could have taken a very different approach. At an earlier stage in my trial, the district superintendent of police investigating the charges against me had observed, 'Sir, it is government policy to prosecute you. You will be held until that policy changes.'

If the DSP Osmanabad could see through the allegations, why couldn't the courts? The only plausible explanation is that the courts did not wish to embarrass the government. Otherwise it would have been the easiest thing to call the government to account on any number of issues, such as the following:

1. Why were the FIRs of the alleged crimes produced so late, not when the alleged crimes took place but several months later, just before the arrest of the accused?
2. Why did the government refuse to share the results of the preliminary police investigation of the alleged crimes, claiming privilege? Was it because the investigation failed to link the accused with the crimes? Would the government produce the files on the investigation now?
3. Why was the Ghatge report on the murder of the nine cart-men not shared with the accused, the government again claiming privilege? Was it because the file did not implicate the accused? Could it be produced now?
4. Was the accused cleared on a technicality by the High Court or on the merits of the case? If the latter, what are the implications of dismissing an officer that the courts have declared innocent? Will the government be still prepared to apply Article 311(2) Proviso (c) of the Constitution after failing to establish guilt of the accused?
5. How can a senior civil servant, cleared by the courts, and willing to accept service under the new regime, be regarded as a threat to the security of the state?
6. Why did the government withdraw its appeals from the Supreme Court, claiming reasons of state? If serious crimes had been committed, why had the government changed its mind about proceeding with them?

If the decision to dismiss me (invoking a special clause of the Constitution) is seen in the context of all the previous occasions when privilege was invoked, then a pattern emerges of systematic obstruction of due process. The government got away with it because the courts allowed it. This says something about the political climate prevailing in Hyderabad as late as 1960, when the final judgement was handed down.

ജ്ഞ

(Document Five: The Court's Decision on the Writ Petition)

IN THE HIGH COURT OF JUDICATURE
ANDHRA PRADESH
AT HYDERABAD

(SPECIAL ORIGINAL JURISDICTION)

TUESDAY, THE TWELFTH DAY OF JANUARY

ONE THOUSAND NINE HUNDRED AND SIXTY

PRESENT

THE HON'BLE P. CHANDRA REDDY, CHIEF JUSTICE
AND
THE HON'BLE JUSTICE NARASIMHAM

WRIT PETITION NO: 148 OF 1957

BETWEEN:

Mohammed Hyder
PETITIONER

AND

The State of A.P.
Rep. by the Chief Secretary to Government
General Administration Department, Hyderabad.
RESPONDENTS

Petition under Article 226 of the Constitution of India praying that in the circumstances stated in the affidavit filed therewith the High Court will be pleased to issue a writ of certiorari or any other appropriate writ, order or direction calling for the records relating to the order of the Government of Hyderabad (now Andhra Pradesh) in No. 300 GAD-I-SRC-C.SP/56 General Administration Department dated 13.10.1956 and to quash the same.

This petition coming on for hearing on Monday the 21st and Tuesday the 22nd days of December, 1959; upon perusing the petition and the affidavit filed in support thereof and the writ and Rule Nisi issued in pursuance of the order of the High Court dated 9-3-1957 and made herein and the counter and reply affidavits filed herein and the papers material in this case and upon hearing the arguments of Mr. M.K. Nambiar for M/s. S. Malakonda Reddy and C. Kulasekhara Reddy Advocates for the Petitioner and of the 2nd Government Pleader on behalf of the Respondent and having stood over for consideration till this day, the court made the following:-

ORDER:-

(by NARASIMHAM, J.)

The Petitioner (Mohammed Hyder), a former Hyderabad Civil Servant, prays for the issue of a writ of certiorari in relation to an order of the former Government of Hyderabad dated 13-10-1956 removing him from service with effect from 18-9-1948, the date on which he was placed under suspension, with a view to get the said order quashed. It is further prayed that a writ of mandamus or any other appropriate writ, order or direction be made by this court to reinstate him into office with effect from 18-9-1948.

The facts leading to the filing of this petition with the said prayers are briefly these:-

The Petitioner was appointed to the former Hyderabad Civil Service in 1937. In January, 1948 he was posted as the Talukdar of Osmanabad District. While he was serving as Talukdar, Osmanabad, he was placed under suspension on 18-9-1948 as he was accused of various grave offences in the course of his employment as Talukdar, Osmanabad. Prosecutions were launched against him in respect of the grave crimes alleged against him: Viz., several murders, looting of property, arson, etc. vide Ex.P-8, the memorandum of the Chief Secretary dated 10-1-1949. It would suffice in this context to refer to the petitioner's reply to the counter-affidavit filed by the State of Andhra Pradesh to have an idea of what followed:

"Thus, of the 24 charges, the petitioner was acquitted of 14 charges, i.e., 12 Apsinga dacoity cases and one murder at Apsinga Village and of the Upla Murder case by the trial court alone. Of the 10 remaining cases, the petitioner was acquitted of Yeet murder case by the High Court on merits as explained above."

"There remained only 9 cases of loot in Kellari which in fact was single case pertaining to a particular date and time and which was split up into three groups which were finally dismissed by the Supreme Court".

It may be stated that prosecutions were launched in the first instance before the Special Tribunal, which was constituted under the Hyderabad Special Tribunals Regulation, for the trial of these cases. The Petitioner was sentenced to various terms of rigorous imprisonment for his offences. He appealed. The High Court, however, without entering into the merits disposed of the Appeals on the technical ground that the constitution of the Special Tribunal was ultravires the Constitution. The State appealed against the said decision of the High Court. The Supreme Court held that the constitution of the Special Tribunal for the trial of cases under the Hyderabad Special Tribunals Regulation No. 5 of 1358 F. was intravires the Constitution. The Petitioner was interviewed by a special committee of the then Cabinet on 12-3-1954 with regard to the cases against him. Even so, the Appeals preferred to the Supreme Court by the State were withdrawn, and the Supreme Court dismissed the Appeals preferred by the State as withdrawn on 25-6-1954. We are not here called upon to enquire into the propriety or otherwise of the said withdrawals. The reference to the said withdrawal may be noticed only as a relevant fact.

Subsequently, on 13-10-1956 the former Government of Hyderabad passed an order removing the Petitioner with effect from 18-9-1948, the date when he was placed under suspension.

In view of the contentions raised before us impugning the said order, we deem it apposite to set it out in extenso:-

"ORDER No. 300/GAD/1/SRC-CSP/56 dated 13th October, 1956, of Government of Hyderabad, General Administration Department, Hyderabad-Deccan.

Shri Mohd. Hyder, Member of Hyderabad Civil Service, who was serving as Taluqdar, Osmanabad, was placed under suspension with effect from 18th September 1948, in view of some serious allegations of a criminal nature against him. Sanction to prosecute him in Court of Law was given, but in view of General Policy of Government in respect of such prosecutions, the Cases against him were withdrawn from Supreme Court. The case against him has been fully examined. The Rajpramukh in exercise of the power conferred on him by Proviso (c) to Clause (2) of Article 311 of the Constitution has satisfied himself that in the interests of the Security of the state, it is not expedient to give Shri Mohd. Hyder an opportunity as required under sub-clause (2) of Article 311 of the Constitution.

3. After considering all the facts, the Rajpramukh is pleased to decide that Shri Mohd. Hyder be removed from service with effect from 18th September, 1948; and on purely compassionate grounds and as an act of clemency, Shri Mohd. Hyder be paid a compassionate allowance for life equal to 50% of the pension that he would have drawn had been retired on medical certificate on 18th September, 1948. The Compassionate allowance will be paid only from the date of this order.
4. For the period from 18th September, 1948 to the date of this order, Shri Mohd. Hyder will receive from Government of Hyderabad only the subsistence allowance which he has been in receipt of. With effect from the date of this order, the subsistence allowance will stop and a compassionate allowance, as mentioned in para 3, will be paid.

Sd/ P.V.R. Rao

Chief Secretary to Government"

It is this order that is called in question now before us.

The contentions raised by Shri Nambiar, the learned Counsel for the Petitioner, are on a two-fold basis:-

It is his primary contention that in as much as the Constitution came into force only on 26-1-1950, pre-constitution misconduct cannot be punished by applying the provisions of the Constitution, to Wit, Article 311(2), Proviso (c).

Para 16 of the affidavit in support of the petition refers to this contention, which may be usefully set out:-

"The removal from service was with effect from 18-9-1948. The constitution came into force only on 26-1-1950. Article 311(2) Proviso (c) was not in force on 18-9-1948. On 18-9-1948 the Petitioner had a vested right not to be removed or dismissed from service except under and according to the then existing law of Hyderabad which required that the charge should be investigated by a Commission after giving the Petitioner an opportunity to defend himself. A true translation of the relevant provisions of Act No. III of 1314 Fasli and the rules framed there under are annexed to the affidavit, marked as Ex.P-2 and P-3 respectively and may be read as part of this affidavit. As can be seen from a perusal of those rules there was no provision in the law of Hyderabad similar to that enacted in Article 311(2) Proviso (c). The Petitioner, therefore, submits that the dismissal as from 18-9-1948 without conforming to the then existing law of Hyderabad, but in conformity with Article 311 of the Constitution which was not in force at that time is void, illegal and without jurisdiction. The Constitution which was not in force at that time is void, illegal and without jurisdiction. The Constitution is not retrospective or retroactive in operation".

Essentially, the argument is that pre constitution misconduct alleged against the Petitioner could be punished only with reference to the rules then in force for punishing the misconduct of officers.

For this proposition, Shri Nambiar seeks to press into his service Articles 372 and 313 of the Constitution.

Article 372 so far as it is relevant may be set out in this context:-

"Article 372(1). Notwithstanding the repeal by this constitution of the enactments referred to in Article 395 but subject to the other provisions of this Constitution, all the law in force in the territory of India immediately before the commencement of this Constitution shall continue in force therein until altered or repealed or amended by a competent Legislature or other competent authority".

It is abundantly clear from the very terms of the Article that all the law in force in the territory of India immediately before the commencement of the Constitution shall continue in force only subject to the other provisions of the Constitution. In other words, it is made clear that the provisions of the Constitution override any law in force prior to the coming into force of the constitution.

Article 313, which is marginally noted as a transitional provisions, is as under:

"Until other provision is made in this behalf under this Constitution, all the laws in force immediately before the commencement of this constitution and applicable to any public service or any post which continues to exists after the commencement of this Constitution, as an all-India service or as service or post under the Union or a State shall continue in force so far as consistent with the provisions of this Constitution".

This Article in terms provides for the continuance of provisions consistent with the provisions of the Constitution only.

There is ample legal authority for the legal position that the provisions of the Constitution only should govern matters in relation to public service after the coming into force of the Constitution. Vide Suyresh Chandra v. Himangshu Kumar Roy AIR 1953 Cal.316; Jagdish Dajiba v. The Accountant-General of Bombay AIR 1958 Bom.283.

In the first of the said cases, it was ruled that Rule 15 of the Police Regulations, 1915, must be held to be ultra virus as infringing Article 311(1) of the Constitution and inoperative under Article 313 of the Constitution. The pertinent observations occur in para 30 of the Judgement at page 318 of the Report and may be set out appropriately:

"But the Petitioner has been dismissed by the order of 6-5-1950 after the Constitution of India came into force. The Petitioner's service is governed by the Constitution and by Article 311 of the Constitution. Rule 15 of the Police Regulations, 1915, which must now be held to be ultra vires as infringing Article 311(1) cannot stand in the way of the Petitioner. The rule must be held to be inoperative under Article 313 of the Constitution. That the Petitioner's service is governed by the present Constitution of India admits of no doubt. See—'NORTH WEST FRONTIER PROVINCE v. SURAJ NARAIN ANAND' 75 Ind.App.343 (P.C.)'

In the second case, it was ruled that

"The Civil Services (Classification, Control and Appeal) Rules cannot be interpreted so as to permit an encroachment on the powers given to the President under Article 310 of the Constitution".

Meeting the contentions, the learned Judges have reasoned thus in paras 8 and 9 of their judgement:-

"(8) It was argued for the Petitioner that under Article 313 all laws relating to services in force before the commencement of the Constitution are continued in force even after the Constitution until other provision is made in that behalf. It was further urged that the Rules are such law and the same having been continued in force under Article 313 of the Constitution should be considered as controlling the exercise of the power of the President under Article 310 of the Constitution.

"(9) It is indeed hard to accept this submission. It is being overlooked that such rules or regulations continue in force so far as they are consistent with the provisions of the Constitution. Secondly, such rules cannot be classed as being "the express provision in the Constitution" simply because they have been continued in force by virtue of Article 313 of the Constitution. All pre-existing rules operate only subject to the provisions of the Constitution".

Shri Nambiar strongly relied on Keshavan Madhava Menon v. The State of Bombay AIR 1951 SC 128; but, we are unable to see anything in the case which would lend assistance to the proposition contended for that the defunct rules are perpetuated as against the express provisions of the Constitution.

That was a case of prosecution for an offence punishable under Section 18(I) of the Press (Emergency Powers) Act of 1931. A Division Bench of the High Court of Bombay held that the proceedings commenced under section 18(I) of the said Act before the commencement of the Constitution could be proceeded with after the Constitution. With that conclusion, the Supreme Court agreed although for different reasons. The concluding portion of the judgement sets out the rationale for the conclusion arrived at thus:

"If, therefore, an act was done before the commencement of the Constitution in contravention of the provisions of any law which, after the constitution, becomes void with respect to the exercise of any of the fundamental rights, the inconsistent law is not wiped out so far as the past act is concerned, for to say that it is, will be to give the law retrospective effect. There is no fundamental right that a person shall not be prosecuted and punished for an offence committed before the Constitution came into force. So far as the past acts are concerned, the law exists notwithstanding that it does not exist with respect to the future exercise of fundamental rights. We, therefore, agree with the conclusion arrived at by the High Court on the second question, although on different grounds."

Shri Nambiar made reference to Section 6(e) of the General Clauses Act as supporting him in his contention that the old rules should be observed in dealing with the delinquent officer. He also made reference to the Adaptation of Laws Order, 1950, made by the President under clause (2) of Article 372 of the Constitution of India stating *inter alia* that the General Clauses Act, 1897, applies for the interpretation of the President's Order as it applies for the interpretation of a Central Act. Section 6(e) of the General Clauses Act saves *inter alia* "any remedy in respect of any such right... as if the repealing Act or Regulation had not been passed".

We have already referred to Article 372 sub Clause (1) of the Constitution. Sub-Clause (2), which is now referred to, states expressly that the President may by order make such adaptations "for the purpose of bringing the provisions of any law in force in the territory of India into accord with the provisions of this constitution".

Here also, the emphasis is on the express provisions of the Constitution and any adaptation is meant only to be in accord with the provisions of the Constitution. We cannot spell out from these provisions referred to by Shri Nambiar, that the old rules of the Hyderabad Government for punishing the misconduct of its officials were perpetuated notwithstanding the express provisions of the Constitution to the contrary. We have said enough to find against the contentions advanced by Shri Nambiar making out a plea for perpetuating the old defunct rules.

Before we formulate our conclusions, we might make reference to an English case, cited by the learned Government Pleader, Re A Solicitor's Clerk (1957) 3 All England law Reports 617. In that case, the appellant, a solicitor's clerk was convicted of larceny in 1953 of the property which belonged to neither his employer nor his client. Such a conviction was not actionable under the Solicitor's Act, 1941; but, by an Amending Act of 1956, the larceny of property of anybody irrespective of whether it belonged to the employer or one of his clients was made actionable. Pursuant to that, action was taken against the Appellant under the Amended Act. A contention was raised on behalf of the Solicitor's clerk that the provisions of the Act of 1956 cannot come into operation in respect of a person convicted before that Act came into operation, as that would have the effect of making the Amending Act's operation retrospective. Lord Goddard, C.J., rejected the contention observing that

"In my opinion, however, this Act is not in truth retrospective. It enables an order to be made disqualifying a person from acting as a solicitor's clerk in the future and what happened in the past is the cause or reason for the making of the order; but the order has no retrospective effect".

It could be seen from this decision that a person has to be dealt with according to the law in force at the time he is dealt with and that the delinquent person cannot invoke rules which ceased to have any operation by a change in the duly constituted authority. There is no force in the contention that by applying the provisions of the Constitution in 1956 when the Petitioner was ultimately dealt with, the authority transgressed by giving retrospective effect to the Constitution.

It is true that the order of removal was to take effect from 18-9-1948. We are not here called upon to decide whether the removal could have retrospective operation having regard to the statement made by the Government Pleader that it could only have prospective operation. But the learned Government Pleader urges that would not make any difference for the reason that the Petitioner was under suspension from that date and that ever since he was being paid subsistence allowance which the Government did not seek to recover from him as could be seen from the order in question. We think that the submission is substantial since the Petitioner is not required to refund the amount which he had received by way of subsistence allowance. That being the case, he has not suffered any injustice and there will be no ground to interfere with that order.

We find, therefore, that we cannot accede to the proposition pressed upon us that pre-Constitution misconduct can be dealt with only with reference to the pre-Constitution rules which ceased to have effect after the coming into force of the Constitution.

The Petitioner was no doubt a member of the former Hyderabad Civil Service. He was put under suspension on 18-9-1948 and continued to be so. Action was ultimately taken against him by an order dated 13-10-1956 by the then Government which was lawfully constituted and functioned within the framework of the Constitution. The rules for punishing the misconduct of Hyderabad officials, which were in force in 1948 ceased to apply at the time when final action was taken against the Petitioner. The Government working within the framework of the Constitution have necessarily to deal with the Petitioner according to the Constitution under which it derived its power and not apply Act No. III of 1314 Fasli, for enquiring into the corrupt practices of Government officials, which ceased to operate.

We are, therefore, unable to find any substance in this primary argument.

Shri Nambiar, the learned Counsel for the Petitioner, seeks to present the Petitioner's case on an alternative footing thus:-

Assuming that the provisions of the Constitution could be applied in dealing with the Petitioner for misconduct in 1948 (pre-Constitution misconduct), he submits that the Petitioner had a vested right to continue in service till his services were terminated under Rules by giving him an opportunity to show cause against his removal and that denial of an opportunity to him under the Proviso (c) to Article 311(2) of the Constitution was malafide.

The learned Government Pleader meets this alternative case by straight answers: that there is no such vested right as the Petitioner contends he had; and the exercise of the power by the Rajpramukh under Proviso (c) to Article 311(2) was not mala fide and further not justiciable in courts of law.

He refers to a Full Bench Decision of the Supreme Court in Rajvi Amar Singh v. State of Rajasthan AIR 1958 S.C.228 wherein in following pertinent observations occur in para 16 of the Judgement at page 230.

Now it is well established that when one State is absorbed in another, whether by accession, conquest, merger or integration, all contract of service between the prior Government and its servants automatically terminate and thereafter those who elect to serve in the new State, and are taken on by it, serve on such terms and conditions as the new state may choose to impose. This is nothing more, (though on a more exalted scale), than an application of the principle that underlines the law of Master and Servant when there is a change of masters. So far as this court is concerned, the law is settled by the decision in State of Madras v. K.M. Rajagopalan, 1955-2 SCR 541 at p.562: {(S) AIR 1955 SC.817 at p.830} (A), which follows the decisions of the Privy Council and the House of Lords in Reilly v. the King, 1934 A.C.176 (B), and Nokes v. Don Caster Amalgamated Collieries Ltd., 1940 A.C.1014 (c). The distinction between rights to property and contractual rights when there is a change of sovereignty was pointed out in Virendra Singh v. State of Uttar Pradesh, 1955-I SCR 415 at p.427: (AIR 1954 SC 447 at p.451 (D)."

This authoritative pronouncement obviously negatives the contention pressed in favour of the Petitioner that he has a vested right to continue in service.

The Constitution provides expressly in regard to the tenure of office of the servants of the Union or a state as the case may be under Article 310. Article 310 Cl. (1) states thus:-

"Except as expressly provided by this Constitution, every person who is a member of a defence service or of a Civil Service of the Union or of an all-India service or holds any post connected with defence or any Civil post under the Union, holds office during the pleasure of the President, and every person who is a member of a civil service of a State or holds any civil post under a State holds office during the pleasure of the Governor of the State".

The words "or, as the case may be, the Rajpramukh" occurring after the work, 'governor' were omitted by the Constitution (Seventh

Amendment) Act 1956. It may be noticed in passing that the order of removal now in question had been passed by the Rajpramukh when those words occurred in the Constitution; that is to say prior to the Seventh amendment Act. It may as well be stated here that the constitutional theory of the tenure of office being during the pleasure of the President, Governor or Rajpramukh, as the case may be, is only a reiteration of corresponding provisions which occurred in the Government of India Act, 1935. The relevant provision of that Act, repealed by the Indian Constitution, was Section 240 which specified the tenure of office as during His Majesty's pleasure.

Our view is consistent with what has been adumbrated by the Supreme Court in Parshotam Lal Dhingra v. Union of India AIR 1958 S.C.36. After referring to the exceptions occurring in the Constitution, the learned Judges have clarified the position thus in para 9 of the reported judgement:- (Relevant portion is extracted).

"Subject to these exceptions our Constitution, by Article 310 (1), has adopted the English Common Law rule hat public servants hold office during the pleasure of the President or governor, as the case may be and has, by Article 311, imposed two qualifications on the exercise of such pleasure. Though the two qualifications are set out in a separate Article, they quite clearly restrict the operation of the rule embodied in Article 310(1). In other words the provisions of Article 311 operate as a proviso to Article 310(1). ...Passing on the Article 311 we find that it gives a two-fold protection to persons who come within the Article, namely, (1) against dismissal or removal by an authority subordinate to that by which they were appointed and (2) against dismissal or removal or reduction in rank without giving them a reasonable opportunity of showing cause against the action proposed to be taken in regard to them. Incidentally it will be noted that the word "removed" has been added after the word "dismissal" in both cls. (1) and (2) of Article 311. Upon Article 311 two questions arise, namely, (a) who are entitled to the protection and (b) what are the ambit and scope of the protection?".

From the aforesaid observations of the Supreme Court, two points emerge: firstly, that the Petitioner could have held office only during the pleasure of the Rajpramukh and that there was no such thing as a vested right in him which is inviolable and inherent in him notwithstanding the Constitution; and secondly, that his removal would be governed by Article 311 of the Constitution.

Shri Nambiar pressed upon us a contention that in any event, the Hyderabad Civil Services (Classification, Control and Appeal) Rules made by the Rajpramukh in exercise of the powers conferred by the proviso to Article 309 of the Constitution of India should be complied with in the matter of his removal from service.

It is to be noted that these rules are only subject to the provisions of the Constitution as expressly enacted under Article 309. Any limitations on the power conferred under Article 310 should be founded on the express provisions of the Constitution and not on the Rules. Moreover, it is to be noted that the Rules in question do not contain any stipulation as to the tenure of services. They only provide for action to be taken against the services in disciplinary matters. They cannot be interpreted so as to permit an encroachment on the powers conferred on the President, Governor or the Rajpramukh under Article 310 of the Constitution. The view we have taken is consistent with what has been expressed in Jagdish Dajiba v. The Accountant-General of Bombay AIR 1958 Bom.283. In para 16 of the reported judgment, the following observations are completely in accord with the view expressed by us:-

"Finally, we have our new Constitution. Article 310 (1) reiterates the constitutional theory of the tenure of office being during the pleasure of the President, the Governor or Rajpramukh as the case may be".

"It is thus clear that any limitations on this power of the President should be founded on express provisions of the Constitution, if any and not on the rules or statues enacted by the Legislatures. Moreover it is to be noted that the Rules in question do not contain any stipulation as to the tenure of services. Among other things they only provide for action to be taken against the services disciplinary matters. The Rules cannot be interpreted so as to permit an encroachment on the powers given to the President under Article 310 of the Constitution".

A Division Bench of this High Court also has expressed the view in similar terms in B. Eswaraiah v. State of Andhra (1958) I an.W.R.132, 136. Subba Rao, C.J. (As he then was) referring to the rules made by the Governor under Article 309 of the Constitution of India, observed thus:-

"It is contended by the learned Counsel for the Petitioner that the statutory rules are as much binding upon the Government as upon a subject, while the Advocate-General contends that a Government Servant holds office during the pleasure of the governor and that so long as the constitutional safeguards provided for him are not infringed, he cannot question the order of the Governor in any Court of Law. The rules were made by the Governor under Article 309 of the Constitution of India and therefore they are statutory rules. But those rules only provide a machinery for working out the constitutional right of a Government Servant to give him the reasonable opportunity vouchsafed to him under Article 311(2) of the Constitution of India. When the safeguard itself is removed by the order of the Governor under clause (c) of the proviso to clause (2) the rules, which only prescribe the mode of giving that opportunity to a particular class of officers, can no longer govern the rights of the Petitioner. The procedure ceases to apply when the substantive right itself no longer exists. We, therefore, hold that the Government was within their rights in dispensing with the services of the petitioner without giving him a reasonable opportunity".

So, we are reinforced in the view we have taken that the Civil Services (Classification, Control and Appeal) Rules do not override the express provisions of the Constitution and that when action is taken under the express provisions of the Constitution, the non-compliance with the Rules referred to cannot be taken exception to. Even so, we might notice that even the rules relied on provide for not giving an opportunity to show cause against removal from service.

Rule 17 (c) (3) of the aforesaid rules is in these terms:

"Where H.E.H. the Nizam is satisfied that in the interest of the Security of the State it is not expedient to give to that person such an opportunity".

This takes us on to the next contention strenuously urged by Shri Nambiar that the exercise of the power of the Rajpramukh under the

Proviso (c) to Article 311(2) was malafide. We have adverted to the reply of the Government pleader in this regard that the exercise of the power was neither malafide nor justiciable in a court of law.

We may now refer to the relevant Article and the proviso:

311.(1) No person who is a member of a Civil service of the Union or an all-India service or a civil service of a State or holds a Civil post under the Union or a State shall be dismissed or removed by an authority subordinate to that by which he was appointed.

(2) No such person as aforesaid shall be dismissed or removed or reduced in rank until he has been given a reasonable opportunity of showing cause against the action proposed to be taken in regard to him:

Provided that this clause shall not apply----

(a) xxx xxx xxx

(b) xxx xxx xxx

(c) Where the President or Governor as the case may be, is satisfied that in the interest of the security of the State it is not expedient to give to that person such an opportunity".

In relation to this proviso, we recall the apposite observations of the Division Bench in Jagdish Dajiba v. The Accountant-General of Bombay AIR 1958 (Born, 283 in para 26 at page 289 of the reported judgment:

"The Constitution in its wisdom has reposed confidence in and invested powers in relation to services on the President who is the highest dignitary of our State and in whom the executive Government vests. The Constitution trusts that the President will always act with full justice to all and in the interest of the State of which he is a caretaker. The integrity and responsibility to carry on the executive Government are the only checks by which the Constitution is satisfied. Moreover, this doctrine of services being at the pleasure of the executive head of the State is not new and is not embodied as a novel theory in our Constitution. This rule is established in English common law and is also recognized in the American Constitution. Shenoy v. Smit (19=895) A.C.229 (E), Myers v. United States, (1926) 272 US 52 (F)".

We are in respectful agreement with the views expressed. We only wish to add that the President or the Governor or the Rajpramukh, as the case may be, as the lawfully constituted authority under the Constitution could satisfy himself in the interest of the security of the State. We cannot subscribe to the theory that the Head of the State acts otherwise than in good faith and satisfies himself in the interest of the security of the State in proper cases.

It has been held by this High Court repeatedly that the satisfaction envisaged in the said provision is 'subjective satisfaction' and cannot be called into question in courts of law. In Mohmmad Azam v. State of Hyderabad (1957) II An.W.R. 464 at page 467, the Division Bench spoke thus:-

"Where the action proposed to be taken against a member of the services specified in clause (1) of Article 311 is under Proviso (c) of clause (2) of Article 311 the satisfaction that it is not expedient in the interests of the security of the State to give that person an opportunity to show cause, is the satisfaction of the Rajpramukh. Is the satisfaction to be subjective or objective? The State of a person's mind cannot be determined by the objective test and as long as the President, Governor, or the Rajpramukh acted in good faith, their satisfaction cannot be enquired into in a court of Law".

The said view was emphasized again in B. Eswaraiah v. State of Andhra (1958) I An.W.R.132, 136 at page 136 of the reported judgment. The pertinent observations are as under:

"Clause (c) of the proviso to clause (2) of Article 311 in terms confers unrestricted power on the Governor in the interest of the State to deprive a particular officer of the reasonable opportunity provided by Article 311 of the Constitution of India. The said power is not circumscribed by any objective standards and therefore, it cannot be questioned in a Court of Law".

Apart from this aspect of the case, we are also satisfied that the Rajpramukh had acted in good faith after examining the whole case of the Petitioner. In the resume of the case, we have set out the details of the charges against the petitioner. We referred to Ex.P-8, the memorandum of the Chief Secretary dated 10-1-1949. In the impugned order, it is expressly stated by the Rajpramukh that the case of the Petitioner has been fully examined and that the Rajpramukh exercised the power conferred on him by the Proviso (c) to the clause (2) of Article 311 of the Constitution. We find ourselves unable to accept the suggestion that the Rajpramukh had not examined the case of the Petitioner fully and that he had not acted in good faith. We, therefore, reject the alternative case presented by Shri Nambiar also for the said reasons.

In conclusion, we find that the impugned order removing the Petitioner from service was made when the Petitioner was a member of the service during the pleasure of the Rajpramukh of the State. We hold that the exercise of the power under Proviso (c) referred to was proper and that there has been no infringement of the express provisions of the Constitution.

We find, therefore, that no case has been made out for interference by way of proceeding in Writ.

In the result, the petition is dismissed with cost; Government Pleader's fee Rs. 250/-

MEMORANDUM OF COSTS

W.P.No: 148 of 1957

Respondents ( )	costs	Rs.	P.
Stamp for Vakalatnama	0	0	
Advocate's fee (as fixed by the Court)		250	0
To be paid by the Petitioner –		250	0
To the Respondent			

Sd/- xxx

SUB ASSISTANT REGISTRAR

//TRUE COPY//

Conclusion

Since we are naturally inclined to look for reasons behind events, I must attempt an interpretation of my experience in Osmanabad. Did I endure a season in hell or was I offered a glimpse of the true condition of the world?

I think a bit of both. It proved impossible to obtain justice not because I had been targeted by some vindictive individuals but because the relationship between the two sides had deteriorated to the point where it was no longer possible to entertain the Hyderabad point of view or to obtain a fair hearing for those identified with it. What should have been a simple matter of setting the record straight, could not be accomplished, because the basis of common values, mutual regard, and ways of communicating that normally sustain notions of fair play and justice had, for the time being, ceased to exist. In its place there had risen up a structure of derogatory attitudes, reminiscent of British or French colonial rule. The same systematic bias of separation and contempt that was applied by the West towards colonial India was applied by free India to an intractable Hyderabad. It was this tendency that opened the way for the injustices visited upon its civil servants.

I got on with my life. I was able to find reasonable employment in Hyderabad, to live comfortably with my family, and to send my children to decent schools there. Life was good. But I keenly felt the break with that validating connection to my profession. There are few jobs in the world that could match the thrill of a collectorship; it offers everything a young and energetic civil servant could want:

independent command, resources, daily encounter with real problems, the possibility of helping the weakest sections of society, of taking effective administrative action over a wide range of public affairs, and of obtaining access, at a moment's notice, to the highest political and executive levels of the state. It was difficult to say goodbye to all that.

There were interesting jobs available abroad. My colleague, Mir Moazzam Hussain, collector of Nalgonda district in 1948, was released a little before me, and was allowed to leave the country. He was keen to help me get a job with UNESCO where he was working throughout the 1950s. My brother, Dr M. Farooq, director of Public Health in 1948, was given the choice of accepting a demotion or an early retirement, despite his unblemished record of service. He chose the latter, and left for England, eventually joining the World Health Organization where he distinguished himself as an epidemiologist. But I could not obtain a passport until 1964, shortly before my fiftieth birthday. Had I pushed, the authorities would have come back with their stock response: that it was not in the best interests of the state to let me go abroad. This put paid to any idea of seeking employment abroad. Incidentally, Pakistan was not an option that I ever considered seriously, either just after the Police Action or later.

I was welcomed back into the social circles of Hyderabad. I am sure some people continued to harbour wild suspicions about me, like one senior civil servant, newly-arrived in Hyderabad, who on hearing my name at a party burst out, 'My God, Mohammed Hyder of Osmanabad! Why, he used to eat little Hindu children for breakfast!'

For others, and especially among the ordinary folk in Hyderabad, I became a figure of quiet admiration. These were mainly people I didn't know, and who did not really know me. Perhaps they needed someone to look up to, in those rather bleak days of the '50s. Or, more likely, knowing what I had gone through, they felt a sort of solidarity with me. I have always been able to sense a connection with ordinary people and it has been a bond between us that has truly sustained me. Perhaps they had a similar fellow-feeling towards me. In any case, as I went about my business, I noticed that the police constables directing the city traffic would salute me; not all, but quite a few. It was a touching gesture; I acknowledged it because it would have been churlish not to.

But I once had occasion to take General S.M. Shrinagesh in my car. He had arrived recently in Hyderabad as principal of the Administrative Staff College. He was a fine gentleman, and it was an honour to claim his friendship. As we drove off, I became aware of a possible awkwardness: the traffic police were saluting me, as usual. I had the wit not to return their greeting. The general, until recently India's Chief of Army Staff, raised his hand automatically once, twice, three times, and then turned to me and observed, 'They can't know me, can they?'

'They obviously do, Sir,' I replied.

'Hmm ...' said the General.

I thus found a certain equilibrium in my life. I was able to pursue my interest in the law, and in 1961 obtained a master's degree – an LLM – from Osmania University in Hyderabad. In 1963, I completed and moved into a house in Asifnagar, in the western suburbs of Hyderabad. It is a lovely house, set amidst vineyards and fruit trees. The land dips to the west and the south of it, and rises again a few miles later, outlining the fortress of Golconda against the sky, and the tombs of ancient kings. There is a road to the north of the house, and across it there are open grounds owned by the army, and beyond that a view of the rocky outcrops bordering Banjara Hills. At dawn and dusk, the strains of the reveille drift up from the military camp. Early in the morning, near four o'clock, long caravans of bullock carts can be heard, slowly winding their way to market; the creak of the carts laden with fruit and vegetables; the cow-bells tinkling; the odd cartman singing, while the rest of his companions dozed at the reins, certain that the bullocks knew the way: a peaceful rural scene in a fast-changing world.

In 1964, my eldest son went abroad to study at the London School of Economics, and my younger son entered a medical school closer to home. A little later, in 1969, my daughter married a likely young scientist and went to live in Zurich. With time, it seemed, things had begun to right themselves.

The court's verdict had not surprised me. My friends in the legal fraternity thought that I had filed the writ too early, while the judiciary was still insufficiently independent of the executive. Perhaps, but I have no regrets: I did what I had to do. Looking back, I find little of redemptive value in what I had endured, little that is uplifting about my experience. Life's trials do not always point to a higher purpose. But I derive some satisfaction from having faced my difficulties squarely. I had lost my career but neither my self-respect nor my faith in mankind. I can imagine worse outcomes.

So much for myself. There is a larger question on which I must conclude: How can we best understand what took place between Hyderabad and India? The confrontation of 1947-48 is usually seen from the Indian point of view, and interpreted in terms of the aspirations of the Indian nationalist movement. I do not find this a useful approach because, seen through that lens, the Hyderabad position appears perverse and illogical, suggesting a futile posture of defiance against the inevitable tide of history that favoured the emergence of a unified India. By now this is the popular interpretation, and the general impression persists that Hyderabad's negotiating position was unreasonable, and that in the end it became the victim of its own miscalculation.

Was Hyderabad mad, bad and irredeemable? There is a natural inclination to doubt the motives of an adversary. But can we dismiss one side's concern with being hustled into accession as irrational, and accept the other's overriding drive towards merger as somehow predestined? This way we end up giving history a discernible direction, by identifying the outcome with the victorious cause. If, instead, we see the Hyderabad response as that of a smaller state, compelled to negotiate with a larger, more powerful state, then what happened begins to make better sense. This is not the place to go into the details of that confrontation but it might be instructive to look for general patterns of behaviour, when two unequal states face each other. A historical analogy might prove helpful.

In 416 BC, in the sixteenth year of the Peloponnesian War, Athens invaded the small island of Melos. The historian Thucydides presents the initial confrontation in the form of a dialogue, which has, since that time, become a classic account of how great powers may treat smaller states. The Melians saw themselves as different, having always resisted the influence of the Delian League (the confederacy led by Athens) and felt themselves closer to Sparta. But now, caught between Sparta and Athens, they wished fervently to remain neutral and independent.

From the start, the negotiations were overshadowed by the Athenian threat of force. The Melians were offered a stark choice: to join the League and pay tribute, or to fight. The first substantive argument the Melians advanced rests on the concept of their rights. This was brushed aside by the Athenians. '…right as the world goes is only in question between equals in power, while the strong do what they can and the weak suffer what they must.' They advised the Melians not to consider what is right but what ensures their security.

Next, the Melians suggested that Athens might consider having a neutral Melos: 'Friends instead of enemies, but allies of neither side.'

'No,' replied the Athenians, 'for your hostility cannot so much hurt us as your friendship will be an argument to our subjects of our weakness.'

The Melians tried a different argument. Since their cause was just, they said, the gods would help them. The Athenians came back with a robust counter-argument, based on the omnipresence of realist behaviour:

'Of the gods we believe and of the men we know, that by a necessary law of their nature they rule wherever they can. And it is not as if we were the first to make this law, or to act upon it when made: we found it existing before us and shall leave it to exist for ever after us; all we do is to make use of it, knowing that you and everybody else, having the same power as we have, would do the same as we do.'

The Melians offered a fourth argument. They claimed that their kin, the Spartans, would come to their aid. The Athenians replied, with irony, that the Spartans were very good at looking after their own interests.

'…Of all the men we know they are most conspicuous in considering what is agreeable honourable, and what is expedient just. Such a way of thinking does not promise much for the safety which you now unreasonably count upon.'

At the end of the meeting, the Athenian delegation withdrew, leaving the Melians to come to a decision, which did not take them long:

'Our resolution, Athenians, is the same as it was at first. We will not in a moment deprive of freedom a city that has been inhabited these seven hundred years; but we put our trust in the fortune by which the gods have preserved it until now, and in the help of men, that is of the Lacedaemonians (Spartans); and so we will try and save ourselves. Meanwhile we invite you to allow us to be friends to you and foes to neither party, and to retire from our country after making such a treaty as shall seem fit to us both.'

The Athenians then began the siege of Melos, and returned in force the next winter to press the attack until the Melians surrendered. All adult men were put to death; the women and children, sold into slavery; and the island, recolonized.

Thucydides is still relevant because he touches on the universal themes of war and peace, and the conduct of men and of states. No exact parallel to the Hyderabad case is intended; for example, there was no standstill arrangement extended to Melos, nor was Hyderabad as dead-set against an eventual merger as Melos appears to have been. But there are some striking similarities: the sense of a separate identity; the preference of both Melos and Hyderabad for remaining neutral; the expectation of support from friendly powers (Melos from Sparta, Hyderabad from Britain and Pakistan); the reluctance to deprive themselves of the freedom they felt they had enjoyed for hundreds of years; the sense of negotiating under duress; the tendency in the admired democracies, Athens and India, towards vindictiveness; and, in both cases, a bloody aftermath to surrender.

This account from classical Greece illuminates the realities of power politics. There is to this day a liberal approach to relations between states and peoples, which emphasizes the rights of individuals and of states, and promotes the rule of law, and there is the realist approach, that rides roughshod and unabashed over them, just as Thucydides describes it. It is the struggle between these opposing forces that continues to shape the destinies of nations and of men.

Appendix

A selection of documents from Mohammed Hyder Vs The State of Andhra Pradesh, Writ Petition 148 of 1957, High Court of Judicature of Andhra Pradesh at Hyderabad.

Note: Legal exhibit numbers (Ex.P.I, etc) refer to the original sequence of legal exhibits as presented in the Writ Petition.

EX.P.11
Case No.8/2 of 1950
Copy of the Note, Revenue Secretary, attached to letter No. 1511, dated Nil.

COURT OF SPECIAL SESSIONS JUDGE, GULBURGA & OSMANABAD

CHIEF SECRETARY,
Mr Mohammed Hyder, H.C.S., 1st Talukdar of Osmanabad has been suspended under the order of Military Governor and the same conveyed to him through his office No. 7, dated 4-1-1358 Fasli. In this connection, the explanation submitted by Mr Mohammed Hyder to this office is sent herewith for the perusal of the Chief Civil Administrator.

It is a fact on two occasions he had submitted his resignation through report, dated 6 August 1948. The report in original is placed below and flagged 'A' and 'B'. As regards his being sent for by the Prime Minister, this office has no record. I remember the then H.R.M. mentioning this to me orally.

From report No. 2990, dated 6 Mehir, 1357, it may be observed that he has taken action against Rohillas and Razakars.

Sd/- A. Hameed Khan,
I-9-1357 F.
REVENUE SECRETARY.

"TRUE COPY"

EX.P.8
SECRET

CHIEF SECRETARIAT
HYDERABAD

No. 78/OSD. Dated the 10 January 1949

SEAL

MEMORANDUM:

To

The Inspector-General of Police,
Hyderabad-Deccan

Sub: - Criminal Prosecution of suspended Officers --
Mr Mohammed Hyder, HCS, ex-Talukdar, Osmanabad.

In enclosing herewith a self-contained note of allegations, against Mr Mohammed Hyder, ex-Talukdar, Osmanabad, I am directed to say that the Government is pleased to sanction the prosecution in the competent Courts of Laws of Mr Mohammed Hyder on all the allegations enumerated therein.

(2) You are, therefore, requested to take necessary action at your earliest and report for the information of the Government the progress of the case fortnightly.

(3) Your report along with other papers is forwarded to you which may please be acknowledged.

Sd/- M.V. Rajwade,
For Chief Secretary.

ՖՕՅ

"TRUE COPY"

(1) Name and designation of the suspended Officer:-
Mr Mohd. Hyder, HCS, ex-First Talukdar, Osmanabad

(2) Charges that can be made against him:-

(a) Active participation in Razakar and Ittehadul Muslimeen movements.

Mr Mohd. Hyder was a close friend of Mr Kasim Razvi and the latter used to visit the former often. A letter sent by Mr Kasim Razvi and dated 5-6-1948 to Mr Hyder is produced in support.

Several witnesses have deposed on solemn affirmation that Razakars used to travel with Mr Hyder whenever he went out on tour.

(b) Murder of Kishen Teke and his wife Godabai.

Mr Hyder accompanied by the Excise Superintendent and several other officers and Muslims visited village Yeet also called 'INT' on 6-5-1948 (6th Thir, 1357) at about mid-day, and caused Kishen Teke and his wife Godhabai to be murdered in his presence.

There is evidence of (9) persons of whom (6) are eyewitnesses. Eyewitnesses include the then Gumasta of the Police Patel. The Excise Superintendent Mohammed Khan s/o Sadat Khan, who in his statement on solemn affirmation admits his presence with Mr Hyder at Yeet on the day of occurrence, has recorded in his tour diary of '6-5-1948' that local Police and Razakars killed (2) Congressmen. From Yeet, I went to Dekrewadi".

(c) Murder of 12 cartmen of village Uppal in Taluk Barsi. On 29-4-1948, 12 cartmen of village Uppal were taking (6) carts of groundnut under a passport, from Uppal to Barsi in the Indian

Union. Twelve of these persons were wearing Gandhi Caps. Mr Hyder who was accompanied by (6) Pathans caused these (12) men to be taken to Osmanabad Police Station and later caused them to be shot dead.

Six persons including a Customs Clerk have deposed in this connection.

(d) Causing loot and arson in village Killari of Taluk Latur.

Sometime in February or March 1948, Mr Hyder accompanied by the Police and Razakars numbering about 400, surrounded the village Killari and looted property worth Rs 60,000 and made away with it. He also arrested (4) persons who were later released by the Indian Army.

(e) Looting village Apsinga and the murder of Shridhar Vari.

There is no evidence of witnesses on this charge.

(f) Advocacy of strong action against the Indian Union.

Evidence is documentary in the form of the weekly confidential reports, dated 20-11-1357 and 6-11-1357.

(3) Does the evidence make out a satisfactory case on the charges enumerated: A satisfactory case appears to have been made out on charges (a), (b), (c), (d) and (f).

(4) Is further inquiry necessary? If so, on what points? How long will it take? Further inquiry is necessary on charge (E)?

(5) Remarks.

(6) Orders.

Sd/- M.V. Rajvade,

7-1-1949.

"TRUE COPY'

EX.P.29

IN THE COURT OF THE SPECIAL SESSIONS JUDGE, GULBURGA & OSMANABAD.

Case No. 8/2 of 1950

Government through Shevarti Shankar Vs: Mohd. Hyder & others
" " Malkarajan Shanker Vs. -do-
-do- -do- Ratanchand Vs. -do-

CHARGE: DACOITY
The Petition of the undersigned accused –
Most Respectfully Sheweth:

That the Investigating Officer, M. Mohd. Abdul Qader in spite of his being present in the Court, has not been produced as witness. For bringing the actual facts of the case to light and for the sake of justice, it is necessary that he should be summoned on behalf of the Court.
HENCE, THE PRAYER:
That the investigating Officer, Mohd. Abdul Qader, Assistant D.S.P., may, for the sake of justice kindly be summoned as witness on behalf of the Court and examined.

MOHD. HYDER
PETITIONER
22 – 4 – 1950

"TRUE TRANSLATION"

22-4-1950
This will be decided in the presence of the Government Pleader. For the time being recorded.
EX.P.21
Case 9/2 of 1950.

To

The Treasury Officer,
Gulburga.

THROUGH: The Superintendent,
Gulburga Jail.

Sir
I require the following papers in support of my defence in this case. I should be grateful if on receipt of this application, you take special

interest to grant through the Superintendent of Jail, the certified copies of the following papers:-

(1) Certified copy of the T.A. Bill of Mr. Hameeduddin Rana, Deputy Director-General of Police, Gulburga Range, pertaining to the town of Osmanabad in the month of Khurdad, 1357 F., together with a complete copy of the entries in the remarks column and certified copy of the diary attached thereto.

(2) Certified copy of the T.A. Bill of Mr. Qutubuddin, Deputy Commissioner of Customs, pertaining to the tour of Osmanabad in the month of Khurdad, 1357 F., together with a complete copy of the entries in the remarks column and the certified copy of the diary attached thereto.

Sd/- Mohd. Hyder

Dated: 20-10-1950

Endorsement of the Treasury Office
It is hereby returned, I am to say that the copies of such irrelevant papers cannot be given without requisition by the competent Court.

ജ്ഞ

"TRUE COPY"

EX.P.26
LETTER
Sholapur

No.A-9627. Dated: 30-8-1950

To,
The Special Judge,
For Gulburga & Osmanabad,
Headquarters Gulburga

Subject: Upla – Dooki incident
Supply of papers in connection with

A file containing pages 1–53, has already been handed over to the Manager, Special Judge Court, Gulburga and Osmanabad, by Shri S.A. Ghatge, ex-District Magistrate, Sholapur at the time of his evidence in your Court on 28-7-1950. There are now no other papers about the Upla incident in this office.

Sd/-
For District Magistrate, Sholapur
O.C. Signed by B.M., C.B.P.: 308.

ຣຄ

Dated: 1st September, 1950
Be filed, be presented on the date of hearing. Should take the signature of the party who called.

Sd/-Judge.
NOTE: 'Kept in Safe'

ຣຄ

EX.P.14
GOVERNMENT OF HYDERABAD
No. 401/GAD/C/50 Dated 25th October, 1950

From
L.C. Jain, I.C.S.
Chief Secretary to Government.

To,

The Special Judge,
Gulburga & Osmanabad.

Subject: - Government through C.I.D. Vs. Mohd. Hyder,
Talukdar Suit no. 22/8 of 1950.

ຣຄ

(Letter quoted in full in Ex. P. 27, para 10 below)

Ex.P.27

IN THE HIGH COURT OF JUDICATURE AT HYDERABAD

Tuesday, the 4th day of December, 1951
Single Bench Judgement
In Crl. Appeals Nos. 1690/6 and 84/6/51 of 1950.
PRESENT: The Hon'ble Shri Justice Vithal Rao Deshpande.

Mohammed Hyder,
Ex-Taluqdar,
Osmanabad. …….. Appellant.

By Mr. Mackenna, Counsel and Mr. Ziaularfin, Advocate.

VERSUS

The State of Hyderabad ………….. Respondents

By Mr. Rajaram Iyer, Advocate General,
AND
Mr. Gopalrao Murumkar, Government Advocate.

Appeal from the judgement of the Court of the Special Sessions Judge, Gulburga and Osmanabad, dated 6.11.1950 in Crl. Case No. 22/2 of 1950, on the file of that Court.

1. The accused in this case is sentenced to death by the Special Session Judge at Gulburga, under section 243 of the Hyderabad Penal Code, corresponding to Section 302 of the Indian Penal Code.
2. Against this judgment the accused as well as the Government have come up in appeal. This came up initially before the Division Bench of this Court, consisting of Sripat Rao and Mohammed Ansari J.J. Sripat Rao J, held the accused guilty of the murder of Kishen Teke and his wife and sentenced him to

life imprisonment instead of death sentence and to a further period of five years and to a fine of Rs. 1000/- under section 368 of H.P.C. corresponding to Section 436, I.P.C. Both the sentences to run concurrently. Mohammed Ahmed Ansari J. held that there are defects in this case and they should be removed by this Court under Section 428 I.P.C. and when that is done proper decision should be given in this appeal. The record as it stands certainly does not justify the conviction of the accused. Due to this difference of opinion the case has been referred to me as the Third Judge. Heard the arguments of both the parties.

3. The brief facts are; on 5th Thir 1357 F., (5th May 1948) the Accused left Osmanabad for the inspection of the village Dhokewadi where two persons, Maruthi and Vishwanath had previously been killed. The accused spent the night at Yermala Camp and in the morning of Thir. 6, 1357 F., (6th May 1949) went to the village INT and thence to Dhokewadi and returned back to Osmanabad. Before leaving for Osmanabad it is alleged that when he was at INT the Pathans informed him that there is one person, Kishen Teke who is not "heeding". The Taluqdar went along with the Pathans to the house of Kishen Teke and told him to lower down the flag of OM. Kishen Take refused; upon which the Taluqdar gave orders to the Pathans to fire and on his orders the Pathans fired, due to which Kishen Teke and his wife died. After this incident the Talukdar ordered the Pathans to burn the corpses, and the corpses along with the house were burnt. On behalf of the prosecution ten witnesses have been examined. The accused denied the charge and examined five witnesses in defence.

4. Before dealing with the facts I shall first of all deal with the legal points argued at the bar. The first point is that the Special Judge failed to question the accused as required by Section 342, Cr.P.C. due to which the trial is vitiated.

Section 342, Cr.P.C. is as follows:-

"For the purpose of enabling the accused to explain any circumstances appearing in the evidence against him, the Court may, at any stage of any inquiry or trial without previously warning the accused, put such questions to him as the Court considers necessary, and shall, for the purpose aforesaid, question him generally on the case after the witnesses for the prosecution have been examined and before he is called on for his defence".

5. Mr Mackenna, Counsel for the accused, argued that the accused was not examined as per provisions of this Section of the Cr.P.C. It is discretionary with the Court to question the accused at any stage of the enquiry or trial but it is compulsory for the Court to question the accused generally on the case after the witnesses for the prosecution have been examined and before he is called on for his defence. Reliance is placed on the case of DWARKANATH VARMA Vs EMPEROR, A.I.R. 1933, Privy Council 124, DURGARAM Vs: EMPEROR A.I.R. 1925 Patna 342 and BHAGWANDAS JAGAN NATH Vs: EMPEROR A.I.R. 1942 Sindh 102. In these three cases it has been held that under Sec. 342 of the code it is not enough to ask the accused: "What have you got to say about the prosecution case or whether you have got anything to say." But, it is necessary that the Court should ask questions which should relate to the whole case and to the salient points appearing in the evidence against the accused. In this case the Special Judge asked the accused: "did you order and cause the murder of Kishen Teke and his wife? ... and made yourself liable for murder and also caused the house to be burnt and thus become liable for damage?" This single question does not cover the directions of the Section. As the provisions are not complied with, the trial is vitiated as is held in the cases referred to above. The contention of the Government Advocate is that every failure to comply strictly with Sec. 342 does not render the conviction of the accused illegal, unless it has in fact caused the failure of justice. This has been so held in Re: ANNAMALAI MUDALI, A.I.R. 1940 Madras, 372. This case does not support the prosecution because in this case the accused was put several questions on every salient points appearing in the evidence against the accused. In A.I.R. 1933, Privy Council 124 DWARAKANATH VARMA Vs: EMPEROR, their Lordships of the Privy Council have held that it vitiates the trial. Therefore,

in my opinion, also the failure to examine the accused for the purpose of enabling the accused to explain any circumstances appearing in the evidence against him vitiates the trial.

6. Secondly, it is contended on behalf of the Counsel for the accused that the stage at which the examination of the accused ought to have been done is, according to Sec. 342, after the witnesses for the prosecution have been examined and before he is called on for his defence. In this case the accused was examined under this Section on 2nd May 1950. On 26.5.1950 and 14.7.1950, the prosecution witnesses were cross-examined. After the cross-examination was finished, the accused was not examined at all. Under Sec. 342, the stage at which the examination of the accused ought to have been taken is after the witnesses for the prosecution have been examined and before he is called on for his defence. It is contended on behalf of the Government that re-cross-examination is not a part of the cross-examination but it is a part of the defence witnesses. But this has not been supported by the Full Bench decision of the Nagpur High Court LOCAL GOVERNMENT Vs. MARIA, A.I.R. 1925 Nagpur 44. In this case it has been clearly laid down that "the expression after the witnesses for the prosecution have been examined", includes their cross-examination after the charge where the accursed has recalled them under Sec. 256 as examination of a witness means his examination-in-chief, cross-examination and re-examination, Magistrate should invariably question the accused generally on the case after the examination of a prosecution witness is over, i.e., they are examined-in-chief, cross-examined and re-examined and before he enters upon his defence". In my opinion, this is the correct interpretation of the section. As the Special Judge has not followed this procedure, the trial is vitiated as it is obligatory to examine the accused before he is called on for his defence.

7. The next argument of the Counsel for the accused is that the failure of the Court to provide the accused with the statement of the witnesses recorded by the Police is a defect which vitiates the trial. It is evident from the docket-sheets that on 28th April, 1950, the Court allowed the request of the defence counsel to

examine the case diary at the first instance, and no copies of the case diary were provided to the accused. This, according to the Counsel for the accused is an illegality which vitiates the trial. In the case of PULUKARI KOTAYYA Vs. EMPEROR A.I.R. 1947 Privy Council 67, their Lordships of the Privy Council have decided that where the statement were never made available to the accused an inference, which is almost irresistible, arises of prejudices to the accused and further it was held that the right to be furnished with copies of statements made by witnesses to a Police Officer given to an accused person by Sec. 162, Cr.P.C. is a very valuable one and often provides important material for cross-examination of the prosecution witnesses. Under such circumstances, the contention of the Counsel or the accused seems to be right and the accused must be given copies of the statements of the witnesses recorded by the Police. It is contended on behalf of the Government Advocate that it is not lawful for the Court to give such order and also it is contended that the accused never asked for any copies of the statements. In my opinion these contentions have got no force. The procedure is that first of all on the request of the accused the court should ask the case diaries to be produced in the Court and after going through them the court should order the copies to be given to the accused. This stage of asking for the copies had not reached as the copies were not produced in Court. Therefore the contention of the Government Advocate is not sound. The cases of EMPEROR Vs. BANSIDHAR I.L.R. 53 Allahabad 458 and BALIRAM TIKARAM MARATHE Vs. EMPEROR A.I.R. 1945 Nagpur Page I, have been referred to in the Privy Council case, cited above and, therefore, I need not discuss them.

8. The next contention of the Counsel for the accused is that the Special Judge failed to attach weight to the written statements of the accused which is against the law. Section 215, Hyderabad Criminal Procedure Code, Section 256, Indian Criminal Procedure Code, dealing with the trial of warrant cases by Magistrate provides that the accused may put in a written statement which shall be filed. In the present case the accused

was tried according to the procedure prescribed for the trial of warrant cases by the Magistrate and this was so required by the provisions of Section 6 of the Hyderabad Special Tribunal and Special Judges Regulations of 1359 F. In the case of EMPEROR Vs: JABBAR MAL A.I.R. 1928 Allahabad 222, it had been held that great weight is to be attached to the written statement of the accused. Similarly in the case of MUHAMMED SALIA ROWTHER Vs. EMPEROR, AIR 1928 Madras 1135, it is held that it is not open to a criminal court to shut its eyes to the statement of the accused when the statement refers to certain documents to which the accused is a party. The Special Judge relying upon EMPEROR Vs. TARAK NATH BAIDYA A.I.R. 1936 Calcutta 687 and MOHAMMED ANIS Vs. EMPEROR A.I.R. 1936 Oudh 405 has observed that the practice of filing written statements by the accused must be discouraged. These cases do not lend support to the Special Judge's observation. The principle enunciated in these cases refers to procedure in cases triable by Sessions Court and not to procedure in warrant cases triable by Magistrate. There is no provision of filing written statements in a trial by a Session Court. Therefore the Special Judge was wrong in holding that such practice must be discouraged and no weight be attached to the written statement of the accused. On behalf of the Government Advocate it is contended that the Special Judge has looked into the written statement and has considered it. The Special Judge in his judgement has held that because it is not a spontaneous written statement and the law does not allow it, hence it should be discountenanced. In my opinion, the Special Judge has not taken a correct view of the law.

9. The next contention of the Counsel for the accused is that the lower Court was wrong in requiring the accused to summon his witnesses before the examination of the prosecution witnesses has been completed. In support of his contention he was cited FEROZE KAZI Vs. EMPEROR A.I.R. 1940 Patna 295, and KESHAB DEV Vs. KING EMPEROR A.I.R. 1924 Allahabad 320. On 2nd May, the Court gave orders to summon the defence

witnesses, while the cross-examination of the prosecution witnesses took place on 26th May and 14th July, 1950. In fact the cross-examination was not complete. So there is force in the contention of the Counsel for the accused that the Court ought not to have required the accused to summon his witnesses before the prosecution witnesses have been completed. Thus the procedure adopted by the Lower Court is not according to the law and prejudices the accused.

10. In this case the accused had filed several applications to the Court requesting that he should be given copies of the Statements recorded by the Civil Administrator and also the statements recorded by the Police in the case diary. Further, he had applied for summoning the file of the departmental enquiry referred to the Memo No. 78/OSD, dated 7th January, 1949. The Special Judge had written a letter to the Chief Secretary to send for the file of the Departmental Enquiry in the Kilari Dacoity Case in which letter 78/OSD, dated 7th January 1949 is filed along with the enclosures of the self-contained notes of allegations. This letter No. 1215 of the Court is dated 16-8-1950. To this a reply was sent by the Chief Secretary which runs as follows:-

"Reference to your letter no: 1215 dated 16-8-1950 and subsequent reminders, I am directed to state that as the documents called for by you in your letter under reply are of a strictly confidential nature and it would be prejudicial in the interest of the Government to disclose them, this office regrets its inability to produce these documents before the Court. The documents relate to unpublished affairs of the State and the production of the same before the Court has not been permitted by the Government. In view of these circumstances, this office claims the privilege of non-production of the documents in question provided for in Section 26 of the Hyderabad Evidence Act and Section 87(c) of the Hyderabad Criminal Procedure Code".

Upon this, the Special Judge has held that the Government is entitled to refuse the production of any document which is final and the court cannot interfere in it. In the first place the Special Judge was wrong in refusing the production of those documents for which the privilege was not claimed, as for instance, the case diary and the statement recorded by the Civil Administrator. On behalf of the Government the privilege was claimed only as regards the departmental file which was called for by letter No. 1215 dated 16-8-1950. So the special Judge ought to have given a chance for the production of the documents. Secondly, when the file itself was produced in the Killari Case, I do not see how a claim for privilege can be made under such circumstances. Thirdly, according to the cases cited at the bar, I do not see any force in the claim forwarded by the Government for privilege. In the case of GOVERNOR GENERAL IN COUNCIL Vs: PEER MOHAMMED KHUDA BUX, A.I.R. 1950 E. PUNJAB 228, the Full Bench had decided clearly that ordinarily the privilege is attached to state papers which are of political or administrative character. The affairs of the State may be defined as matters of public nature in which the State is concerned and the disclosure of which will be prejudicial to the public interest, or injurious to the national defence or detrimental to good diplomatic relations. Privilege is not to be claimed on the mere ground that the documents are state documents or are official or are marked confidential, or if produced it would result in Parliamentary discussion or public criticism or it will expose a want of efficiency in the administration or tend to lay a particular department of Government open to claim for compensation. Indeed, it is not sufficient that the Minister of the department concerned does not want to have the documents produced. But the sole objective of this privilege is that the disclosure would be injurious to national defence or to good diplomatic relations or for the proper functioning of the public services, and it is necessary to keep that document or the class of the document secret.

11. Further, it has been held that under Evidence Act it is either the Minister or the permanent head of the department who has the right to grant or withhold permission of the production of a document relating to affairs of State. If the authority of the person claiming privilege is called into question the matter can always be

proved by evidence. This case was followed by the Bombay High Court in the case of LADY DINBAI DINSHAW PETIT Vs. THE DOMINION OF INDIA A.I.R. 1951 Bombay 72. The Bombay High Court held that the privilege under Section 123 in respect of any document only applies to unpublished official records relating to any affairs of state and before the privilege can be claimed there must be adjudication that the documents in respect of which privilege is claimed are official records relating to affairs of State. Further, it has been held that it must be left to a responsible Government Officer, either a Minister or the person at the head of a Department, to look at the document, to consider it, and to decide for himself whether the document falls in the category of the affairs of State referred to in section 123. If, therefore, having considered the documents, he tells the Court that the documents is one relating to the affairs of State and that its disclosure will be injurious to public safety, the court ordinarily would accept his statement if made on oath. But a privilege of this nature should be rarely claimed and should only be claimed after the responsible Minister or the Head of the Department has fully satisfied himself that the document whose disclosure is being resisted is really a document relating to the affairs of State and whose disclosure will result in injury to public interest. In this case their Lordships have held that the Judgement of the House of Lords in DUNCAN Vs. CAMELL LAIRD & CO. 624, does not in any way overrule or disagree with the Privy Council case of ROBINSON Vs. STATE OF SOUTH AUSTRALIA 1931.A.C.704. It has been observed that no arguments were advanced before the House of Lords as to the sufficiency of the Affidavit. The only contention which was considered by the Privy Council was whether it was open to the Court to inspect the document and the House of Lords rejected that contention and to that extent held the P.C. decision to be erroneous. [...] But really I see no irreconcilable difference between the two judgments except on the one point as to whether the court can or cannot inspect a document in respect of which privilege is claimed by the State and on the point there can be no question that as far as our country is concerned we are bound by the statutory provision contained in Sec. 162 of the Evidence Act and the Court is precluded from looking at the documents. Thus this is the State of law so far as Indian Courts are concerned. As in these two cases the other cases cited at the bar have been discussed, I need not discuss them again.

12. Coming to our Hyderabad Evidence Act, it will be seen that Sec. 126 of the Hyderabad Evidence Act corresponds to Section 162 of the Indian Evidence Act. The first parts of both Sections are nearly the same but in the Hyderabad Evidence Act, sub-section 2 has been added which is not to be found in the Indian Evidence Act. Sub-section 2 is as follows:-

"From the provision of Sub-Section (I) no Court is entitled of itself or on the application of any party, to compel the production of any document or its copy from any Government Office by which some official secrets are divulged or there is a probability of any occurrence of the breach of the peace".

There is no explanation to this Section which provides that for the purposes of this Section the decision of the Head of the Government Department and in case of Secretariat, decision of (Madar-ul-Moham), the Prime Minister will be final as regards the production of the document in this respect.

13. In this section the prime minister in case of the Secretariat Departments and the Head of every Government Department in other cases have been given the power to give a decision as regards the production or non-production of the document and it is provided that this decision will be final. Therefore, according to the Hyderabad Section it is not the decision of the Court but the decision of the Head of the Department that has been made final. This sub-Section was inserted by an amendment of the Evidence Act No. VI of 1317 F. It has been argued that this amendment was repealed by the enforcement of section I of the Hyderabad Civil Procedure Code passed in 1323 F., and it has been so held in the case of ABDUL ALI Vs. ZENITH ENGINEERING CO. 12 Nazaire-e-Osmania Adalat Aliah, 216. In my opinion, this section stands as it is and is not repealed by Section I of Hyderabad Civil

Procedure Code. [...] Therefore, I agree with the opinion of M.A. Ansari J., that the amendment to section 136 stands and is not repealed. Under Section 86 of the Criminal Procedure Code the Court is entitled to issue summons to produce documents. The exception of this section is provided in Section, 87. It provides that the provisions of the above Section will not apply to clauses (a) (b) and (c). We are here concerned with Clause (c) only, and that Clause (c) reads as follows:-

"Any document which is in the custody of the Public Officer in his official capacity as a confidential document, and the disclosure of which will in his opinion be detrimental to the Government purposes."

Thus to claim privilege under these two sections it is necessary to prove that the document was kept in the custody of the Public Officer as a confidential document, which, if disclosed in the opinion of the officer, would be detrimental to the Government purposes and secondly, there must be a decision of the Prime Minister or the Head of the Department about the production or non-production of the document. Unless and until these two conditions are proved the Government cannot claim any privilege at all. It has not been proved in this case that the document was kept with the Secretariat Department as a confidential document and as the document was in the custody of the Secretariat it was necessary to prove that it was a decision of the Prime Minister not to produce the document in Court. Unless and until these two things are proved it is for the court to determine whether the production can be resisted, under the plea of privilege. In this case the letter of the Secretary has been filed but in this letter there is nothing to show that there was any such decision and that the decision was made after looking into the papers. So, the sections under which the privilege is claimed are not at all applicable to the case under consideration. Therefore, the plea that the documents are privileged ones cannot stand.

14. It is contended on behalf of the accused that there cannot be an appeal by the Government as there was no acquittal under

section 368, Hyderabad Penal Code, and corresponding to Section 436 of the I.P.C. The special Judge has given no finding as regards this charge. He simply sentenced the accused under Sec. 243 Hyderabad Penal Code and as there is no acquittal nor conviction there cannot be any appeal by the Government. On behalf of the Government Advocate relying on PADTAL BUCHAM Vs: SARKAR-E-ALI, 36 Deccan Law Report 4, it is argued that this should be treated as an acquittal. In my opinion, this argument has got no force. Unless and until a clear finding as regards the acquittal is given there cannot be any appeal. Under section 342 of the Hyderabad Criminal Procedure Code, the Government can appeal only against the decision of Judgement of acquittal and not otherwise. Therefore, unless and until there is a judgement of acquittal there cannot be an appeal. In 36 Deccan Law Report 4, the facts were that the accused was challenged under Section 243 for murder and charge was also framed under the same section. The accused was committed to the Sessions. The Sessions Court after trial gave a finding that the offence proved against the accused was a culpable homicide and that the accused has not committed the offence of murder. The file was sent for confirmation and the High Court decided that it is proved that the accused had committed murder. It was contended on behalf of the accused that as there was no appeal by the Government against the acquittal under charge of murder, the High Court was wrong in convicting the accused under that charge. The Judicial committee held that this contention was right. This case is of help to the contention advanced by the Government advocate, because there was a clear judgement given by the Sessions Judge that the offence of murder was not proved and the accused was convicted under culpable homicide. Therefore, there can be an appeal against this acquittal (In this case the Special Judge has not given any finding either of conviction or acquittal and therefore, it cannot be held that the accused was acquitted of the charge under Section 368, Hyd. Penal Code. In my opinion, the appeal is not competent and is therefore dismissed.)

15. It is argued on behalf of the Counsel for the accused that the Special Judge was wrong in not summoning documentary evidence of the Accused. The refusal by the Special Judge has materially caused injustice to the accused and, therefore, he should be given a chance to produce the evidence. Mr M.A. Ansari in his judgement has dealt with this aspect of the case and under Sec. 428 of the Cr.P.C. has ordered that the defects in the case should be removed by this Court by calling for documentary evidence. In my opinion also there are defects in this which could be removed by calling further evidence but when on the facts on record the conviction cannot be sustained there is no need for further enquiry. Therefore, I need not consider this aspect.

16. Having disposed of the legal arguments, I now come to the factual side of the case. The incident took place on 6th May, 1948. It is admitted by the accused that the accused was present on the date of the incident at 'Int' the place of the occurrence. But his defence is that at the time when the occurrence took place he was not there but had returned to Osmanabad. It is to be seen whether the accused was present at the time of the occurrence. In order to prove this on behalf of the prosecution four eyewitnesses have been examined. The first and the most important witness in this case is P.W. 2 Kishen Rao. He is in the employ of the Police Department for six years. He has deposed that he went to 'Int' along with the Pathans for disbursement of the salary to the Police Force and the pickets stationed on the border of the State; the accused came there on the 6th May 1948 at about 10 or 10.30; from there the Talukdar went to Dhokewadi as there was disturbance and as there were two or three dead bodies found; to see them the Talukdar had gone; from that place the Talukdar returned to 'Int' about 11.30 or 12; the Razakars parade was held and the Talukdar gave them some rewards; a Pathan from the locality came there and told the Talukdar that Kishen Teke make much mischief in the village; the Talukdar asked Hakim Khan and Feroz Khan to go and see what it was; so both of the them went to the house of Kishen Teke and returned and said 'He does not heed'. At this the

Talukdar and all others assembled there, went to the house of Kishen Teke; but he replied from the courtyard that he would not come, then the Talukdar asked to remove the flag; when Kishen Teke refused to remove the flag, the Talukdar ordered the Pathans to open fire, which killed Kishen Teke and his wife; thereupon the Talukdar ordered the corpses to be burnt; at the time of kindling the fire the Talukdar was there only, a local Pathan entered the room in the house of Kishen Teke and carried away a girl there from; the house was burnt; then the Talukdar went towards Osmanabad. In his cross-examination this witness has stated that it was 12 o'clock or half past twelve when this event occurred. In the statement of this witness, I find that there are several discrepancies which are very important ones. This witness deposed that after the order was given by the Talukdar to fire, from among Taj Mohd. Khan, Hakim Khan, Feroz Khan, Abdul Wadood Khan, Naeem Khan, Sankya Khan, Rasul Khan, a few went with the Talukdar inside the house and a few more were in the courtyard. Further, he stated that the Talukdar was standing outside near the door; he did not go into the door; he was nearby. He had stated that after the Pathans fired, Kishen Teke and his wife died. Further, in the cross examination he has stated that from the place where the deponent was, nothing inside the house could be seen and he did not see Kishen Teke and his wife from the place where he was standing. He also said about the Pathans firing, who was seen in the courtyard, and he said that the Talukdar did not go into the door. Further, he said that at the time of the kindling the fire the Talukdar was there only; a local Pathan entered into the room in the house of Kishen Teke and carried away a girl there from; he could not tell his name; his house is near the Police Station; the Pathan carried away the girl to his house, the house was burning. Further, he has deposed that when Sher Mohammed came out with Rukmani Bai, the house was not on fire. These contradictory statements of the witness are such that they detract the importance of the witness. The most important criticism that can be made on this witness is that the documentary evidence belies his presence at 'Int' on the day of the occurrence. The witness is a Head Constable of Second grade stationed at Osmanabad at the time of the accused's visit to 'Int'. His travelling allowance bill has been produced on behalf of the accused which shows that on the day of the occurrence he left Umerga and reached Tuljapur at 5.00 p.m. It further showed that he did not go to 'Int' until 13th May. From the contents of this bill it follows that Kishen Rao's evidence is false and that he was not present at 'Int' on 6th May. Kishen Rao in his cross-examination did not suggest that there was any other Head Constable stationed at Osmanabad in May 1948 of the same name. This suggestion was made for the first time in the High Court by the Public Prosecutor. The High Court sent for the register of the Police Stationed at Osmanabad in May 1948 and it was found from that register that there was only one Kishen Rao, who was a Second Grade head Constable. Therefore, it is proved that the T.A. Bill refers to this witness. This T.A. Bill is a genuine document. It was summoned by a letter to the Head of the Treasury Office, Osmanabad on the 27th June, 1950. It was sent by the Government Department in response to this letter. One of the witnesses for the prosecution Syed Khayamuddin, the auditor at the Talukdar's office at Osmanabad P.W.6 verified this T.A. Bill. He deposed that the T.A. Bill was submitted to his office by the Police Dept., with the signature of the Superintendent of the Police which he identified.

17. Objection is taken on this T.A. Bill by the Public Prosecutor viz., that it was not the T.A. Bill of P.W. 2; secondly, that it was not proved; and thirdly that the nature of the document showed that it was a false document.

18. As regards the first objection I have shown above that the Register of he Police Force summoned in the High Court conclusively proves that this T.A. Bill refers to Kishen Rao, P.W. 2. This register showed that on the 6th May 1948 there was only one Kishen Rao stationed at Osmanabad with the rank of Head Constable, Second Grade, that is the rank of Kishen Rao mentioned in the T.A. Bill and that was the rank of P.W. 2. Incidentally, if there had been two persons with this name and

rank, one would have expected P.W. 2 to have mentioned this fact when he was cross-examined on the T.A. Bill. He did not do so because as the register shows there was only one.

19. The second point that the T.A. Bill was not proved has got no force in it. There was the document proved by P.W. 6 who identified the signature of the D.S.P. upon it and he said that it was submitted to his office by the Police Department. Further the document was sent to the court on the 4th July 1950, by the Treasury Office at Osmanabad in answer to the Judge's letter on the 7th June, 1950. The D.S.P.'s letter of the 11th August 1950 and the District Accounts Officer's letter of the 8th September 1950 are further proofs that the document is an official report. There is no necessity that the contents of the document should be proved. Section 53 of the Evidence Act provides that an enquiry in official record stating a relevant fact is itself a relevant fact. This means that the statements in official records are sufficient to prove the facts stated. [...] .

20. There is no strength in the third objection raised by the Public Prosecutor. It is argued that the document described the purpose of the tour as patrolling and Kishen Rao said that he was an Accountant, therefore, the document is false in itself. But the argument is not sound. The Clerk preparing the T.A. Bill may describe the purpose of the tour as patrolling, in the case of the Accountant as in the case of others, who may accompany. There is nothing to show that P.W. 2's duty did not include patrolling. Thus the objections on the T.A. Bill are without foundation and in my opinion the T.A. Bill is proved. If the T.A. Bill is proved then this witness becomes a false witness and when once this witness becomes a false one, P.W. 3 who states that P.W. 2 was present also becomes false.

21. P.W. 3 is Said Sanadi. As P.W. 2's deposition is shaken by the documentary evidence, the evidence of this witness also collapses because this witness clearly states that he met Kishen Rao at 'Int' on the day of occurrence. If P.W.2 was not at 'Int' as is evident from the above discussion then this witness must have lied deliberately in order to corroborate P.W. 2. [...] This witness

said that at the time of burning the Talukdar was inside the door. The whole house was burnt and Sher Mohd. Rohilla took away the girl. After the house was burnt, the Talukdar and all others went towards the Police Station. This witness said that Kishen Teke came out of the house and refused to lower down the flag. This is contrary to what Kishen Rao said, viz., that he refused to come out. This witness also said that Pathans loaded their rifles with cartridges and fired at the door which means that the Pathans were outside, while Kishen Rao said that the Pathans had entered the house. Moreover, this witness further said that at the time of burning, the Talukdar was inside the door while Kishen Rao deposes quite contrary to this. This witness said that from the place where he was standing the courtyard inside the house could be seen and further he said that Kishen Rao P.W. 2 was standing by his side. While Kishen Rao. P.W. 2 said that from the place he was standing nothing could be seen inside the house and further said that the deponent was behind the Talukdar outside the door and that he had not seen Kishen Teke and his wife before they were burnt by the bullet as they were inside the house only. From the deposition of this witness it seems that Sher Mohammed, Rohilla took away the girl Rukmani Bai P.W. 8 after the house was burnt but this is not substantiated by another evidence. This witness like P.W. 2 does not give any sufficient explanations as to the reason why Kishen Teke was a scoundrel or makes mischief. This witness had said that he had gone to the Talukdar, Osmanabad, along with Raghunath, son of Kishen Teke, P.W. I and the then Talukdar had taken his statement. This statement was not produced in spite of several attempts made by the accused to summon the same. Had it been produced, it is likely that it would have gone against the prosecution. So this witness also is not of any help to the prosecution.

22. The next witness is Dinanath P.W. 4. This witness is not an eye-witness to the incident. He was present with the accused during the earlier part of the incident until Hyder went to Kishen Teke's house. He did not accompany Hyder to Kishen Teke's house; he went to his own house which is within a few yards

of Kishen Teke's. This witness is a businessman and instead of accompanying Hyder he went to his business. This witness was frightened. In this respect he does not resemble P.W.s 2, 3 and 7. Although the house of this witness was within a stone's throw of Kishen Teke's house, where Kishen Teke and his wife were murdered and the house was burnt down. When the deponent came there afterwards the house was burning and had fallen down. If these things happened as P.W.s 2, 3 and 7 said that they did it is surely incredible that this witness living so close should have seen nothing and should have heard no gun-shots. In his statement to the Investigating Officer he said the he mentioned to this officer the names of Chitamber Niverthi, Vishwanath and Shanker, but he does not say that he mentioned the name of Hyder. He further said that after the Police Action he along with Raghunath had been to the Collector. He had already made his statement and he did not remember to have mentioned the names of all the accused. In spite of the accused's several attempts to get the copies of these statements he could not get the copies in order that he might cross-examine this witness on that basis. This witness contradicts himself when he said that he did not remember on what the flag was fixed and after a few seconds said that it was fixed on a bamboo.

From his shop he saw Sher Mohammed carrying away a girl, Rukhmani Bai (P.W. 8). From this statement it seems that Sher Mohammed took away this girl after the death of Kishen Teke and before the burning of the house. This witness deposed that he came to the Police Station at 1 o'clock. Half an hour must have passed in making the statement of the deponent. After the statements the deponent stayed there for 5 or 10 minutes. Thus this witness too is not very helpful to the prosecution.

23. Coming to P.W. 7 who is a Carpenter, it is stated in his disposition that the motor-car of the accused came after the motor lorry with the Police Force, while the other witnesses said that they reached first and the Talukdar came afterwards. This witness has deposed that he saw the accused present but when asked to identify him he said that he appears to be like him. Thus he could not clearly

identify the accused. Further, he stated that the Talukdar was there but "what do I know?" In spite of the fact that the other witnesses were there, this witness deposed that the Talukdar was there inside the door but did not know who were with him. Contrary to P.W. 2, this witness stated that the inside portion of the house of Kishen Teke can be seen even from outside the house. He further said that he did not remember who was at the side of the deponent; which means that he had not seen P.W. 2. His statement was recorded by the C.I.D. Inspector, which the accused could not get in spite of his several attempts for the sake of cross-examining the witness. Thus this witness also is of no great help to the prosecution.

24. Then the next important witness is Rukmani Bai, P.W. 8. She deposed that she was in the house when first some two to four Pathans entered the house and enquired where Kishen Teke had gone; they fired two to four shots at the flag; she did not know where they went because she remained inside the house; the Rohillas came again; the Talukdar and others of his party all came; the whole house was full and called 'Kishen; Kishen' and went to the other side; a Pathan approached the deponent and carried away by holding her hand. The story that is told by this witness is quite a different one from what the others said. She deposed that the Pathans came twice and not on the occasion as the other witnesses deposed. So, either this witness is false one or the other witnesses are false. When the Talukdar along with the Pathans came, the other witnesses deposed that he called Kishen Teke, who refused, and then there was a conversation between Kishen Teke and the Talukdar about the lowering down of the flag. This witness did not say anything about the conversation. She only said that the whole house was full and said Kishen, Kishen, and went that side. Where was the need to call for Kishen, when Kishen Teke was there speaking to the Talukdar. As to the time when she was carried away by the Pathans, there also the others witnesses did not support what she said. She said that when the Rohilla caught the hand of the witness, she cried and shouted. They were firing shots from outside. So, at the time

when the shots were fired, Sher Khan caught hold of this girl. This girl said that, that is the same Pathan who told her that Kishen Teke had been murdered. If at the time when the shots were fired she was in the house she must be knowing that Kishen Teke was dead. But she said that she heard it from the Pathan. She further stated that she was not present when Kishen Teke was killed, which is, it seems, strange. Further, she said that she did not know when the Razakars of the village and the Pathans of Osmanabad entered the house and whether the accused was there or not. But, in her examination-in-chief, she has stated that the accused was there outside, which is contradictory. Thus from the statement of this witness also it seems very doubtful whether the accused was there or not at the time of the incident.

25. The next witness is Raghunath s/o. Kishen Teke, P.W. I He was at Kherda at the time of the incident. He stated that Niverthi, the carpenter gave him information of the occurrence. This witness is not an important witness. He has been examined because he is the son of the deceased. At the time of the inquest the statement of the brother of this witness was taken and he has not alluded to the presence of the accused; while this witness stated that he got the information that the accused was present. The brother of this witness is not produced. Therefore, this witness also is not of very much help to the prosecution.

26. The next witness is Manohar P.W. 5. He is a Punch. This witness does not need any criticism. Then comes Khyamuddin, P.W. 6. He was the Auditor and had identified the T.A. Bill of the accused. In his cross-examination he had stated that Ex-A the T.A. Bill of Kishen Rao, P.W. 2 was submitted in his office by the Police Department with the signature of the Superintendent of the Police. He had verified the signature of the Superintendent of the Police. So, from the statement of this witness it can very well be said that the T.A. Bill of P.W. 2 is a genuine one.

27. P.W. 9. is Mohd. Abbas, who is a Police Head Constable. He was working at Wasi in Kallam Taluk and the village Int is within its jurisdiction. He stated that the information of the murder was received from the Nakadar of Int. He had made investigation of

this case. The accused had called him at Yermala and directed him to take the report of the Police Patel regarding the murder of Kishen Teke and his wife at Int and to take action since the Pathans had gone over to Kishen Teke's house and killed him. This witness reached Int on 8th May and obtained the Police Patel's report and forwarded it to the Police Station for recording the case. The Police Patel reported that the Congress Arya Samaj flag was hoisted in Kishen Teke's house; when he refused to lower it down, the Rohillas came back and reported to the Talukdar thereupon both the Talukdar and the Rohillas went together and as Kishen Teke refused, the Talukdar gave orders to kill him; hence he says that the Rohillas killed Kishen Teke and his wife. In his investigation he says that he came to know that the Pathans had killed him. When the investigation was completed, he further stated that he was trying to arrest the Pathans when he was transferred to Aurangabad. The Rohillas became inimical towards him, therefore, the Rohillas on 17th Mehir, 1357 Fasli attacked the deponent with rifle and hurt him. In his cross-examination this witness said that the Police Patel's report was enclosed and forwarded with the information report; but the report was sent to the Munsiff court at Kallam; he had also sent his diary and the information report to the Superintendent's office; he was shown the report of the Police Patel sent by him which is in the File No. 100/1, dated 10th Thir 1357 F. There is a copy of this report on the record which shows that the evidence previously given by this witness about the contents of the report was wholly untrue. It is urged that this witness has stated that the accused ordered him to prepare a false first information report. The statement that he had given does not substantiate this, what he has told is that the accused directed him to take the report of the Police Patel regarding the murder of certain persons. Kishen Teke and his wife at Int and to take action since the Pathans had gone over to Kishen Teke's house and killed them. However stretched, these words cannot be interpreted as the directions to the witness to prepare a false First Information Report. If he was told to prepare such a report it seems that he behaved very strangely if his evidence is true. He filed a First Information Report stating that Kishen Teke had shot at a Constable and that Constable had killed him and his wife in self-defence. According to his evidence he had found that the Pathans had killed Kishen Teke in the presence of Hyder. He must, therefore, had knowingly filed a false First Information Report. This witness said that he was given instructions to investigate the case by Hyder and the D.S.P. and that the instructions were given at Osmanabad on 7th May. He fixes the time when the instructions were given at about 12 or 1 PM. Reference to Hyder's T.A.Bill shows that Hyder left Osmanabad for Nanaj on 7th May at 11 AM. This shows that this witness is telling a lie. The accused did his best to get the investigation file and the case diary kept by the witness during the investigation but without success. Had these documents been produced, probably they would have gone against the prosecution. So this witness also is of little help to the prosecution.

28. The last witness is Syed Ali Naqvi, P.W. 10. He is a C.I.D. Inspector. But he denied the fact of seeing the case diary of Abbas Khan P.W. 9. He said that the case diaries are not with him. He also denied the fact about the statement being taken by the Government which is very strange. Thus, this witness also is of no importance in support of the prosecution.

29. As regards the defence witnesses, Counsel for the accused states that he does not rely upon these witnesses in order to prove the story as told by Zaman Khan, but his main defence is that the accused was not present at the time of the occurrence and in order to prove this he has examined these witnesses and not to prove the truth or falsity of Zaman Khan's story. The first witness is Abdul Ghani, who was working as a personal clerk to the accused. He has deposed that he was with the accused on the tour of Int and when they returned to Osmamnabad, Zaman Khan stayed at Int. He came on the third day; Zaman Khan returned and informed the accused that the Pathan, Feroz Khan by name was attacked by some person and the bullet passed touching his belt; thereupon Feroz Khan fired and Kishen Teke and his wife both were killed. His being with the accused is supported by the fact

that his name was included in the list of witnesses enclosed with the Challan. From the statement of this witness it can be seen that had the incident occurred in the presence of the accused, there was no need for Zaman Khan to give the report of what happened at Int. As he was the personal clerk of the accused he heard the report of what Zaman Khan had told the accused. The next witness Mohd. Ahmedulah, D.W. 2 is a Major in the Army and was posted at Osmanabad at the time of the occurrence. He was posted with the 3rd Golconda Lancers. There used to be meeting between the accused and this witness in connection with the border raids as this witness used to take part in the Advisory Committee. This witness has deposed that he remember that in Thir, Zaman Khan made a report. He had perhaps returned from Int and said that some people had gathered in Patel's house and had some arms with them. Zaman Khan went there for enquiries and he was fired upon, and he produced a bullet, a belt and cartridges. The deponent saw a mark of bullet on the belt and also a revolver with it. He had also heard that the Pathans fired in self-defence and due to this firing a man and a woman died. So, this witness supports the statement of D.W. I, Viz., that Zaman Khan had given a report to the Talukdar. Had it been a fact that the Talukdar was present at the time of the occurrence it is impossible that Zaman Khan would have given such a report.

30. Then I come to D.W. 3 Syed Mohd. Khadri, the Tehsildar. He went to the Collector to give a report about the Nanaj incident. At that time Zaman Khan had come there and there he got the information that Zaman Khan gave report of the Int incident. D.W. 4 Gulab Khan is an inhabitant of Int. He has deposed that the accused had come in a motor-car on the date of the incident and went to Dhokewadi and after his return from Dhokewadi he distributed money to the survivors of the deceased who had come from Dhokewadi and went away to Osmanabad; nobody reported to the accused regarding Kishen Teke and his wife, Godabai, so long as he stayed there. The incident occurred two or three hours after the accused left the place. D.W. 5 is Abdul Jaleel, who was the Peshi Clerk of the accused. Zaman Khan was

telling this witness when he was writing the report that the two local inhabitants of Int were killed and the Pathans had killed them. From these statements, the accused has tried to prove that he was not present at Int when the incident occurred.

31. Taking into consideration the statement of the witnesses, which I have referred to and non-production of important documents, and also considering the fact that the eye-witnesses, Bhojan, Joshi, Niverthi, the blacksmith, Govind, Vishnu, the two Ramoshis and Vishwanath are not produced, in my opinion, a doubt is created as to the commission of the offence by the accused as alleged by the prosecution, and when a doubt is created, benefit of doubt must be given to the accused.

Under these circumstances, giving the benefit of doubt to the accused, I acquit the accused of the charges of murder and allow the appeal of the accused. So far as the appeal by the Government is concerned, I dismiss the same for the reasons set out above.

32. In view of my finding there is no need for me to discuss the contention that the Special Judge's judgement was unconstitutional.

33. In the result, the appeal of the accused is allowed and the appeal of the Government dismissed.

Sd/-V.R. Deshpande,
JUDGE.
4-12-1951

"TRUE COPY"

(In the judgement cited above, text has been shortened in four places – in paras 11, 13, 19 and 21 – without influencing argument. Deletions marked by square brackets – editor)

EX.P.28
TOP SECRET

GOVERNMENT OF HYDERABAD
HOME DEPARTMENT.

No. SPL/IP/39/51. Hyderabad. D/-6-2-1952

From

Nagendra Bahadur Esq., I.A.S.
Secretary to Government,
Home Department.

To,

The Inspector-General of Police,
Hyderabad-Deccan.

Subject:- Cases against ex-Government Officers.

ജ്ഞ

Sir,

With reference to your letter No. 312/4-INT/51, dated the 24-10-1951, on the above subject, I am directed to enclose a statement showing the details of cases against the ex-Government Officers and to inform you that the Government have decided to withdraw these cases pending in various Courts.

I am, therefore, to request that the Public Prosecutors in the respective Courts may kindly be instructed to present petitions to the Courts concerned for their withdrawal for reasons of State.

I am also to enclose herewith a statement showing the action to be taken in respect of cases in which appeals are pending in the High court and to request that necessary action in the matter may kindly be taken at an early date and this Department informed of the action taken. As regards the rest of the cases your recommendation have been approved by the Government.

Yours faithfully

Sd/-A. Ganpat Rao
Dy. Secretary (HOME DEPARTMENT)

Copy forwarded for information to:-

1. Dy. Inspector-General of Police, C.I.D. Hyderabad
2. The Registrar, High Court of Judicature.
3. Collectors concerned.

ജ്ഞ

<u>TOP SECRET</u>

Criminal Investigation Department
Crime Branch, Hyderabad-Deccan.

No. 312/4-INT/51 Dated: 9th February, 1952

Copy, together with a copy of a list of cases to be withdrawn to the Public Prosecutor, Osmanabad.

The cases mentioned in the list may please be withdrawn forthwith and a compliance report sent through the Special Messenger of the C.I.D. who is bringing the letter for favour of information of Government, through I.G.P. Hyderabad.

Sd/- Dwarkanath,
Superintendent of Police, Crime Branch, C.I.D.

"TRUE COPY"

LIST OF CASES (OSMANABAD)								
No.	Name of Officer	Fir	No	Offence	Place of occurrence with District			
10	Mohd. Hyder ex-Talugdar, Osmanabad and S.M. Qadri ex Tahsildar	35/49	395	P.C.	Apsinga			
11	same as above	36/49	395	P.C.	Aspinga			
12	-do-	39/49	454	P.C.	Aspinga			
13	-do-	38/49	454	P.C.	Aspinga			
14	-do-	30/40	454	P.C.	Aspinga			
15	-do-	34-49 Osmanabad	380	P.C.	Aspinga			
19	Ghulam Samdani Headmaster of Ther School and (7) others	64/48 Osmanabad	302	I.P.C.	Ther			
20	Bhurhanuddin ex-clerk Naldurg Post Office	30/31 32& 36/49	409	I.P.C.	Naldurg PO Osmanabad			
21	M.M. Shaik ex-Postmaster Osmanabad	16 & 17/49	409	I.P.C.	Osmanabad			

EX.P.30

IN THE HIGH COURT OF JUDICATURE AT HYDERABAD

Copy of Order
Case No. 4/6 of 1951 – 52. (Full Bench)
Mohd. Hyder VERSUS The State of Hyderabad

IN THE SUPREME COURT OF INDIA
CRIMINAL APPELLATE JURISDICTION, THE 9TH JULY 1954

CRIMINAL APPEAL 10 of 1953.

The State of Hyderabad --------- Appellant

VERSUS

MOHD. BAQUER HUSSAIN QURESHI
S/o. GHULAM ALI. Ex.Talukdar
KARIM NAGAR DISTRICT. Respondent

CRIMINAL APPEAL NO. II OF 1953

THE STATE OF HYDERABAD ------ APPELLANT
VERSUS
MOHAMMED HYDER
Ex-FIRST TALUKDAR OF OSMANABAD
Now residing in Hyderabad City. RESPONDENT

CRIMINAL APPEAL 12 OF 1953

THE STATE OF HYDERABAD ------- APPELLANT

SYED MOHAMMED QUADRI
Ex-TAHSILDAR
TULJAPUR
DISTRICT OSMANABAD.
RESPONDENT

CRIMINAL APPEAL NO. 13 OF 1953

THE STATE OF HYDERABAD -------- APPELLANT

SYED MOHAMMED QUADRI,
Ex-TAHSILDAR
TULJAPUR
DISTRICT OSMANABAD ----------
RESPONDENT

ꙮ

Appeals under Article 132 (1) of the Constitution of India from the judgement and Order, dated the 21st of July, 1952 of the Hyderabad High Court in Criminal Appeals Nos. 3/6, 4/6, 12/6 and 17/6 of 1951 - 52

ꙮ

AND

IN the matter of withdrawal of the Appeals above mentioned.

25th June, 1954

CORAM:

The Hon'ble Mr. Justice S.H. Bhagwati.
For Appellant (in all the Appeals)
Mr. P.G. Gokhale, instructed by Mr. R.H. Debar, Agent
For Respondent in Cr.As.Nos. 11 and 12
Mr. Rajinder Nary, Advocate.

WHEREAS the Appeals above mentioned were preferred to this Court under Article 132(1) of the Constitution and the High Court of Hyderabad was requested by this Court to prepare the Paper Books of the Appeals and WHEREAS the Appellant state in all the four Appeals subsequently made applications before the High Court praying for leave to withdraw the Appeals and WHEREAS the High Court by its orders, dated 8th December, 1953 and the 26th April, 1954 granted the Applications and issued certificates purporting to be under Order (13) Rule (4) Supreme Court Rules AND WHEREAS the appeals above mentioned were filed and registered in this Court the matter of the withdrawal of the Appeals mentioned above was called on for hearing before this Court on the 25th day of June, 1954 UPON hearing Counsel for the Appellant and Counsel for the Respondents in Criminal Appeals Nos. 11 and 12 Respondents in Criminal Appeals Nos. 10 and 13 not appearing either in person or by Counsel THIS COURT DOTH ORDER THAT the Appeals above mentioned be and are hereby dismissed as withdrawn.

WITNESS THE HON'BLE Mr Mehar Chand Mahajan, Chief Justice of India at the Supreme Court, New Delhi this the 25th day of June, 1954.

Sd/-S.D. Goswami
REGISTRAR

8th July, 1954.

"TRUE COPY"

Ex.P.I
GOVERNMENT OF HYDERABAD
General Administration Department,
Hyderabad – Deccan.

No. 300/GAD/I/SRC-CSP/56. Dated: 13th October, 1956

ORDER

Shri Mohd. Hyder, a Member of Hyderabad Civil Service, who was serving as Taluqdar, Osmanabad, was placed under suspension with effect from 18th September, 1948, in view of some serious allegations of a criminal nature against him. Sanction to prosecute him in Courts of Law was given, but in view of the general policy of Government in respect of such prosecutions, the cases against him were withdrawn from the Supreme Court.

Full text of this Order is quoted in Chapter 12, I File a Writ, under Affidavit of Mohammed Hyder, para.9.

Glossary

ASP: Assistant Superintendent of Police

CID: Criminal Investigation Division of the Police

Challan: Charge sheet. After receiving an FIR (First Information Report), the police conducts an investigation and, if satisfied, files a criminal case before a Magistrate based on a charge sheet or challan.

Collector: The administrative head of a district, also known as a Talukdar.

Collector and District Magistrate: Although judicial and executive powers are separate, Collectors retain some of the former powers under the Land Revenue Act and are therefore designated as Collector and District Magistrate. See also Talukdar.

Dacoity: Armed gang robbery. In India, a dacoit is a member of a band of robbers.

Diwani: Excluding the administration of the areas under Sarf e Khas Paigah and Jagir, the administration of the remaining areas of the state under the direct jurisdiction of the Diwan or Prime Minister was termed Diwani.

DSP: District Superintendent of Police, the highest police officer in a district. The DSP has concurrent jurisdiction with the Collector (Talukdar).

Fasli: Official calendar of Hyderabad State. The Fasli calendar, which is linked to the harvest cycle, was introduced by the Mughals and later adopted, with some modification, by the Nizams, and served as a convenient guide for the collection of revenue. The Muslim Hijri calendar was lunar, whereas Fasli was solar.

Gomashta: Agent, representative.

HCS: Hyderabad Civil Service. The senior administrative service of Hyderabad, entry to which was through a competitive exam.

HEH: His Exalted Highness. Selected Indian Rulers had the title of His Highness conferred on them by the British Government. After World War I, the Nizam of Hyderabad was recognized as the premier prince of India, with this distinctive title.

ICS: Indian Civil Service. The senior civil service in British India subsequently replaced with the IAS or the Indian Administrative Service. The Nizam's Hyderabad had its own Hyderabad Civil Service (HCS).

Jagir: Grant of villages by the Nizam, free from assessment. Holders of Jagir were authorized to collect agricultural tax from the farmers in their Jagir.

Majlis e Ittehad Ul Muslimeen: Leading Muslim Party in Hyderabad during 1947-48. Its origins may be traced back to 1927 when the Union of Muslims was created with the objective of bringing together Muslims of different denominations on a single religious and cultural platform. Its politicization, which became evident by 1938, grew with the rise of the anti-Hyderabad sentiment, against which it assumed the role of the defender of Muslim rule in Hyderabad. The two most prominent Majlis leaders of the time were Bahadur Yar Jung and Qasim Razvi.

Paigah: Grant of Jagir villages to high ranking families, regarded as second only to the Nizam and his family in status, who were in turn expected to maintain men at arms to protect and defend their feudal lord.

Pathan: Person belonging to a distinct ethnic/linguistic group, the Pashtuns, originating from the North-West Frontier Province in present-day Pakistan, and from East and Southern Afghanistan. Given their reputation as fighters, the Pathans were employed as irregulars in the Nizam's Hyderabad.

Police Action: The military invasion of Hyderabad State by the armed forces of India in September 1949. Also known as Operation Polo and Operation Caterpillar.

Rajpramukh: According to the original constitution of India, the erstwhile British Indian Provinces had the Governor as the head of the state, while a Rajpramukh headed the former princely states. This distinction was abolished with the reorganization of the states in 1956.

Razakar: A volunteer militia, created by the Majlis e Ittehad Ul Muslimeen Party of Hyderabad, in response to the threat of border raids. Literally, 'volunteer'.

Rupee: Hyderabad had its own currency, the Rupee, which was – confusingly – also the name of the currency in circulation in British India. In 1948, the Hyderabad Rupee was worth about a third of an American Dollar (or three Rupees to the US Dollar).

Sarf e Khas: Personal estate of the Nizam, comprising 6,536 villages. After the Police Action, when all the jagirs, including Paigah and Sarf e Khas, were reabsorbed by the state, the Nizam was compensated with an annual grant of Rs 2.5 million.

Talukdar: The administrative head of a district. A district was (and remains) the basic unit of administration in both Hyderabad and India. He is usually known as Collector in India. Each district is subdivided into 10-12 Taluks.

Tehsildar: Revenue Officer, in charge of a Taluk, which is a sub-division of a district. Each taluk consists of 100-150 villages.

Vakil: Advocate, pleader, or counsel.

Working week: The working week ended on Thursday in old Hyderabad, and Friday was the official day of rest.

Timeline

1936: Hyder receives BA degree from Osmania University.
1937: Hyder is admitted to the Hyderabad Civil Service.
15 August 1947: India achieves Independence.
29 November 1947: India and Hyderabad sign 12-month Standstill Agreement.
30 November 1947: Laiq Ali ministry formed in Hyderabad.
5 January 1948: Hyder assumes Collectorship of Osmanabad.
31 January 1948: Gandhi is assassinated.
11 September 1948: Jinnah dies.
13 September 1948: Indian forces invade Hyderabad ('Police Action')
17 September 1948: Hyderabad surrenders.
2 October 1948: Hyder suspended with effect from 18 September 1948, under orders of the military governor
10 January 1949: Government sanctions criminal prosecution of M. Hyder.
18 February 1949: Hyder is arrested.
22 March, 1949: Hyder is transferred to Osmanabad jail.
30 May 1950: Transferred to Gulbarga jail.
1 April 1950: Trials begin in Special Court, Gulbarga.
1951: The High Court of Hyderabad overturns all Special Court convictions in appeal; government appeals in all cases to the Supreme Court.

6 February 1952: The government withdraws the only remaining undecided case against Hyder (Apsingha) from the High Court, citing reasons of state.

29 February 1952: Hyder is released from prison.

25 June 1954: The government withdraws its appeals from the Supreme Court.

13 October 1956: Hyder is dismissed from government service under a special proviso of the Indian constitution.

7 March 1957: Hyder files a writ petition in the Hyderabad High Court against the State of Andhra Pradesh (successor state to Hyderabad in the Indian Union).

12 January 1960: The High Court of Andhra Pradesh at Hyderabad rules on the writ petition filed by Hyder.

Acknowledgements

Quotations from Thuycidides in the final chapter originally based on the Benjamin Jowett translation of 1883, have been replaced with the Richard Crawley translation, which employs less archaic language.

I should like to acknowledge the encouragement and guidance of Dr Hasanuddin Ahmed, IAS (Retd), who shared his extensive, first-hand knowledge of the last days of the Nizam's Hyderabad.

I should also like to thank Mr R. Venkatraman, who, over a humid summer in Chennai, entered the entire manuscript into the computer, while taking an enthusiastic and critical interest in what he was typing.

My stay in Chennai in 2006 was made possible by my mother-in-law who, with extraordinary generosity, turned her smoothly-functioning household over to me, during her trip abroad.

My family, as usual, has been a total distraction, which is, in fact, quite healthy, and keeps me living in the present, as no doubt the author of this work would have liked me to do.

Masood Hyder

Index

About the Author and Editor

In 1948, when the princely state of Hyderabad was going through difficult times, **Mohammed Hyder** was Collector of Osmanabad, one of the most politically sensitive districts of the state.

Masood Hyder is consultant at World Food Programme and Adjunct Professor, Department of Public Administration at Syracuse University.